W9-AGV-077

THE SERPENT'S EYE
Shaw and the Cinema

DONALD P. COSTELLO

The Serpent's Eye

SHAW AND THE CINEMA

Foreword by Cecil Lewis

University of Notre Dame Press • Notre Dame & London

FRONTISPIECE:

Shutter-bug Shaw at a garden party in Malvern, 1932

Courtesy of Radio Times Hulton Picture Library

NOTRE DAME, INDIANA

LIBRARY OF CONGRESS CATALOG CARD NUMBER: 65-23512

MANUFACTURED IN THE UNITED STATES OF AMERICA

DESIGNED BY KLAUS GEMMING

FOR CHRISTINE

FOREWORD
George Bernard Shaw: A biographical footnote

HE WAS TALL, thin, and erect. His habit of wearing a "Norfolk" jacket and trousers that fastened just below the knee exposed a pair of rather spindly stockinged shanks, which, for some reason or another, always reminded me of Malvolio. The fashion of these suitings had gone out with the turn of the century, but Shaw continued to wear what was actually "fancy dress" right through to the day of his death. His head was squarely carried on the shoulders, the chin somewhat drawn in, and this gave an impression of keen attention and at the same time a sort of lofty detachment from everything going on around him. The back of his head was conspicuous; his neck had no nape. Broad lobes ran down from the crown, as it seemed right into the shoulders. He attributed his remarkable intelligence to this extra cervical capacity. A life-long vegetarian ("I have not eaten meat for twenty-seven years: the results are before the public!"), he gave the impression, even in extreme old age, of exceptional health. The skin was clean, pink, and fresh; the eyes, clear and sprightly; and the white hair and beard, always groomed and fine in texture. In repose the face was composed and thoughtful as if contemplating some problem. In animation his lively wit, exploding like fireworks, was accompanied by a high abrupt laugh and sudden jerky movements of his hands and arms as he made his points; but these high-spirited sallies were never malicious; they were rather an extremely acute and impartial light on the topics of the conversation. "What the public calls genius," he said, "is only an unaccustomed way of tickling it."

His was the unique combination of a fine perceptive mind allied to a gorgeous sense of fun. He went straight to the heart of a problem and exposed it in a joke. What you had followed with serious attention was suddenly capped with a truth—and the truth seemed always hilariously funny. He was no tragedian. Even in *St. Joan,* basically a heroic and terrible story, the audience feels it is participating in a view of history, and the denouement is so inevitable and monumental that it passes beyond tragedy into pity at the folly of man. When Trebitsch, who had translated all Shaw's plays into German, sent one of his own, a turgid domestic drama, for Shaw to put into English, he turned the whole subject to farce. "But," Trebitsch wailed, "you have made of my tragedy, a comedy."

When I first met Shaw he was seventy; I was twenty-four. We had just started broadcasting in the U.K. I was one of the founders, and I had invited him along to see if I could get him to let us broadcast one of his plays. After totting up the royalties due from the huge audience, he suddenly said, "It is clear you cannot afford to pay me, so—I will do it for nothing," and a fortnight later he came to the microphone and read the whole of *O'Flaherty V.C.,* with impeccable verve and artistry.

From that day on he allowed me a certain intimacy. First at Adelphi Terrace and later at Whitehall Court, I was invited to lunch almost every week for many years. These lunches were works of art in themselves. The guests were never more than four in number, and lunch was always formally served. Shaw presided at the head of the table, Mrs. Shaw at the foot. The four guests were surprising in their variety. There I met H. G. Wells, Lawrence of Arabia, Elgar, Gene Tunney, Aldous Huxley, the Webbs, besides every star in the theatrical profession and many who asipired to be so. The conversation was almost always a monologue of comment and reminiscence by Shaw, and I never heard him repeat himself. Asked, I remember, on one occasion if his characters were all invented, he replied that sometimes they were taken from life. Shotover, for instance, was moulded on Gordon Craig's father, who, on his death bed, had refused to eat the bread of Extreme Unction unless he could have some cheese with it.

But behind the wit, the anecdote, and the magic of his plays, the clarity and style of the beautiful English, the insight into character and situation, lay a wealth of practical commonsense about any problem that came his way. He would settle your private affairs, the education of your children, or your future career over a cup of detoxicated coffee; but it was in the theatre that I most clearly remember his professional acumen. An ambitious young artist wanted to play *The Millionairess*. Shaw at once replied, "She has not enough experience. A star part requires the artiste to be able to sustain a scene of twenty minutes in each act. *The Millionairess* demands more than that." Of a play I sent him in which there was a difficult hysterical part in the first act for a character that did not appear again he commented, "You have written a scene that no 'small part' actor can tackle. You cannot have a star who only appears for ten minutes. It is uneconomic. Cut the scene; it is too early in the play anyway." Or to an actor-manager with a small theatre in Chicago offering to pay a 10% author royalty on one of his plays. "You cannot afford to pay 10% with a theatre of your capacity. The royalty will be 5%." Or, when an actor, who habitually drank too much, set fire to his bed and perished in the flames: "This is evidently a case of spontaneous combustion."

During his lifetime it was the fashion to say that Shaw had no sense of character—they were all puppets spouting Shaw. But the actors were not of this opinion. In fact, each character is so loaded with individuality that I have known artists in despair at how to speak his lines, finding layer under layer of characterization in the words. When he sent *Capt. Brassbound's Conversion* to Ellen Terry, her maid read the play aloud to her. Suddenly she stopped and laughed, "It's so exactly like you, Ma'am!" Ellen Terry played the part.

Shaw's plays were not just bright ideas, good stories, or dramatic situations; they arose from quite another source, a desire to show up the false values, inequalities, or stupidities of the age in which he lived. The sense of situation, the taut dialogue (try to cut it), and the fun were all, in a sense, merely technical aids to his aim. But it happened that his theatrical genius was such that the plays took on a life of their own and will last long after the windmills at which he tilted are no longer social issues. When his first play, *Widowers' Houses,* was presented at a Sunday Society for one performance, Shaw took a curtain call. Among the enthusiastic applause was one loud, long boo from the gallery. But Shaw was equal to the situation. "I quite agree with you, sir; but what are we two among so many."

In 1930 he agreed to let me make the first film ever of his plays. We chose his one act comedy *How He Lied to Her Husband*. With one set and three characters it was about as unmovielike as anything could be. The contract drawn by Shaw himself (in *Who's Who* was the laconic announcement "Agents: none. Capable of managing his own business.") forbade any cuts or alterations in the text, and Shaw had two hundred such contracts printed for future use. (He also offered to print two hundred more, substituting my name for his!) I had never directed a film in my life, but this was clearly nothing more than a licence to film a stage play. He attended some rehearsals, posed for photographers, pronounced the film a huge success when it was nothing more, I fear, than a cinematograph curiosity; but, as he intended, it launched me on a film director's career.

Next year I attempted a full-length feature of *Arms and the Man*. His scribbled notes on the script and his curt letters and postcards during production were, perhaps, the most interesting part of a picture that failed miserably. I had them bound and thirty years later sold this unique folio to America.

It was in Hollywood in 1937 that Gabby Pascal came to me and asked me to script *Pygmalion,* which Shaw had licenced him to turn into a motion picture. I had previously met Gabby at lunch with GBS in London and admired his Hungarian wit and style. Of course he was a showman; but Shaw, so often surrounded by serious and worthy people, had a fairground streak in him with an engaging weakness for the confidence trick or the peepshow. Often at lunch amongst people of "established reputation" you would find black-belted women Judo wrestlers, clairvoyant sleep healers, or high-wire acrobats, who had somehow or other managed to get themselves invited to that very exclusive table. Gabby, who confessed to not having half a crown in his pocket on the day I first met him, had talent, of course, but more he had dreams and something basically irresistible—a genuine admiration and affection for GBS. I had not seen him since that day, but had heard, of course, of his Shavian success. When he turned up at my house in Coldwater Canyon, I was surprised that he wanted me to script Shaw's play. I attributed it then, and still do, to a suggestion from GBS himself and Gabby's concern at the outset to fall in with whatever the great man wished.

Of course there was the same problem as with all the Shaw films, the author's insistence on sticking to his dialogue. But as I began to work, I saw deeper into the play to its central failing. *Pygmalion's* plot revolves round a bet to pass a flowergirl off as a duchess at a fashionable ball. But, in the play Shaw bilks the issue: the scene at which the bet is won is never shown. So the whole climax of the plot is sidestepped and the audience frustrated.

I wrote to Shaw at some length, pointing this out to him. He might as well, I said, have written *St. Joan* and left out the trial scene. The sparks began to fly as GBS retorted, and it soon became clear he thought the scene of no importance. The development of Liza's character and Higgins's precious phonetic alphabet were the twin pillars of the play, and it needed Samson (in the shape of Gabby) to pull them down. I completed the rather sad task of breaking down the dialogue into endless "shots," knowing full well that if this were transferred to the screen, it would suffer the same fate as *Arms and the Man*. But I finished it, delivered it to Gabby, wished him luck for the, so I thought, hopeless enterprise, and left for the South Seas.

That Gabby did succeed in blarneying GBS into alterations and getting a film onto the screen was a major success for him: nobody else had come near it. However, I personally thought that the result in this and both the other films he made was no more than a bodge. As films they creaked at the joints, and it remained for Lerner and Loewe to achieve that magical free adaptation of which GBS would certainly have sternly disapproved.

We are apt to forget that Shaw was at this time in his late seventies. Why should he accept the younger generation who were only anxious, as far as he could see, to castrate his plays of the parodox that had made them world famous and turn them into conventional "valuable properties" with his name on them? We forget he was an "original," a socialist, a reformer, a thinker, and, as such, unique. Plenty of people could write good stories with witty dialogue to pass an evening. That was not his object. He had something to say and said it with consummate skill, calculating every scene for maximum originality and effect. Even the laughter was calculated. "Human nature such as it is," he used to say, "can stand serious conversation for about twenty minutes. It is then necessary to relieve the tension and make them laugh." This was his technique at public meetings, where he always made a joke in the first minute, not to get a laugh, *but to listen to where the laugh came from.* If it came from the back of the gallery, he was being heard all over the hall and it was *that* that mattered.

Now, in old age myself, I think of him as one of the great influences in my life, for he set standards of generosity, integrity, and professional craftsmanship which I have never met elsewhere. His life was cast in a large mould, and he thought and acted with a natural magnanimity that made other men seem petty and vain. There was a severity approaching Olympian grandeur about his later years, but it was always tempered by his mischievous and rapierlike humour. I remember sitting in his study one morning when Maurice Chevalier was announced. Then at the height of his career, charming and debonair, this great professional, then a young and extremely attractive man, sat at his ease and chatted of this and that, while Shaw, arms folded and smiling, listened attentively. Came a pause in the conversation, and Shaw leaned forward in the most innocent way, "Tell me, Mr. Chevalier," he remarked inquiringly, "You act, don't you?"

Great writers are always surrounded by swarms of critics and commentators appraising or denigrating their work. But I cannot bring much critical faculty to the man who, in my early youth, gave me the largesse of his company, the benefit of his wisdom, the hilarity of his wit, and the encouragement and generosity of a father at the outset of my rather mercurial career. Trips to Hollywood, the South Seas, the Second World War, and then farming in Africa separated me from him for many years. But three months before his death at ninety-six I returned to visit him at

Ayot. He greeted me as though I had not been away a week. His mind was as clear as ever; but he was not much interested in the world around him. He was past writing, he said, but he was spending the days meticulously putting in order a complete edition of his works with all the alterations and additions that had accrued over the years. Alone now in the modest house, for Charlotte was dead, his faithful housekeeper served the usual impeccable lunch. Still walking erect with the aid of a stick, he waved my car away down the lane when I left him, never to see him again.

ACKNOWLEDGMENTS

I AM GRATEFUL to The Public Trustee and The Society of Authors for permission to quote from the play versions, printed screen versions, and sound-track versions of *Pygmalion, Major Barbara,* and *Caesar and Cleopatra;* from the unpublished Shaw screen plays for *Arms and the Man* and *The Devil's Disciple;* from Shaw's "My First Talkie" and "Arms and the Man on the Screen"; and from *Meeting at the Sphinx.* I am grateful to the Estate of Gabriel Pascal for permission to quote from the sound tracks of *Pygmalion, Major Barbara,* and *Caesar and Cleopatra,* and to quote from the final shooting script of *Caesar and Cleopatra.* I am grateful to Mr. T. E. Hanley for materials from his Shaw collection, now at the University of Texas in the Humanities Research Center. For helpful correspondence I am grateful to Arthur L. Mayer; Blanche Patch; Cecil Lewis; J. A. Barrier of Rank Film Distributors; Brenda Davies of The British Film Institute; film director Christopher Mann; Marjorie Plant of the British Library of Political and Economic Science; T. J. Brown of The British Museum; The Shaw Society of London; The Shaw Society of Chicago; The Shaw Society of Los Angeles; The Shaw Society of America; Professor Stanley Weintraub of *The Shaw Bulletin;* Mr. John Foster White of MacDonald and Company; The Theatre Collection of the New York Public Library; and The Museum of Modern Art Film Library.

For permissions to quote from published works, I gratefully acknowledge the following:

Mrs. Hesketh Pearson, for permission to quote (on page 78 of this book) from Hesketh Pearson's *G.B.S. A Postscript.* London: Collins, 1951.

Film Production Division of The Rank Organisation, for permission to quote (pages 17, 46, 115–116, 124, 132–134) from Marjorie Deans' *Meeting at the Sphinx.* London: MacDonald and Company, Ltd.

E. P. Dutton and Company and The Hutchinson Publishing Group, for permission to quote (page 77) from Stephen Winsten's *Jesting Apostle*. London: Hutchinson and Company, 1956.

The Viking Press and Macmillan Company of Canada Limited, for permission to quote (page 28) from Gene Fowler's *Good Night, Sweet Prince*. New York: The Viking Press, 1943.

Miss Blanche Patch, for permission to quote (page 26) from her *Thirty Years with G.B.S.* London: Victor Gollancz, Ltd., 1951.

Dodd, Mead and Company and The Hutchinson Publishing Group, for permission to quote (page 48) from S. Winsten's *GBS 90*. New York: Dodd, Mead and Company, 1946.

Hansom Books, Ltd., for permission to quote (page 39) from Walter Charles Mycroft's "Shaw—and The Devil to Pay," *Films and Filming*, V (February, 1959), 14, 30, 31.

Illustrations have been reproduced through the courtesy of

National Film Archive: pages 34, 35, 38, 41, 43, 44, 45, 57, 58, 61, 63, 91, 94, 96, 98, 120, 121, 125, 130, 139.

The Museum of Modern Art Film Library: pages 33, 94, 137.

Mrs. Valerie Pascal Delacorte: pages 47, 81, 87, 88, 114, 115.

Metro-Goldwyn-Mayer: pages 56, 63, 64, 67.

New York Public Library: pages 87, 117.

United Artists: pages 87, 117.

Radio Times Hulton Picture Library: frontispiece.

Culver Pictures, Inc.: pages 85, 89.

Clarkson N. Potter, Inc.: page 118 (from *To A Young Actress* [New York, 1960], page 183).

I must especially thank Professor Dan H. Laurence, Miss Marjorie Deans, and Mrs. Valerie Pascal Delacorte for aid beyond the call of scholarly duty. I am grateful to Professor John Meagher of the University of Notre Dame for research assistance in London, to James Wolff for research assistance in New York, and to Professor Elder Olson of the University of Chicago. And to The Danforth Foundation for my profession. And to my wife.

CONTENTS

ILLUSTRATIONS

INTRODUCTION

"I AM VERY FOND of the movies," wrote Bernard Shaw. "I am what they call in America a 'movie fan.'" His interest in motion pictures was a long-standing interest, developing out of an early fascination with photography. Long before anyone thought of putting the pictures together to make them move, Shaw had become a fanatical devotee of photography, appearing wherever he went with a camera around his neck. By 1901, Shaw had made himself enough of an expert on photography that he was writing reviews of exhibitions at the Royal Photographic Society. When the pictures finally did begin to move, Shaw's interest heightened, and he developed consistent theories about the motion picture both as a social force and as a means of artistic expression. He was never a professional motion picture critic, as he was a critic of the drama, of music, and of art. But, characteristically, he did have much to say about the cinema, and he said it loud and often. Finally, he turned from theory to practice, and became himself a movie writer as well as a movie fan. Out of his work as a movie writer has come a significant body of Shaviana, representing a considerable part of the Shaw canon.

Neither Shaw's cinema theories nor his cinema practice has ever been subjected to close study. That is what this little book intends to do. From it, we hope to be able to determine what Shaw thought about the films and what he did about them: what changes his plays underwent as he brought them from the stage to the screen, and what effect Shaw's cinema theory had upon the quality of his own cinema practice.

The Fascination of the Serpent's Eye

To Bernard Shaw, the silent cinema was "a much more momentous invention than printing." This extraordinary significance was due not to the artistic value of the motion picture, but to its social force. Shaw the propagandist, the dramatist who insisted that great art can never be anything but intensely and deliberately didactic, had never had any patience with the doctrine of art for art's sake. Art was for the sake of society. And now, with the advent of the cinema, Shaw saw a chance for reforming the whole world through communication. That prospect excited him; the birth of a new art form did not.

The Cinema as a Social Force

The social power of the cinema lay primarily in the fact that it, unlike books, could reach everybody. In a *New Statesman* article of 1914, Shaw explained:

Before printing could affect you, you had to learn to read; and until 1870 you mostly had not learned to read. But even when you had, reading was not really a practical business for a manual laborer. Ask any man who has done eight or ten hours' heavy manual labor what happens to him when he takes up a book. He will tell you that he falls asleep in less than two minutes. Now, the cinema tells its story to the illiterate as well as to the literate; and it keeps its victim (if you like to call him so) not only awake but fascinated as if by a serpent's eye. And that is why the cinema is going to produce effects that all the cheap books in the world could never produce.

The effects to be produced by the fascinating serpent's eye of the cinema were monumental. Shaw enumerated some of them: "The cinema is going to form the mind of England. The national conscience, the national ideals and tests of conduct, will be those of the film."

If the mind of England was going to be shaped, Shaw wanted to be in on the shaping. He announced publicly in 1914 that he would be happy to contribute a few sample scenarios to any movie maker who wanted them. This would be the first step, he hoped, in the establishment of a cinematic movement devoted wholly "to the castigation by ridicule of current morality." He was, of course, calling for the establishment of a specifically Shavian cinema, a cinema which, he added, could exist only if the state would endow the cinema so as to place it above the needs of competition. But there were no takers. Shaw the scenarist was not to be born for two decades. In the meantime, to his growing displeasure, Shaw had to limit his attacks on current morality to his plays, his pamphlets, and his speeches. He had to do without the potent social force of the cinema.

Shaw, of course, exploded into wrath at the idea of all that cinematic power being employed for decidedly un-Shavian ends. Indeed, the silent cinema, far from attacking the current conventional morality, was helping to form it and to spread it. The great danger of the cinema was its morality. In his contribution to a symposium on "Education and the Cinematograph" in a 1914 issue of a London journal called *The Bioscope*, Shaw complained that because a film had to go around the world unchallenged if a maximum of profit was to be made from it, the silent cinema was in actuality "not merely ordinarily and locally moral, but extraordinarily and internationally moral." The cinema was the great moral leveller. And, he added, levelling, though excellent in income, is disastrous in morals. Everyone, the London boy and the mining camp denizen, people in cathedral towns and Chinese seaports, everyone was force-fed and fascinated by the same desolating romantic morality. No superman would thus be formed to rise up above the moral level. He was worried that national characteristics and individuals would all be blended: "The next generation of English-men will no longer be English: they will represent a world-average of character and conduct, which means that they will have rather less virtue than is needed to run Lapland." Looking around, Shaw discovered that "the nameless exponents of a world-wide vulgarity (vulgarity is another of the names for morality) have complete possession" of the silent cinema, a cinema without Shaw.

But Shaw's early enthusiasm for the motion picture was not easily crushed. He recognized, even in the silent days when the cinema was under the control of world-wide commercialism and morality, that many indirect advantages kept seeping through the movies. One of the advantages that he admitted was the exposure of the movie-going public to certain principles of beauty: "The cinematograph, by familiarizing us with elegance, grace, beauty, and the rest of those immoral virtues which are so much more important than the moral ones, could easily make our ugliness look ridiculous."

After the introduction of the synchronized phonograph and cinematograph, this aesthetic function became more obvious. Now beauty, with its civilizing powers, could be brought by the motion picture and phonograph, with heightened powers of effectiveness, into those outlying districts where, heretofore, the people had to grow up as cultural savages. He wrote in a 1915 *Metropolitan Magazine* article:

> I once saw an excellent film in which Sarah Bernhardt figured as Queen Elizabeth. It was in a small town on the Welsh border, to which it could never have paid any manager to bring so expensive a star; and I realized that if the people there were ever to hear great plays handsomely mounted and spoken by famous actors (an absolutely necessary part of high popular culture), the synchronized cinema and gramophone was their only chance. Already they can hear the singers of Westminster Cathedral singing the Masses of Palestrina. . . . When they can see and hear Forbes-Robertson's Hamlet equally well produced, it will be possible for our young people to grow up in healthy remoteness from the crowded masses and slums of big cities without also growing up as savages.

While lamenting the moral levelling of the cinema, Shaw praised its social levelling. Indeed, the *best* work of the pre-Shavian cinema was the simple exposure of the masses of poor children to the habits, dress, manners, and surroundings of people who could afford to live decently. Eventually, he hoped, the poor would thus become so discontented with squalor and poverty and savage manners that they could force a change in the social structure. Until that happy day, the poor were at least entertained while they were being exposed to higher standards, and the children of the poor, locked out of their house by working mothers, had a harmless refuge in the movie house. Shaw published a nicely Shavian suggestion with respect to those pious members of society who were agitating to have children excluded from the cheap cinemas: "They should be executed without pity."

Aside from its power in aesthetic education and social levelling, Shaw saw the early cinema as a potentially effective means of spreading valuable social and political doctrines. Very rarely, individual movies—like the controversial silent film *Dawn* (1928), a picturization of the life and execution by the Germans of nurse Edith Cavell, and the M-G-M pacifist film *The Big Parade* (1925)—could break through the ordinary commercialism of the movies and bring such vital social messages as the peculiar horror of war to thousands of people who, in their provincial isolation, could never be reached by the medium of the stage.

Shaw's strong belief in the social power of the cinema embroiled him in numerous censorship controversies. In 1928, Shaw attacked the "dozens of films which carry the art of stimulating crude passions of every kind to the utmost possible point—aphrodisiac films, films of hatred, violence, murder, and jingoism." Two years later, the sexual immorality of the cinema had become so shocking to Shaw that he told *The Times:* "Scenes of what is politely called exhibitionism have become cinema specialties: One which I cannot describe in your columns was shown recently in a first-rate West End picture-house." Still, no matter how shocked he was, and no matter how loudly he attacked such films, Shaw remained stoutly opposed to official censorship because, he felt, censorship was both useless and pernicious. Censorship succeeded not in stopping the offenders, but only in harassing the serious author. Censorship was also pernicious because of its dangerous tendencies to suppress works which the authorities guarding the *status quo* disliked. Shaw gave to *The British Film Journal* in 1928 "two glaring instances" of films which were banned by the censor for political reasons. Sergei Eisenstein's *Battleship Potemkin*, which Shaw called "one of the best films ever produced as a work of pictorical art," had been banned as "simply a move in class warfare." And the antiwar *Dawn* was "suppressed on the ridiculous pretext that it might offend Germany."

One of Shaw's many attacks on film censorship, his 1930 letter to *The Times* defending the censored *Night Patrol*, a film which warned about the activities of white slavers who lured country girls to London under the pretext of offering them domestic jobs, actually resulted in a special meeting of Parliament, called to discuss the problem of official censorship. But no action was taken on censorship, and only three days later, on February 25, 1930, the Lord Chamberlain refused to give The Masses State and Film Guild permission to show the Russian film *Mother*, created by the great theoretician of the cinema, V. I. Podovkin. Shaw joined in the angry protests which arose over the banning. He issued a public statement in which he appealed "to public opinion to sweep this official—that is, the censor—and his powers and department into the dustbin."

In 1935, Shaw proposed his own alternative to film censorship, the licensing of all places of public entertainment by local authorities, with power to remove licenses remaining in the hands of a local committee. Now the tables were turned, and Shaw was attacked by the National Council on Freedom from Censorship, in a statement issued through the American Civil Liberties Union. "Censorships," Shaw concluded in desperation, "are the very devil."

Obviously, one of the major ways that the cinema could spread vital social and political doctrines—if it could adequately free itself from morality, commercialism, and censorship—would be to take up the doctrines of Bernard Shaw. This was possible only after the introduction of sound, when Shaw rhapsodized about the prospect of telling his audience what he really thought of them "without having the platform stormed by an infuriated mob." Shaw was fascinated, reported theatrical producer Jed

Harris in 1928, by "the idea that simply by talking at a machine he can not only be seen but heard by everybody in the world." His social message could now reach all the way across the ocean: "I can say what I want to say to Americans, sitting quietly in my study, and pocket $50,000 without any physical discomfort. Those who want to see and hear me will be able to do so as well as if I were before them in the flesh." But Shaw still did travel with his social doctrine. In Leningrad, in July of 1931, Shaw delivered a speech incorporated in a documentary film devoted to Lenin. In a news dispatch headlined, "Shaw Hails Lenin as a Pathfinder," *The New York Times* reported on Shaw's role in the film. But the prose of Shaw's speech, as given to newsmen by the Russians, was hardly Shavian: "He was a man, several of whom are in one point." And, later, "I simply testify myself as a revolutionist, but have no right in notifying your time now."

Garbled language or clear Shavian speech, the cinema of the 1920's and the 1930's was *not* ready for the dangerous plays or speeches of

Shaw talks into a microphone—about the art of talking into a microphone—in an early talkie newsreel. Photographed from the screen.

G. B. Shaw; but it was certainly ready for Shaw himself. Shaw was now able to enlarge the equipment of his personal publicity plant even though he could not yet deliver his doctrines. In 1926, a dispatch from London announced that Shaw had agreed to appear in a test film at the studio of the DeForest Phonofilm Company. But of course—as the beleaguered movie producers who were to try later to deal with Shaw the scenarist were to find out to their exasperation—Shaw was to have the final say. The film would be released only if it confirmed what Shaw himself thought he ought to look and talk like in a film. Shaw was apparently satisfied with the finished product, for in 1927 a five-minute film was released which pictured Shaw, Sybil Thorndike, and Lewis Casson discussing a projected film version of *Saint Joan*. This was Shaw's first appearance in a talking picture. His debut was soon followed by two Movietone appearances, each of which proved to be heady bits of self-advertisement, with Shaw artfully blowing his nose, making little speeches about Mussolini, and attacking the habit of beach-going. For all the rest of his years, Shaw appeared in short subjects and documentaries and news films, all the way up to a ninetieth birthday film in which he said goodbye to the public.

Shaw saw some value in what we now call "documentary" films, both because he felt them to be a precious relief from the stifling romantic fiction films of the day, and because he recognized the technical excellence and educational effectiveness of a directly educational cinema. He particularly noted the value of accelerated motion, as when the camera pictures the gradual opening of flowers. "One of the things that you are going to see on the film today," he announced in an introduction to a 1927 film called *Secrets of Nature*, "is how, when a flower falls in love, that flower opens its arms and invites embraces, and it is a beautiful thing to see. Miss Pickford could not beat it, if she went in for that sort of thing." Shaw also recognized the educational value of the cinematic technique of slow motion and suspended motion. He saw a direct educational use of the cinema in athletics, in dancing, and in art classes, where the figure in action can be stopped at the most expressive moment.

Throughout the many years of Shaw's comments on the cinema as a social force, he kept his eye on its potentialities—for spreading social and political and aesthetic values, and for direct education. Shaw saw the cinema, most of all, as a means to force people "to see farther than their own noses and their own nurseries, [then] people will begin to have some notion of the sort of world they are living in; and then we, too, shall see—what we shall see." He seemed to be always waiting for the cinema to develop itself into that means of social revolution through communication which he had envisioned in the early years. But this revolution never took place. Shaw was never satisfied with a cinema which for all its potentiality only indirectly and intermittently worked toward the overthrow of conventional morality. Eventually, Shaw began to examine seriously the potentialities of the motion picture as a form of artistic expression. Maybe all that potentiality, all that serpent's eye fascination, could be exploited by feeding into it the *art* of Bernard Shaw.

The Cinema as an Art Form

From the very beginning, Shaw looked with some interest on the *art* of the cinema, and thought of his own entry into that art. But he hoped for not nearly so much from its artistry as he did from its social force. He liked, it is true, the entertainment quality of Charlie Chaplin and Harold Lloyd, of Edna Purviance, Bill Hart, Alla Nazimova, Douglas Fairbanks, and Mary Pickford. "Clever" and "witty" was the faint praise that he gave to their "dramatic dumb show and athletic stunting." But all possible variations on such pantomime were quickly played out, and soon the "silent drama" had exhausted the resources of silence.

Although Shaw occasionally talked about the "beauty of the picture" in the silent films, and saw filmic possibilities for plots and adventures and romances, he never appreciated the silent film as an art distinct from the theatre, as plastic-art-in-motion, with unique creative functions to be found in the moving camera or in the basic silent film concept of creative montage. Instead, Shaw saw the history of the cinema as a constant striving toward the perfection of the theatre, a perfection which it could never attain while it remained dumb.

Shaw's basic criticism of the art of the silent film and the basic reason for his staying out of it was this: "A play with the words left out is a play spoiled." Shaw, indeed, always spoke of the silent films as "film drama"; and he concluded quite clearly: "Drama in its highest reaches cannot exist without speech." To Shaw, a silent movie was stage business without the dialogue. Shaw asked his readers to imagine how intolerable the stage business in Moliere's *Tartuffe* would be without the language that carries the moral meaning of the drama, or to try to imagine the scene in which Iago poisons Othello's mind against Desdemona conveyed by dumb show, or to imagine the difference between Shakespeare's Lear and anyone else's Lear if there were no language. "The omission of the words and the presentation of the mere scenario," Shaw contended, "is very much as if you offered the wire skeleton which supports a sculptor's modelling clay as a statue."

The silent cinema was crippled not only by its wordless nature; it was the victim of money and stupidity. Probably the most famous quotation concerning Shaw and the movies is the legendary Shaw quip to Samuel Goldwyn: "The trouble with you, Mr. Goldwyn, is that you're interested only in art; while I'm interested only in money." But, Shavian as it sounds, it is not Shaw. It is Hollywood Press Agent—one Howard Dietz, who was working for Goldwyn at the time of his well-publicized visit with Shaw. In contrast with the legend (although the legend *is* more in keeping with Shaw practice!), Shaw told Archibald Henderson, "You cannot combine the pursuit of money with the pursuit of art." Capitalistic, commercial control had two immediate effects upon the movies: artistic levelling and the preponderance of the vulgarly spectacular.

The "colossal proportions" of the silent cinema industry, said Shaw, "make mediocrity compulsory." Artistic levelling was inseparable from moral levelling and resulted from the same cause: the commercial necessity of a film's interesting "a hundred per cent of the globe, barring infants in arms." The result, by 1914, could be studied at any picture palace:

You have what an agricultural laborer thinks right and what an old-fashioned governess thinks properly sentimental. The melodramas are more platitudinous than melodrama has ever been before. The farces, more crudely knockabout than any harliquinade ever enacted by living performers. . . .There is no comedy, no wit, no criticism of morals by ridicule or otherwise, no exposure of the unpleasant consequences of romantic sentimentality and reckless tomfoolery in real life, nothing that could give a disagreeable shock to the stupid or shake the self-complacency of the smug.

The international silent movies were no more Shavian in their art than they were in their morals.

In ten years, by 1924, the state of the movies had not improved:

The result of the fact that movies must go everywhere and please everybody is that the movie play has supplanted the old-fashioned tract and Sunday School prize: It is reeking with morality, but dares not touch virtue. And virtue, which is defiant and contemptuous of morality, is the lifeblood of high drama.

The silent films—without words and in the grip of commercialism—were *not* high drama.

As the movies sought to level out their art in an effort to bolster up the box-office, they hit upon a popular formula which exploited their own unique ability: spectacle. The movie producers not only became too money-seeking for Shaw's approval, but, in order to make larger profits, too money-spending. They busily produced what Shaw called "a glut of spectacle." Shaw recognized as well as the producers against whom he railed that "people who understand nothing about art, and that is the vast majority, judge a thing by its cost and the cost of the film will determine its popularity." The result was so much spectacle that any dramatic imagination was overwhelmed:

Take an opium eater's dream to Los Angeles, and they will realize it for you; the more it costs the more they will believe in it. You can have a real Polar expedition, a real volcano, a reconstruction of the Roman Forum on the spot; anything you please, provided it is enormously costly. Wasted money, mostly. . . . Oh, those scenes of Oriental voluptuousness as imagined by a whaler's cabin boy! They would make a monk of Don Juan.

Shaw did have a piece of advice on how to handle the money-making, money-spending producers: "If the United States Government put a limit of $25,000 to the expenditure on any single noneducational film, the result would probably be an enormous improvement in the interest of the film drama, because film magnates would be forced to rely on dramatic imagination instead of on mere spectacle."

But the film magnates were hardly in a mood to take advice from Bernard Shaw, especially after he accused them of packing their films "full of the stupidest errors of judgment." These errors of judgment were not inherent in the art of the films; they were simply caused by the artistic incompetence of businessmen who had "imperfectly developed artistic instincts and ideals, who have their eyes fixed primarily on financial rewards." Shaw collected an oppressively long list of specific errors of judgment:

> Overdone and foolishly repeated strokes of expression; hideous make-ups; close-ups that an angel's face would not bear; hundreds of thousands of dollars spent on spoiling effects that I or any competent producer could secure quickly and certainly at a cost of ten cents; featureless, over-exposed faces against under-exposed backgrounds; vulgar and silly sub-titles; impertinent lists of everybody employed in the film from the star actress to the press agent's officeboy.

"Film people," Shaw finally exploded, "simply don't know how to behave themselves."

So the silent cinema was crippled by its essential dumbness, and was made still worse by its succumbing to commercial pressures which levelled it out to blandness in both morals and art, and which engulfed it in spectacle and in the stupidity of business-minded magnates. There is thus no point, complained Shaw, in hiring skilled dramatists to write movies. Without words, no great drama; without great drama, no great dramatists; without great dramatists, no Shaw. "Asking me to write a dumb show," he suggested in 1924, "is rather like asking Titian to paint portraits in black and white."

A dumb show could not engage a loquacious Shaw. It would not only offend his artistry but it would offend his pocket-book as well:

> Consider the reaction on the box-office. People see a *Macbeth* film. They imagine they have seen *Macbeth*, and don't want to see it again; so when your Mr. Hackett or somebody comes round to act the play, he finds the house

empty. That is what has happened to dozens of good plays whose authors have allowed them to be filmed. It shall not happen to mine if I can help it.

So Shaw found himself helpless with regard to the silent films. Although he recognized their extraordinary social force, he could not contribute to them with his most potent weapon—his art. He could do little else but attack the silent films for not being Shavian. He could not *make* them Shavian because his art depended upon words—which they did not possess. He had to bide his time until the revolution of the talkies.

In the meantime, Shaw could speculate on the ways in which this new art of the cinema would affect his own old art of the theatre. He was certain that the silent cinema would have a most significant effect on the spoken drama. The cinema was, in fact, already relieving the drama of two elements which Shaw felt held the stage back from its true glory. First, the silent film was taking away from the stage the well-made play of the French school, the kind of play on which, to Shaw's consternation, the English theatre had long been dependent. These plays of "ingenious and exciting" plot but of "worthless and superfluous" dialogue could now be shorn completely of their talk and made into silent films. They would thus be, announced Shaw happily, "finally lost to the spoken drama." Second, and also to Shaw's pleasure, "the elaborate art of scenic illusion will be hopelessly beaten and exposed by the pictures." Thus the stage would be able to return to the conditions under which the drama in the past reached its highest peaks, as in Greek tragedy and Elizabethan melodrama. The theatre would no longer attempt "the would-be deceptive realistic scenery" of the nineteenth century, for the movie-goer would soon be so accustomed to "genuine realism in scenery" that any attempt to duplicate it on the stage would look absurd. The modern dramatists thus would be given "a way of escape from the eternal realistic modern interior" and could, instead, "indulge their imagination with a rapid succession of scenes in the open air, on the sea, in the heavens above, in the earth beneath, and in the waters under the earth" with no attempt at "realistic historical pretending." The film, then, would be a kind of savior of the drama, for it would remove from the stage that "impossible scenic verisimilitude" which Shaw had been attacking ever since his theatre reviews of the 1890's.

Without the elaborate plot and the realistic scenery getting in the way of the talk, the drama—driven to higher ground by the competition of the silent film—could return to its real role:

> Film Drama will compete so successfully with the spoken drama that it will drive it to its highest ground, and close all paths to it except those in which its true glory lies; that is, the path of high human utterance of great thoughts and great wit, of poesy and of prophecy. Or, as some of our more hopelessly prosaic critics call it, the path of Talk.

Shaw had made a happy discovery. Although he could not make the silent film Shavian, that crippled art would help the *drama* to become more Shavian than ever, by clearing the anti-Shavian elements out of his path. The value of the silent film as artistic expression was thus, to Shaw, found not in what it could achieve in itself, but in what, by collecting the refuse, it left behind for the theatre. The silent cinema performed for Shaw the important function of the artistic dustman.

The explosion of sound, with *The Jazz Singer* on October 6, 1927, and with the first full-length, all-talking picture, *The Lights of New York*, in July of 1928, was a total explosion. "The silent film," says movie historian Arthur Knight, "died with alarming suddenness." And it died amid disorder, amid what Knight has called "the head-shaking of industry leaders" and the "shocked protests of the film aestheticians." But Shaw was not shocked at the death of an art which could not be Shavian. The addition of words to the pictures did not toll, to Shaw, the death of the films as plastic-art-in-motion; it merely completed the destiny of an art which had been creeping lamely toward this fulfillment. The films *could* now be Shavian, for they were now clearly literary; there was most obviously now no basic distinction between the stage and the screen. Shaw never accepted the accommodation which cinema theorists eventually made to the introduction of sound, an accommodation which viewed the talking film as a distinct art whose medium is a fusion of visual and aural elements. The talking pictures were never, to Shaw, a separate art in which sound and pictures merged into a unique cinematic expression. At this point Shaw and all cinema aestheticians part company, never to meet again.

The clearest and most definite fact about Shaw's views of the talking motion picture as artistic expression was this: the motion picture is filmed theatre; it is an extension of the literary art of the stage, with some limitations removed. The talking picture was not essentially distinct from the theatre in dramatic technique, in dialogue, or in action. This view determined Shaw's future course through the mazy world of cinema.

Shaw could not have been more definite about the identical nature of the dramatic technique shared by stage and screen. An interviewer asked him in 1937: "Do you suggest that the screen has not a dramatic technique of its own, differing from that of the stage?" And Shaw replied: "I don't suggest. I tell you flatly and violently that there is no difference whatever. The dramatic technique is precisely the same."

Shaw considered screen dialogue, too, exactly the same as stage dialogue. Now that "the importance of words in the film is recognized," words could become the basis of film art. He was ready to defend this view with some heat. A questioner at a public discussion boldly contended, in the face of Shaw: "The main function of the screen is to relate the stories in terms of moving images. Strictly speaking, speech should be secondary, whereas on the stage speech is primary." Shaw snapped back at him: "It is all very well to say, 'Now we have got the talk and we are losing the movement.' That is not the purpose or point of the drama. When you get the talkie you are in for drama and you must make up your mind to it."

Both the stage and screen, then, were drama; and drama depended upon words as its basis. Neither the stage drama nor the screen drama used natural speech such as people speak in real life. But theatrical language on the stage was the same as theatrical language on the screen, for no matter whether it was spoken alive in an auditorium or reproduced through a microphone, it was still language, and not pictures, which carried the burden of the drama. Shaw never recognized what cinema aestheticians call the greater economy of screen language, based on the cinema's ability to cut into the middle of a conversation and to cut it off after enough has been revealed; nor did he recognize the possibility of greater naturalness and sparseness in cinematic dialogue which didn't *need* to visualize by rich verbal imagery. On the contrary, Shaw lectured on the great possibilities of reproducing explicitly poetic speech—especially Shakespearean speech—on the screen, precisely as effectively as on the stage. So basic was speech in the Shaw aesthetic of the cinema that he gave to *it* the role of producing the rhythm and variety and dynamism for which the cinema theorists looked to the moving camera and the editor's shears. Rhythm and variety and dynamism of the screen was, for Shaw, not a matter of montage but a matter of "a contrast of voices." As a playwright, he contended, he had always known the importance of getting performances vocally right and varied, and this necessity should be equally basic and essential to the talking pictures.

Shaw was so convinced that the stage and the screen were not distinct arts that he often became impatient with interviewers who pressed the point. As with dramatic technique and language, Shaw was convinced that action could be identical on both stage and screen. To an inquiring journalist, Shaw wrote, categorically and crisply, all that was worth discussing on the subject: "It has been established already that stage action can be reproduced effectively on the screen." Similarly, a questioner who suggested that the screen should emphasize the pictorial, should create a kind of action—through cutting and motion and a new dynamics that would keep the movie from becoming a mere photographic replica of a stage play—was told with some pique: "Now that you have got the talkie and can have real drama you must not cling to the old techniques of the silent film. You must get rid of it." Real drama, then, meaning drama of *talk*, was the ideal of the film; and this meant creating in the film the stagelike kind of action which would keep out of the way of the language, which would not waste time showing, as Shaw put it, "gulls and cliffs and all that." Simply, concluded Shaw, "if you want to do a drama, then it must hold the audience as drama."

There is not much point in multiplying quotations. Everything that Shaw said about the talking film confirms his iron-clad conviction that stage and screen were not distinct in form or in essential technique. They were just two different methods of presenting drama, and whether conveyed by "handwriting, typewriting, cinematography, photophonography, telepathy or what not, does not matter a rap." "There is nothing new," Shaw insisted, "in the art of drama." The cinema is merely "like an instrument added to the orchestra."

But this instrument, the talking cinema, for all of its essential identity with drama as a whole, did appeal to Shaw—and even excite him—for its few minor but unique virtues. The great point about the talking picture, Shaw told his friend Adolph Menjou, is its permanence, its unchangeability. He went on to explain:

> When I am rehearsing a play I go and see it thirty or forty times—not once do they ever get it *all* right, but each time there are one or two bits which I feel are just right, but it never happens that everything is right at the same performance. . . . But in films, I suppose that with a sufficient number of trials you can get it all right?

The films were perfectible, but that did not mean they were perfect. As always, the incompetence of men interferes with the possibilities of art. "I suppose you do not always have good directors," Shaw suggested to Menjou. "Some directors may like all the bad bits and cut out all the good bits. That cannot happen on the stage, and so you never have a real atrocity as you can in a film with a bad director."

Although he failed to recognize its implications for the birth of a new, distinctive, primarily visual art, Shaw noticed obliquely one of the uniquely cinematic qualities of the motion picture: its destruction of the spatial continuum of reality. Thus the cinema could, by realistically reproducing varied settings, give the spectator the illusion of moving about in a space where distance is meaningless:

> The film can take you into the open air, over the hills and far away, up the mountains and over the seas. It can show you horses galloping down vistas of half a mile of road, or over moors and prairies, not to mention motor-cars and aeroplanes and all sorts of conditions of life which the theatre can only imitate clumsily and distressingly when it dare attempt them at all. The film transports the spectator to the very place that has been photographed.

Shaw also noticed the ability of the cinema to destroy the unvaried distance between the spectator and an object or person to be viewed: the cinema, although Shaw never quite articulated it, could magnify one object, or person, or part of a person, and thus intensify the interest of the spectator on precisely that which the author wished to emphasize. Shaw vaguely noted that the cinema could "magnify" and "intensify," and he implied that this ability applied to things heard as well as to things seen.

Shaw also seemed to recognize something of the freedom of the cinema from temporal limitations as well as from spatial ones. Although he failed to see many of the implications of the cinema's powers of exposition, of its abilities to move about freely in the present and the past like a novel, he did note—and in his later practice, he often exploited—the obvious possibility of the actual representation on the screen of certain narrated incidents which had to take place off-stage in a play. He even noted briefly the cinema's greater closeness to the novel than to the theatre in narrative technique: "The film," he said, "lends itself admirably to the succession of events proper to narrative and epic, but physically impracticable on the stage." But Shaw did not follow through on these observations as subsequent observers and theorists of the cinema have done; he did not explore the contribution of the cinema's destruction of time and space for the creation of a new artistic expression.

Shaw was, however, well aware of economic implications; he always recognized the enormous financial resources of the screen, resources which relieved the playwright of crippling restrictions on his imagination. "The resources of the screen," he admitted, "are enormously larger than those of the stage. In writing for the screen you can disregard time and space and money to an extent that would make a play impossible on the stage." He never got over the excitement inherent in the fact of unlimited money. As late as 1945, while his *Caesar and Cleopatra* was being filmed, Shaw, impressed by the huge crouching Sphinx silhouetted against a background of desert sand and sky, exclaimed:

What scope! What limitless possibilities! When I look back on my work as a young man with my colleagues in the theatre, it seems to me we were like children playing with wretched makeshift toys. Here you have the whole world to play with!

And in 1949, a year before he died, Shaw was still excited over this playing with the world. In modern films, he said, "there is no limit to scenic possibilities; and directors may spend millions of pounds profitably instead of a few thousands."

All of these freedoms enjoyed by the cinema—from change, from spatial, temporal, and financial restrictions—would certainly affect the traditional drama. We have already seen that before the introduction of sound, Shaw had thought that the silent film would drive the drama to higher ground, to the path of Talk. Now the talking film had free access to that path; and Shaw was sure that the "poor old theatre is done for." The movies were drama, but they were drama plus: "When, as at present, there is practically no limit to scenic, vocal, and financial possibilities, or to magnification, illumination and audibility, the film leaves the stage nowhere." Shaw contended that travelling drama companies, with all their burdens, could not possibly compete with the films, with all their freedoms. If the stage drama were to survive at all, it would become merely a minor institution at which people were taught to act. "Apart from that," concluded Shaw in 1930, "there will be nothing but talkies soon."

But before the freedom of the films could replace the limitations of the theatre, certain demands had to be met. The inhabitants of the dramatic world had to *prepare* themselves for their new position in life. Except for the writer: He was already a dramatist and so he needed no special preparation. Original stories could be written for the screen, provided only that the writer was a dramatist. If he was a "born playwright" the screen technique would not have to bother him. (If he was not a born playwright he "should peddle baked potatoes.") Any small adaptations that had to be made in the filming of an already existing play would, of course, be made by the playwright himself, just as he prepares his own prompt copies for the theatre. The writing of screen plays—whether original or adaptations—thus demanded, thought Shaw, not a new kind of writing. It was the actors, the producers, the directors and photographers who had to bow to the new freedoms—and the consequent demands—of the cinema.

"The ordinary actor—as such—is unsuitable for the talkies," contended Shaw. He is unsuitable because he has not mastered the "special technique of motion, speech, and song required for reproduction by instruments which greatly magnify them and intensify them." For the same reason, the reverse is true: Talkie actors are not suitable for the stage:

> The screen magnifies and intensifies and the clever movie actor knows this and does not appear on the ordinary stage. Mary and Douglas prefer to remain as the glorified beings that have been magnified by the camera. To see them as they really are would be like looking at them through the wrong end of a telescope.

Shaw knew first hand of the result of this cinematic magnification of ordinary stage movements. He told Adolph Menjou of the time he was interviewed in a talking film: "I behaved just as though it was on the stage. Everything was exaggerated to a ludicrous degree. They ought to have told me that before." Even so luminous a figure as Mrs. Patrick Campbell had to learn how to behave as a screen actress. She had a screen test but, said Shaw, "she was no good in it at all. The reason, of course, was that she had not been told to minimize every movement, because it comes out in so emphatic a way on the screen." There was only one solution if the demands of screen acting were to be met: "For the new medium we shall have to breed a race of talkie actors who have mastered the technique of moving and talking," a technique of "diminution instead of exaggeration."

Just as they demanded a new race of actors, the talkies demanded a new race of producers. Knowing movie magnates as well as he did, Shaw seemed to have little confidence in discovering or breeding such a new race, but he nevertheless demanded that before plays could be successfully reproduced as talkies, "a race of artistic producers who understand the new technique involved by magnification, and who know good work from bad when they see it and hear it, *and who don't prefer the bad*, must be discovered and placed in control of the originating performances."

Screen technicians, too, had a special job under the new freedoms and new demands of the film drama. They had to do nothing so active and difficult as becoming a whole new race. Their job was a negative one: They merely had to start their cameras, and then get out of the way. The great difficulty was "to keep the camera in its place." Shaw lamented: "It is extraordinary how much can be spoiled, if you let the photographer get the upper hand." Film techniques were constantly interfering with the words, which, after all, were the whole point of drama, even film drama. Unless these techniques are kept out of the way, argued Shaw, "they not only spoil the verse but they spoil everything else." He saw no reason why such cinematic techniques as the close-up, the fade, the wipe, the quick changes of scene and distance, could not be imposed on top of the stage play, provided only they did not interrupt the verbal drama. "You have to remember," after all, warned Shaw, that you are speaking words, "not giving an exhibition of photography."

Once the demands placed upon the actors, the producers, and the technicians were met, the film drama could assume the role that best suited it: to present "great plays handsomely mounted and spoken by famous actors." Then, when the cinema turned to its specific job of photographically recording stage plays, every corner of the country would witness performances which in the past had been limited to a few locations and a few people. There would be no need to hunt about for special screen plays because the stage and screen are the same, and thus "all good plays are suitable" for filming. Shaw himself would not be adverse to taking part in this coming of the millenium: "There is nothing I should like better than to have all my plays added to the repertory of the picture theatre."

Many advantages would result if only the cinema—"still too much obsessed with the movie tradition"—would turn to its true role. The audience, the actor, the producer and writer would all benefit from widespread photographic records of stage plays.

There was no doubt, contended Shaw, that the audience would prefer first-rate movies over third-rate plays, which, in the past, was all they could get:

I cannot imagine any provincial theatre audience being satisfied with a £50 touring production when a £50,000 talkie is being shown in a cinema. People won't accept third-rate actors when they can see and hear "stars" on the screen.

These stars, too, would gain mightily by the photographic reproduction of plays. No longer would the actor "be condemned to the inhuman task of playing Hamlet for hundreds of consecutive nights." Shaw lamented that the great actors of the past "might have been creating a thousand new parts while they were repeating old ones in tedious long runs that only wasted their talents and staled their enthusiasm!" But, perhaps more important, under the reign of the cinema the great actor would be immortal: "We shall hear no more of the fugitive fame of the actor's art which perishes with himself; for Robertson's Hamlet, filmed and recorded, may delight posterity." Or is money more important than immortality? "What prodigious fee he will get for his filmed and recorded performance," Shaw seemed to gasp, "I dare not conjecture."

The same advantages of money and fame which would flow in upon the actor, when the cinema takes up its true function, would flow as well upon the producers and writers. As early as 1928, Shaw noticed that authors were turning more and more to the screen. "What is really dawning upon them," said Shaw, "is that the screen is far more lucrative than the book." Shaw himself, of course, was not unwilling to join his fellow authors in the march to the cinema (and to the bank): "I am extremely anxious," he said in 1933, "to have all of my plays filmed before I die."

But, although Shaw was ready for the films, they were not ready for him. As he put it: "The studios aren't yet doing the class of work my plays require." The film makers did not accept Shaw's belief that the talkie was the same as the play, and that the author need make no changes in dramatic technique, in language, or in action. That was Shaw's theory about what the film *should* do, but the hard reality about what the film *did* do was quite another story.

Shaw's theories were faced with facts: the actors, producers, directors were not becoming a new race; the theatre itself was refusing to give up its ghost; the movies were not becoming mere filmed plays. The facts did not force Shaw to question his theories, to wonder if the destiny of the film perhaps lay along its own path, not the path of the theatre. Instead, he clung to his theories and attacked Hollywood for refusing to accept its "true" function.

Shaw was not the only one to attack Hollywood in the days of the early talking films. Film theorists attacked Hollywood because the talkies did not separate themselves sufficiently from the theatre, were not "cinematic" enough; Shaw attacked Hollywood because it strewed the "path of Talk" with obstacles of movie technique. Hollywood, Shaw repeated, refused to see its function as the recording of verbal stage plays; instead, it kept the techniques of the silent film, with pictures primary, and merely spoke the sub-titles. The theorists wanted the cinema to become an independent art; Shaw wanted the cinema to become an extension of the stage. No one was satisfied by the middle ground which Hollywood took.

If Shaw had assailed what he called the stupidities of silent film makers, he all the more violently assailed the talkie makers. He turned his scorn against the whole crew of them: the producers and directors, the screen writers, and the exhibitors. "Can you do nothing to stop them?" he pleaded to his friend Archibald Henderson.

Upon the head of Hollywood, Shaw alternately heaped scorn ("I do not concern myself with Hollywood. I write for America, a quite different country.") and patronizing contempt ("I see I shall have to educate Hollywood. It means well."). Shaw kept this up throughout his life. As late as 1946, William Saroyan told of Shaw "scoffing at the producers of moving pictures."

Shaw saved his most lofty, lively, and lovely scorn for the screen writers of Hollywood. In an interview in the 1937 issue of a movie-trade annual called *FAME*, his victims were the screen writers and adaptors who wanted to adapt Shaw's plays to the cinema, a process for which Shaw had little appreciation: "I object to having my plays adapted to the screen by unqualified and unknown bunglers who do not know the A.B.C. of the art of telling a story dramatically." The Hollywood procedure for adapting plays, according to Shaw, is to "send for the office boy." But he had second thoughts, and then went on to expand on his personal complaint:

> It is too evident that the adaptor could not hold down a job as office boy for a week. I perhaps should have said the bell boy. The bell boy's vision of life is a continual arriving in motor cars and going upstairs and disappearing through doors that immediately close and leave life a blank. The film firms have therefore made a rule that ninety-five per cent of a film must consist of going up and down stairs and getting in and out of motor cars. Not even the success of Chaplin has taught them that staircases are not interesting unless the hero falls down them. My plays do not depend on staircases for their interest. I am therefore told that I do not understand the art of the screen.

Screen writers, according to Shaw, had only one job to do: they had to become playwrights.

The exhibitors, too, received a Shaw lashing. These people who choose the films which the audience shall see gave them no variety; the exhibitors were, contended Shaw, "an incurably romantic" lot. "Their heads are full of the most amazing things. They believe that the public is entirely occupied either with wild adventures of the most extravagant kind, or—this they believe to be at least nine tenths of the whole attraction—with something that they call 'sex appeal.'" In fact, these exhibitors were so singleminded that Shaw suggested: "They are extremely morbid in their tastes and ought to see a doctor."

Shaw's views of the motion picture as artistic expression were, obviously, very different from the view of the movie makers and theorists. What was Shaw to do? His scorn could have only limited effect. He was not about to stand back forever from this new power "much more momentous" than printing and writing. He was itching to enter the fray.

GBS the Screen Writer

IN INTERVIEWS, at press conferences, in the midst of speeches and conversation, Shaw repeated, for many years, his willingness to allow his plays to be filmed. "My shop is open," he reminded the public in 1928, "and people can come and negotiate with me." And—big and little—the negotiators continued to come. "People seem to have been negotiating with me for many years," he concluded gloomily, "but nothing has come of it." Nothing came of it because the negotiators found that Shaw's mind was not as open as was his shop. He remained adamant: the art of the talkie did not differ from the art of the stage. Anyone who was to film a Shaw play had to film a Shaw play. The whole subsequent history of Bernard Shaw and the motion picture is the story of how closely Shaw adhered to and how far he departed from his stated philosophy of the cinema. Was Shaw a good and successful screen play writer when he was true to his beliefs or when he betrayed them? The constant attempt of movie makers was to force Shaw to abandon his theory that a good film is only a filmed play, that the film is primarily a literary art. All of the explosions in the course of Shaw's long connection with the motion pictures were caused by this basic clash in ideology: Are the movies a distinct art from that of the stage? Or are the movies merely an extension of the stage?

Movie-making visitors to Shaw used many lures in an attempt to get him to release his plays, with no strings, for movie adaptation. Shaw's secretary, Miss Blanche Patch, remembers constant skirmishes between Shaw and movie men who were "forever angling for one of his plays." Shaw himself wrote that in one of these skirmishes over film rights a visitor threatened to murder him.

Shaw must have been sorely tempted to succumb, if not to physical attack, then to the attack of Hollywood money. "It is surprising," he admitted, "what high prices Americans will pay. At first their offers made me almost ill and I couldn't believe them. When I told my friends they advised me to see a doctor." But the offers were real. Long before any Shaw film was produced, offers poured in from a *Who's Who* of entertainment luminaries: from, among others, film magnates Jesse Lasky, Sam Goldwyn, Louis Mayer, Alexander Korda, and Harry Warner (who found himself unable even to get a hearing); from actors Louis Calvert, Reginald Denny, Adolph Menjou, and John Barrymore; from actresses Mary Pickford and Pola Negri; and even from heavyweight boxing champion Gene Tunney. The most common bait was money: Louis Calvert wrote in 1915: "Will you accept one thousand pounds each for the cinema rights of *John Bull's Other Island* and *You Never Can Tell?*" By 1921 Shaw reported that he turned down ten-thousand-pound movie offers "about three times a week." On February 18, 1920, Shaw wrote to a New York lawyer: "I have already an offer of a million dollars for the cinema rights of all my plays." When, in 1926, Jesse Lasky offered Shaw $75,000 for the screen rights to *Cashel Byron's Profession*, to star Gene Tunney, Shaw replied that he thought the novel was worth $250,000 and that he wanted a hand in the casting, suggesting that Jack Dempsey should appear as the villain. Shaw established, in these early days, two rigid financial principles which he followed throughout his many years of cinema negotiation: he would not consider selling all his rights in one huge package because of income tax problems, and he always demanded royalties on a percentage of the gross income. But financial principles or money itself counted for little; the negotiations always broke down because of the clash between Shaw's cinematic theories and the movie makers' practice.

Where money proved too weak a lure, something more potent was tried. *The New York Times* reported on Pola Negri's 1928 visit to Shaw:

Pola Negri has come, seen, and conferred with GBS. Emerging triumphant from a luncheon party in Shaw's apartment here today, she announced that the first time a Shavian play is to be screened it will be *Caesar and Cleopatra* and that she will play Cleopatra. . . . Apparently, what all of Hollywood's aureate allurements could not accomplish has been achieved by the wit and perhaps the charm of woman. Not only did Shaw consent to release his play, but he made the even more astounding concession that he might alter it to suit the film. Pola Negri could scarcely talk under the strain of excitement when she returned to her hotel. "Such a g-r-r-reat man!" she exclaimed.

Secretary Blanche Patch later confirmed the luncheon and reported that Shaw's "schoolboy escapade was to write a report of the visit in newspaper English and offer it to an evening paper [*The Daily Mail*] where it duly appeared as a gossip feature." Miss Patch quotes the Shaw notice —which managed to get in some good Shavian self-advertisement—as she transcribed it from Shaw's shorthand:

It is an open secret that Pola Negri saw great screen possibilities in *Caesar and Cleopatra* when it was produced by the Theatre Guild in New York three years ago. It is equally well known that Mr. Shaw's plays have been dismissed so often by the critics as "all talk" that he has confessed to an impish desire to let them have their way by showing them his plays with the talk omitted. On other grounds, too, Mr. Shaw is known to be a movie fan. Therefore, though the official report is that nothing has been settled, it seems not impossible that Pola Negri's hurried visit to London will not have been in vain.

Pola Negri's attempts to break down Shaw's opposition to adapting *Caesar and Cleopatra* for the silent screen proved ultimately as much in vain as Mary Pickford's similar attempts two years later. Following a Mary Pickford visit to Shaw's home at Ayot St. Lawrence, Shaw accused her of being simply a "temptress." He would not succumb to her pleas for a talkie version of a Shaw play, he assured her, because she insisted on a specially written scenario instead of working from the play itself. "Is the play not good enough?" he asked. "I am waiting until the talkies are through with scenarios and are ready for me just as I am—without one plea."

The producers of motion pictures were not ready to take Shaw just as he was—without one plea. Consequently, all early negotiations between Shaw and movie emissaries broke down. The series of battles between Shaw and film makers regarding just one play—*The Devil's Disciple*—is representative of the whole Shaw versus Movies war. As early as 1926—still in the silent film era—the name of *The Devil's Disciple* came up for serious film consideration. Shaw had already had enough trouble with that "one plea" for wild adaptation that he had made a policy of turning down all film offers, lucrative or otherwise tempting as they might be. It took friendship to reawaken his serious interest. J. E. Vedrenne, manager of London's Court Theatre and long-time friend of Bernard Shaw, had become interested in the artistic possibilities of the silent film. When Vedrenne, who had presented, along with Granville-Barker, the first Shaw dramatic successes in London, appealed to Shaw for cinema rights to *The Devil's Disciple*, the appeal was taken seriously. Nobody else on earth, Shaw told Vedrenne in July of 1926, could have induced him to reconsider the whole business of films. But even so, Shaw decided to release the rights to *The Devil's Disciple* to Vedrenne *only* if he could guard against having it spoiled by its being turned into a love story. A year later, in June of 1927, the negotiations, floundering on the rocks of story adaptation, still had not been completed, and Shaw wrote to Vedrenne wondering whether an agreement ever would be reached. It wasn't.

Six years later, in 1932, now in the talkie era, RKO began an assault upon Shaw for movie rights to *The Devil's Disciple*. But negotiations had a hard time getting under way. RKO flew an executive across the Atlantic to talk with Shaw personally. Time after time, visit after visit, Shaw refused even to see the RKO man. Impatient, the executive finally demanded a reason, and Shaw sent back word: "Tell him I've seen an RKO picture."

When John Barrymore teamed up with RKO in the assault upon Shaw, negotiations did at least get started. On October 30, 1933, Barrymore wrote to Shaw that he was thinking of coming to England with his wife and children and "would love to do" *The Devil's Disciple* in an

English film production. Shaw rejected the Barrymore suggestion for a Shaw film in England, contending: "I am out of the film world here, being Victorian and very old, and yet too advanced for the poor things." But about a Hollywood *The Devil's Disciple* for Barrymore, Shaw was more cooperative, and eventually, through Kenneth Macgowan of RKO, plans were begun for a film of *The Devil's Disciple* with John Barrymore as Dick Dudgeon. A cable in the RKO archives, dated November 6, 1933, reveals the terms: Shaw was to receive 10 per cent of the gross receipts from the exhibitors, with RKO retaining a five-year lease on the rights. Shaw, of course, demanded approval of the final script.

On November 25, Shaw gave an interview to the press, announcing: "I never go about offering my plays. They are there if anybody wants them. Hollywood had the intelligence to want *The Devil's Disciple.* I am very pleased that John Barrymore is to play the lead." Shaw added that he did not intend to go to California to assist in the production, unless some fee in the neighborhood of 20,000 pounds [about $104,000 at the rates of exchange at that time] were offered as inducement, for, he explained, "Money is useful, even to an old man like me, in his seventy-seventh year." He then repeated his position about the filming of his plays: "I never objected to film producers tackling my plays. On the contrary, I like them to, for I need the money. What I always objected to was the way they wanted to film them."

And, once more, "the way they wanted to film them" was to clash with the way Shaw wanted to film them. Shaw wrote to John Barrymore:

> There is one stipulation which I have sprung on them too lately to receive a reply. This is, that Dick must not be represented as being in love with Judith. If you have read the play you will understand that Judith is a snivelling little goody-goody, as pathetically pretty as she pleases, and spoilt and conceited enough to imagine that Dick has faced the gallows for her sake instead of "by the law of his own nature." But the least suggestion that he was prowling after her instead of standing up to her husband would belittle him unbearably, and reduce the whole affair to third-rate Hollywood sobstuff. Unless I can knock this into RKO, the bargain may fall through.

And fall through it did—for the same reason that all Shaw-Movie deals had fallen through. They refused to film his plays as is; and he stuck firmly to his position that his "original text," as his secretary phrased it, "was Holy Writ."

Although Holy Writ could never be abridged (Shaw once wrote to Ellen Terry: "When you propose to cut me, I am paralyzed at your sacrilegious audacity!"), new Holy Writ could be written when required, but obviously only by the Inspired One. Many years later, after Shaw had succumbed to the magical allurements of film producer Gabriel Pascal, Shaw did admit the desirability of himself adding introductory and linking scenes when transferring *The Devil's Disciple* from stage to screen. But he refused to remake the play into a conventional movie "scenario." "I undertook to make a scenario of *The Devil's Disciple* according to the conventions," he once wrote with good Shavian sarcasm. "After I had written a practically complete history of the causes leading up to the American Revolution, together with vivid scenes from the Boston Tea Party, a close-up of Indians, and so forth, I found that the amount I'd written already needed about 50,000 feet of film and I hadn't got to the beginning of *The Devil's Disciple* itself." But, when he laid aside the Hollywood conventions, he did eventually, in the late 1930's, get to the beginning of *The Devil's Disciple.* Although no film of this play was ever completed during his lifetime, Shaw wrote for Pascal's producing firm two brilliantly Shavian introductory movie scenes, both of them in perfect harmony with the mocking tone of the original play. One of the new scenes was to show a fussing, gabbling King George III, blissfully unconcerned about "the Colonies," and even unaware of their location. The other scene was to show a foppish Lord Germain in his room in Whitehall, off to a country holiday, not bothering to send a vital military dispatch to General Howe in America. These two new scenes would have introduced the historical situation of the play in actual representation, instead of in subsequent dramatic exposition. This film project was laid aside for other matters, but, many years later, in January of 1946, when Gabriel Pascal was filled with multitudes of plans for Shaw films and was issuing almost daily news flashes to the press about detailed schemes, the old plans for *The Devil's Disciple* were revived.

Shaw searched about for his new introductory scenes and sent them to Pascal, where they were buried in the mountains of Pascal ideas. Shaw and Pascal both died before any version of *The Devil's Disciple* could be filmed. But Miss Marjorie Deans, script writer for Pascal's producing firm, has kindly sent me the previously unpublished introductory scenes which Shaw had written for *The Devil's Disciple,* an addition to the Shavian Holy Writ which I have reproduced as Appendix B at the end of this book.

Bernard Shaw won almost every battle in his war with the movies. He did not let the studios take his plays and, as he put it, "mutilate them, murder them, give their cadavers to the nearest scrivener" so that they could be turned into movies. But the price of his victory was a cinema without Shaw. Unless there could be a Shavian *The Devil's Disciple,* Hollywood would have to get along without any *The Devil's Disciple* at all. Which is precisely what Hollywood had to do—until Shaw was no longer around to carry arms in the defense of Shaviana. When, in 1959, Hollywood's Hecht-Hill-Lancaster decided to film *The Devil's Disciple,* they were offered Shaw's own introductory scenes, but they refused, saying they were not interested. The result was the mutilation and murder which Shaw feared—a love story, a traditional adventure romance, which, as he had once prophetically warned, would some day be "presented to the public with my name attached, and an assurance that nobody need fear that it had any Shavian quality whatever, and was real genuine Hollywood."

Throughout years of on-again, off-again negotiations, Shaw, in his battle against movie makers, remained victorious—and off the screen. Other Shaw plays had no more success in transferring themselves to celluloid than did *The Devil's Disciple.* Anytime someone suggested that some of his dialogue be replaced by a picture, Shaw called off negotiations. "One sentence of mine," he steadfastly contended, "is as good as any visual feast." If movie makers would not transfer his plays to the screen just as they stood, perhaps the way to create a Shavian cinema would be to write specifically for the screen? He toyed with the idea throughout his life. As early as 1926 he admitted that he was "absolutely badgered by requests from America" to write original scenarios. In fact, he added at another time, "I should say without exaggeration that twice a week for the last five years I had offers from all sorts of people, American and English, begging me to write a scenario for the films." But this he couldn't do until he was "satisfied that there is a producer who also knows his job." The producer to satisfy Shaw was hard to find. An Englishman, Charles Graves, representing Famous Players, once offered Shaw $150,000 for an original silent film scenario "of the type of *Four Horsemen* or *The Big Parade* or *The Ten Commandments.*" Yet Shaw was never convinced that the trouble of writing something specifically for the screen was really justified: "Nonsense," he replied to Graves, "I can get that much without raising my little finger. If I wrote a new scenario I should want $150,000,000." Although he didn't rule out entirely the possibility of some day writing "a play especially for the talkies," he found it difficult to face the task when he was convinced that a mere transference from stage to screen was possible: "I see no reason why *The Apple Cart*, for instance, should not be produced exactly as it stands." So no original Shaw screen drama was ever born; he just bided his time until, in 1927, he found a producer willing to lift a scene from one of his plays and to flash it, unchanged, upon a screen.

Shaw had made his debut as a film personality in that 1927 five-minute Phonofilm—synchronized picture and phonograph—of Shaw, Sybil Thorndike, and Lewis Casson discussing a projected film version of part of *Saint Joan.* Shaw the screen writer was born immediately after Shaw the screen performer—when Phonofilm producer Vivian Van Dam and director Widgey Newman recorded with this scratchy, flickering medium the cathedral scene from Shaw's *Saint Joan*, starring Sybil Thorndike herself. Except for a pirated screen treatment of Shaw's novel, *Cashel Byron's Profession*, produced in Czechoslovakia in 1921, the scene from *Saint Joan* was, as is noted in Appendix A, the first Shaw work to be filmed. And it was filmed in Shaw's way, not Hollywood's way. It was not an adaptation; it was filmed drama. Shaw had won the first round; now he was determined to bring to the movies the full-fledged glory of Shaw. It was time for his theory to be put into practice.

A dispatch from London dated August 7, 1930, broke the news of the final showdown between Shaw and the movie forces. Shaw had finally found a movie producer willing to screen an entire Shaw play just as it had existed on the stage:

George Bernard Shaw signed his first film contract this afternoon in Wardour Street, London's film centre. Although Americans had been negotiating for a long time, an English company, British International Pictures, obtained his work. The play selected is *How He Lied to Her Husband,* a work published in 1904. A start on filming it will be made at Elstree, the Hollywood of Britain, almost immediately. The cast will be all-English and Shaw will be present while the film is being made.

Shaw certainly was present while *How He Lied to Her Husband* was being filmed. He was out to prove by this film that talkies could successfully reproduce his plays exactly. Cecil Lewis, who directed this first authorized Shaw film, recently wrote to me: "You are right in assuming that Shaw considered the screen an extension of the stage. He refused to have any cuts made in the dialogue. . . . He was, in effect, not a screen writer himself; but he insisted on vetting the scripts that were made and meticulously reinserted any dialogue that was cut." The actual contract between Shaw and British International Pictures, dated August 18, 1930, was perfectly specific on this point. The movie makers, in signing the contract, bowed completely to Shaw's theories. What finally succeeded in getting Shaw's signature on a film contract was neither money nor feminine persuasion. It was total submission:

The films produced under this Agreement shall be faithful reproductions of the Play as written and designed for ordinary theatrical representation by the Author according to the current authorized published editions of the same without transpositions interpolations omissions or any alterations misrepresenting the Author whether for better or worse except such as the Author may consent to or himself suggest.

When Frank Launder, a writer for British International, tried to add a little cinematic touch to the film of *How He Lied,* he discovered that Shaw meant what the contract said. Launder thought up a scene where the young lover, in his eagerness to meet his lady, dashes into the apart-

Shaw on the set of Cecil Lewis' *How He Lied to Her Husband,* with Vera Lennox as Herself and Edmund Gwenn as Her Husband, 1931.

Edmund Gwenn, Vera Lennox, and Robert Harris in *How He Lied to Her Husband,* 1931.

ment and places his opera hat on the head of a piece of sculpture. He suggested that the camera show in a close-up that the piece of sculpture is a bust of Shaw himself. Shaw was not amused; and British International stuck to the contract, and to the script.

Throughout the actual filming, Shaw continually, in the words of director Cecil Lewis, "imposed his wishes." He did this not only by contract limitations but by his actual physical presence. Shaw had once told Archibald Henderson: "Every author should be his own producer. The production of a play is an essential part of it, and cannot be done by anyone else without an alteration of values." Shaw did not abandon this

Vera Lennox, Robert Harris, and Edmund Gwenn in *How He Lied to Her Husband,* 1931.

insistence upon his own personal supervision now that a play of his was being transferred to film. Some of the rehearsals for the film version of *How He Lied to Her Husband* actually took place in Shaw's own home, with Shaw, age 74, rolling on the floor to show star Edmund Gwenn how he wanted a fight-scene to be staged, and Shaw supervising the decoration of a Victorian drawing room, and Shaw instructing the heroine on the correct clothing of the period. Once, at the studio, Shaw even interrupted the shooting to admonish an actor that he should "look more serious."

When the completed *How He Lied to Her Husband* was shown at the Malvern Festival in August of 1931, Shaw wrote, for the *Malvern Festival Book,* a defense of the film. This article is a good summary statement of Shaw's experience with film makers, and is the closest Shaw ever came to putting his theory of screen writing into one complete statement. Until now Shaw had delivered only bits and snatches of cinematic theory, scattered in a hundred different places. Now he takes on directly the whole horde of cinema theorists. Here is the entire Shaw article, called "My First Talkie":

> To the uninitiated general patrons of the Talkies the little film entitled *How He Lied to Her Husband* is a talkie like any other talkie. To those behind the scenes it is an experiment. Like all playwrights, I have had many proposals from the great film corporations for the screening of my plays, some of them tempting enough commercially. In the days of the Movies the objection to these proposals was that my plays were made to be spoken and could be of no use as silent plays, no matter how ingeniously they were patched by scraps of printed dialogue thrown on the screen as "sub-titles." When the Talkies arrived the situation was changed. It became possible for the screen not only to shew my plays, but to speak them. The rejected proposals were renewed.
>
> But when we came down to the tacks, I found that the film corporations were nearly as far as ever from real play screening. The only business they had mastered was the Movie business; and their notion of a screened play was really only a Movie with spoken sub-titles. The only use they had for a play was to re-arrange it as a Movie in which the actors were occasionally heard as well as seen; and the movie stars, instead of putting drama into their voices, put it, as they were accustomed to, into their facial expression and gesture, and then repeated the words by rote, unmeaningly and often very discordantly. Though they had acquired to perfection the special art of moving for the lens, they had no idea of the equally special art of speaking for the microphone.
>
> In this phase the talkie art was quite useless to me. My plays do not consist of occasional remarks to illustrate pictures, but of verbal fencing matches between protagonists and antagonists, whose thrusts and ripostes, parries and passados, follow one another much more closely than thunder follows lightning. The first rule for their producers is that there must never be a moment of silence from the rise of the curtain to its fall. Hollywood would not hear of such a condition: it was, they said, impossible. To cut out half my dialogue, in order to insert dozens of changing pictures between the lines of

what was left, seemed to them quite indispensable. So we parted with reciprocal assurances of the highest consideration, but—nothing doing.

It was, I think, the great success of the talking films in which Mr. George Arliss appeared that first shook the Hollywood superstition. Mr. Arliss's performances proved that a good play could be a good play, and good acting good acting, on the screen exactly as on the stage. British International Pictures resolved to try an experiment in the new manner; and I placed *How He Lied to Her Husband* at their disposal for the purpose. Mr. Cecil Lewis, a playwright and stage producer, keen on developing the talkie dramatically, and free from Hollywood superstitions, undertook the direction.

The result can be seen and heard at the Malvern Picture House during the Festival. The points for connoisseurs are (a) that the dialogue is continuous from end to end, except when Mr. Gwenn purposely makes a silence more dramatic than words could be, and (b) that as the entire action takes place in the same room, the usual changes from New York to the Rocky Mountains, from Marseilles to the Sahara, from Mayfair to Monte Carlo, are replaced by changes from the piano to the sideboard, from the window to the door, from the hearth rug to the carpet. When the husband arrives he is not shewn paying his taxi, taking out his latchkey, hanging up his hat, and mounting the stairs. There is no time for that sort of baby padding when the action of a real play is hastening to its climax. Yet I do not think anyone will miss it. It will seem incredible that only the other day Hollywood declared that such things are the life and soul of the films.

When *How He Lied* was produced in London the young film fans complained that the conversation of my characters was such as had never been heard except in old-fashioned nineteenth century super-literary books. The poor fellows had never read anything but a Hollywood sub-title. They could not be persuaded that English people really talk like that. My Malvern patrons will know better.

Shaw now thought of himself as a screen writer: he joined the Screenwriters' Association. But he never did think of himself as a cinematician: he always refused to join The Association of Cine-Technicians, stating: "I am not a cinetechnician. I am a playwright."

Shaw felt triumphant now that he was at one and the same time and with one and the same skill both a screen writer and a playwright. He was convinced that the "experiment" of *How He Lied to Her Husband* had proved that his theories were right—and he said so in both public and private. Immediately after the film was first shown, in early 1931, he issued a public statement asserting that dramatic work is essentially the same for the screen and for the stage. "Hollywood doesn't think so," he said, "but we have proved it." Later, Shaw said the same thing in private. "He told me," writes Marjorie Deans, "that he had *proved* that you could make a film in one set, using the entire text of the original play as it stood." But apparently no one but Shaw thought the film of *How He Lied to Her Husband* was a success or felt that it proved Shaw

Barry Jones as Bluntschli, Margaret Scudamore as Catherine, and Anne Gray as Raina in Cecil Lewis' *Arms and the Man,* 1932.

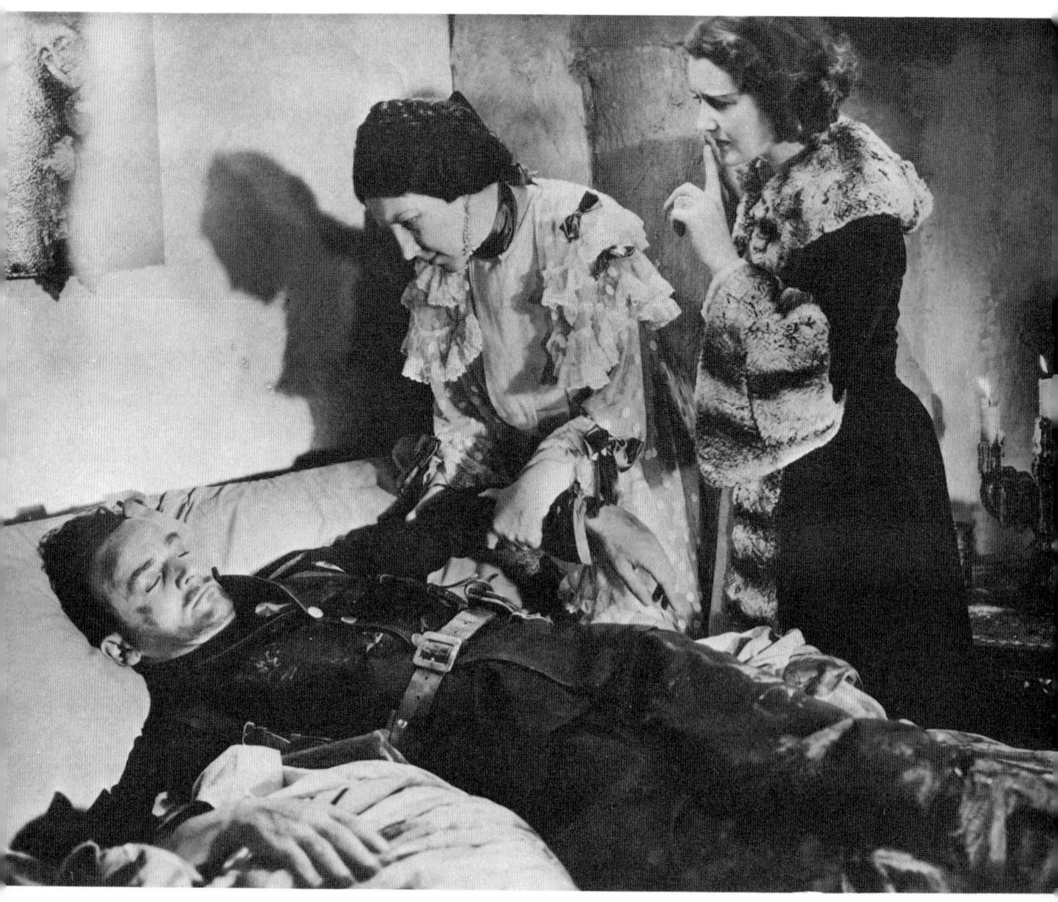

right. Although the short film cost only 5,000 pounds to produce, it still lost money. *The New York Times*, after surveying the British film critics, concluded that everyone agreed that the film "is a dull, disappointing effort." Noted critic Alexander Bakshy, writing in *The Nation,* assessed the trouble: "The film was produced under Shaw's personal supervision; and it is rather a pity, for Shaw's ideas of direction, which cramp his plays even on the stage, are little short of disastrous when applied to the movies. He evidently does not feel the difference between the movies and the stage." One New York newspaper summed up the matter by calling *How He Lied to Her Husband* "the world's biggest flop." This brought out the most delectable Shaw wrath. The newly born screen writer shot back:

> Of course the movie fan critics, who are incapable of following closely-knit dialogue and know no other dialect than Californian, are hopelessly left behind after three sentences, and fill their papers with their dismayed bleatings in that tongue.

Not a bit daunted by the icy reception given *How He Lied to Her Husband*, Shaw insisted that British International follow the same policy of exact textual fidelity in filming the next Shaw play—*Arms and the Man*. This time the movie makers were not totally submissive. Walter Charles Mycroft, scenario editor for British International, described the continuation of the same old Shaw-Movie battle:

> We set out to exploit all the possibilities of the play to make *Arms and the Man* into an exciting movie. Shaw intervened. He would not agree to a single cut or change. All he would concede was the introduction of visual action, without dialogue, between the stage scenes, as it were.
>
> I argued and pleaded in vain. The white beard glinted frostily on this fine spring day as he said, finally: "Mr. Mycroft, you are a clever man, and you are not the first to think you can improve my plays; but my plays can't be improved."

Shaw won again, and, as before, he felt elated. "Shaw was as delighted with the new film," says secretary Blanche Patch, "as a boy with a toy train." *Arms and the Man* remained a play, a literary creation, with the dialogue primary and uncut, but in this filming Shaw put into practice not just his contention that the cinema was drama—which he had "proved" with *How He Lied to Her Husband*—but he put into practice his contention that the cinema was drama-plus, that the camera freed the stage from certain restricting physical and economic limitations. Shaw exulted when the film was shown before the Malvern Festival audience in August of 1932:

> Following up the experiment shewn last year at Malvern with the little film of *How He Lied to Her Husband*, I have this year repeated it on a larger scale with the screening of a full-length comedy. It may interest those who have seen the play on the stage to note how the physical and economic limitations of the theatre are expanded by the possibilities of the picture house. In the play the incident in the battle of Slivnitza, on which the story turns, is not seen: it has to be described in a lady's bedroom. The whole action of the play has to be confined to three scenes, two of them indoors. In the picture the battle is shewn, and the flight of the fugitive whom the heroine shelters. There is no pinning of the characters to one spot: they pass in and out of doors, upstairs and downstairs, into gardens and across mountain country, with a freedom and variety impossible in the room with three walls which, however scene-painters may disguise it, is always the same old stage.
>
> As to the economic limitations, British International Pictures have, without thinking twice about it, spent as many pounds on this picture as any manager could afford to spend pence on the plainest and cheapest performance of the play.

But, once more, Shaw was alone in his enthusiasm. "We, at Elstree," wrote Walter Mycroft, "surrendered unconditionally. The film lost real money this time, and our chairman was not having any more." Neither the audience nor the critics were any more pleased with *Arms and the Man* than they had been with *How He Lied to Her Husband*. "As the reels rolled on and on," wrote Mr. Mycroft, "festivity ceased to reign" at the Malvern Festival. Drama historian Allardyce Nicoll concluded that "no more dismal film has ever been shown to the public."

British International was having no more of Shaw. And with their loss of money burned deep into the minds of all movie-making businessmen, Shaw was never again to meet a film production company which would so completely meet—and be faithful to—his demands. But, being Shaw, he remained unbowed, always contending that the two filmed plays

Frederick Lloyd as Petkoff, Margaret Scudamore as Catherine, Angela Baddeley as Louka, and Maurice Colebourne as Sergius in *Arms and the Man,* 1932.

had proved him right. "My stuff is as good on the screen," he wrote, "as on the stage."

The year after the disastrous film version of *Arms and the Man,* in 1933, an airplane with Shaw aboard was forced down near Hollywood. In a surprise visit to the place he had attacked so consistently, Shaw continued his accustomed role. He insulted actress Ann Harding, criticized another actress' hat, and, after short conversations with John Barrymore and Charlie Chaplin, left Hollywood with the promise to return some time in order to "show you how to make pictures."

But few men were willing to take picture-making lessons from Shaw.

For an acceptable film offer, on his own terms, Shaw had to turn to Germany. Throughout 1934 Shaw had a long correspondence with Klagemann Films of Berlin, planning a German-language film version of *Pygmalion*. Finally, after much bickering, on February 16, 1935, the contract to produce the film was signed. In the contract, Shaw guaranteed that he himself had written the talking-film scenario. This scenario was, of course, to be filmed exactly as written. Klagemann Films had no more contractual freedom than had British International, for all transpositions, interpolations, omissions, and alterations were again specifically forbidden. But this German *Pygmalion* was made far away from Shaw and his ministrations, and the director—in opposition to the contract—adapted freely to cinematic demands, adding several especially visual scenes. One of these added scenes might well have been the germ for the Ascot Gavotte from Lerner and Loewe's later *Pygmalion* adaptation, *My Fair Lady*. As a trial, after Eliza has had a few lessons in manners and phonetics, Higgins and Colonel Pickering take Eliza to a socially distinguished outing at the race track. From the grandstand Eliza spies an old Covent Garden friend, now an ice-cream vendor, getting the worst of a row with a customer. Eliza jumps up and gustily enters the fray, skirts up and parasol flying. Clever as such scenes might have been, they were not Shaw. It is no surprise that when Shaw finally saw the finished German *Pygmalion* film, he exploded into his own lovely prose:

There is a German film called "Pygmalion, by Bernard Shaw." The makers were bound by their contract and their most solemn promises to follow my scenario exactly. They took the most extraordinary pains, and spent huge sums, in altering it out of all recognition. They spoiled every effect, falsified all the characters, put in everything I left out and took out most of what I had put in. They thought they knew better than I. If they had, they would have been Super-Shaws. As it was, they were in the position of a yokel who buys a hat for the Coronation in Piccadilly and, finding it not to his taste, brushes it the wrong way, jumps on it half a dozen times and then proudly walks down the street in it to show how well he knows what's what in the way of a gentleman's headgear. So now you know why my plays are still waiting to be filmed.

Two years later, the same basic story was repeated, but this time the

Pygmalion film was a Dutch version. Ludwig Berger's cinematic adaptation of Shaw's play again departed from the original Shaw dialogue and staging. And, although the film was successful at the box office, the unauthorized changes again infuriated Shaw.

One would think that Shaw would have despaired of movie making and movie makers. But by this time Shaw had been captivated by a figure almost as colorful as Shaw himself, a figure who had descended upon him in a whirl-wind, leaving behind a trail of legends.

Gabriel Pascal, described by interviewer C. A. Lejeune, as "short, bull-necked and swarthy, with eyes like burnt raisins," arrived in London in 1935, virtually unknown and broke. He had been a some-time film producer and a dealer in continental films, but he had his eager eye,

Anton Edthofer as Colonel Pickering, Jenny Jugo as Eliza, and Gustaf Gründgens as Higgins in the German *Pygmalion,* 1935.

Jenny Jugo as Eliza and Eugen Klopfer as Doolittle in the German *Pygmalion,* 1935.

Facing page, above, Johan de Meester as Higgins, Lily Bouwmeester as Eliza, and Edward Verkade as Colonel Pickering in the Dutch *Pygmalion,* 1937.

Below, Lily Bouwmeester and Johan de Meester in the Dutch *Pygmalion,* 1937.

his romantic Hungarian heart, and his fervent soul—dedicated to what he called "The Miracle of Art," complete with capitals—pitched toward higher things. He had come to London to fulfill his destiny:

From my early youth I struggled to discover my own way to work miracles: whether as a scholarly vagabond; or as a pilgrim follower of Saint Francis; or as a creative artist. I tried the first two ways, and failed. After long wandering and searching, it was my predestination to meet the man who from my boyhood seemed to me to have, since Shakespeare, the greatest God-given gift of expressing the truth through art. This man was G.B.S.

Pascal had first met Shaw, according to Pascal's wife, while bathing at Cap d'Antibes on the French Riviera during the mid-twenties. In a memorable scene, as Shaw and Pascal clung to the same red life buoy, Pascal had boasted to Shaw of his artistic integrity, "fighting under the banner of Beauty and Truth." Pascal talked on, mostly about his mystical dreams, and apparently fascinated Shaw, who invited the struggling film producer to come and talk in England someday, whenever he was utterly broke, about making a film of a Shaw play. It was in 1935 that Pascal finally went to see the Master.

He had come to London, Pascal said, directly from India, where, while searching his way to become a mystic, he had been told by his guru that he had been especially chosen to spread the works of Shaw through the medium of films. Pascal described the scene of his London meeting with Shaw:

I went to Shaw and asked him to let me make *The Devil's Disciple.* This play had revolutionized our minds when I was a student, and I believe there's a great message in it. Shaw said to try *Pygmalion* first, because he thought it too dangerous to attack the masses with such strong meat. So we decided to start with *Pygmalion.* . . .

I used no arguments. I talked dramatic art with him. I told him what I wanted to do. Other producers had waved checks at him. But I spoke his [sic] spirit. My modern, spiritual, romantic way was not the dry, stuffy way that others had spoken to him. You see, I have no inferiority complex—not before geniuses or kings or anybody. I said that I would make no picture with box-office compromises. And I think the old man believed in my love of art, that's all. There's no mystery about it.

Gabriel Pascal and Bernard Shaw, in Shaw's study.

It was perhaps, in actuality, just a bit more than Pascal's love of art. "Pascal," said a neighbor and friend of Shaw's, "could beat every one in flattery. To him Shaw's eyes were as blue as the sky reflected in the two lakes in his home in Hungary, his beard as soft and white as the snow on the mountain peaks of his native land."

Even Shaw was capable of being swept off his feet. "GBS never," says Miss Patch, "met a man who entertained him more." Gabby was "a delightful creature," Shaw himself admitted, "but quite outside all ordinary rules."

"After several visits," Pascal explained, "we became friends; he was convinced that I had something to say in the artistic world. But I knew that if I did not do something drastic, our short and delightful relationship would go on for months without getting down to brass tacks." With, no doubt, much of the showman shining through the facts, Pascal describes the Shaw capitulation:

I had nothing in my pocket but an invitation to make pictures in China. I therefore said to him, on the 8th of December, 1935: "Look here, GBS, if you don't give me your rights, I am leaving 15th of this month for China, but I am ready to wait until Friday, 13th, four o'clock—which would be an admirable day to sign a contract."

He said to me: "What: Is this an ultimatum!"

I said: "Yes, an ultimatum!"

I did not hear from him for five days and the 13th came. . . . It was a quarter past three . . . it was half past three . . . it was a quarter to four . . . still no telephone call, no contract. At quarter to four, I started to pack my toothbrush and some imaginary luggage; imaginary because I had nothing. . . . Suddenly, Big Ben struck, and the door bell rang. A messenger boy entered.

"Are you Mr. Gabriel Pascal?"

"I am." And just as Big Ben was sounding the fourth stroke, he handed me a big envelope. I opened it. It was the contract of *Pygmalion* and the photo of GBS signed and inscribed: "Auspicious Day, Friday, 13th December."

The long Pascal-Shaw partnership had begun—a partnership that was to produce three Shaw films, some art, much controversy, and the banishment of Gabriel Pascal. And it had begun with the contract to produce a film version of *Pygmalion*, the film which was to depart most drastically of any approved film from the original Shaw play, and the film which was to prove by far the most successful of any Shaw film ever.

Pascal glowed mystical in his triumph: "So G.B.S. entrusted me with the magic flute of his art, which he knew I could play." The destiny of Gabriel Pascal had been fulfilled:

> To persuade G.B.S., in spite of his first unfortunate experience of pictures, to entrust me with the difficult task of adapting his plays through the medium of the screen for a world-wide audience. This was my role, given to me by God.

Providence or not, Gabriel Pascal had carried off the greatest *coup* in cinema history.

The rest of the story of Bernard Shaw and the motion picture is the story of the screen plays Shaw wrote for three films produced by Gabriel Pascal, films in which Shaw was forced to depart in varying degrees from his theory of the cinema. We can make no final conclusions about Shaw's skill and success as a screen writer until we have examined the changes Shaw made—under the influence of Gabriel Pascal—in transferring these plays from stage to screen, and the degree of success which these three films achieved.

Pygmalion

In 1937 a statement signed by Bernard Shaw appeared in a motion-picture trade journal: "We are to have a British *Pygmalion* film presently. Pascal Films have announced it. Wait and see. At all events, this time it will be an authentic Shaw screen version." Behind that "authentic Shaw screen version" lies a tale, a tale of a three-year tug of war between two mighty wills and two mighty egos. Shaw and Pascal worked with one another and against one another, but they were united in purpose in one mighty crusade: to bring Shaw to the cinema.

After that "auspicious day" when Gabriel Pascal received from Bernard Shaw the cinema rights to *Pygmalion,* the penniless Hungarian all but moved heaven and earth to get the work of the Master on the screen. His first problem was a financial one. The money did not begin pouring in the moment Shaw signed the contract. Pascal had the job of getting money from financiers who remembered only too well the financial disasters which had struck the backers of Shaw's two previous filmed plays. No one, of course, had confidence that Pascal would be able to squeeze, charm, and pressure enough changes out of Shaw to make *Pygmalion* an acceptable film. Columbia Pictures wrote Pascal that they could enter into contract only if they could "have the right to make changes in the scenario and to omit portions thereof and make alterations therein, to transpose parts of the same and interpolate therein parts of other works;

and that we shall have the right to recut, re-edit and reassemble and reconstruct said photoplay in such manner as we in our sole discretion shall deem advisable." Shaw, it need hardly be mentioned, said "No."

Eventually, others joined Pascal in the hunt for money. They heard objections that nobody was interested in the classics, that Pascal was too inexperienced, that Shaw would never cooperate in the necessary adaptations, that *Pygmalion* didn't have enough sex to become a successful film. But a financier named Nicholas Davenport formed a syndicate among friends of his in London and managed, in spite of the objections, to get together 10,000 pounds. Richard Norton, the head of Pinewood Studios, used his vast influence to round up backers. A successful flour miller named J. Arthur Rank was just getting interested in films and decided to add his support. Finally, production was arranged at Pinewood Studios in England, with Gabriel Pascal as producer, and with a young director named Anthony Asquith, who had not yet made his mark on the cinematic world, sharing the direction of the film with actor Leslie Howard. Loews was signed to become the American distributor. But financial matters never were serene. Throughout production, *Pygmalion* clung tenuously to life, threatened every day with financial collapse.

Casting was not nearly so big a problem as money. Shaw at first told Pascal that he should pay a visit to Covent Garden and pick, for Eliza, the first flower girl he came across. But, in a more serious mood, Shaw had seen a new young actress named Wendy Hiller in a play called *Love on the Dole*; he saw her as the perfect Eliza. "This is your fate," Pascal later told her. "I will make you famous." Pascal was determined to have Leslie Howard as Henry Higgins, but Shaw was suspicious of Howard's screen image as a romantic idol. "The public will like him and probably want him to marry Eliza," said Shaw, "which is just what *I* don't want." Shaw wanted, instead, a determined antiromantic in the role, and even suggested that Leslie Howard, who was "hopelessly wrong," should change roles with Cecil Trouncer, a villain-type stage actor who was cast for the small new role of a constable. But Pascal, in the first of his many victories over Shaw, signed Leslie Howard both to play Professor Higgins and to co-direct the film. Romance had won its first round. Bit parts were all filled by Pascal with unusual care and extravagance. A first glimmering of that unconcern for money which was eventually to get Pascal into much trouble now shone through: "I hired the very best actors in London," boasted Pascal, "even for extra roles. Instead of two pounds a day I paid them fifteen. And I told them, 'All right, it is an honor for you to be an extra in a Shaw picture.'"

But both money and personnel were, after all, only preliminaries. The central problem was the one that persisted throughout all of Shaw's connections with the cinema: How much would the movie depart from the play? Who would win the battle, Shaw or the film makers? "Our understanding," wrote Pascal, "was that I should put his plays on the screen as they were." Shaw wrote confidently: "Mr. Gabriel Pascal will produce the author's scenario." Shaw insisted, of course, that no additions or omissions be made in that scenario without his express permission. But the difference between *Pygmalion* and the previous Shaw films was precisely that—permission *was* given. A neighbor of Shaw's, who had many conversations with him about the making of the film, exclaimed in surprise: "He agreed to almost all of Pascal's suggestions!" "What Gabby did," Blanche Patch has written, "was to persuade Shaw to make the play presentable in the new medium. It was the biggest concession Shaw ever made to anyone."

The assembled hordes collected by Gabriel Pascal descended upon Shaw, pressuring him constantly for changes and adaptations. He complained that Pascal's studio was "immediately infested with script writers" and with "about twenty directors who spent their time trying to sidetrack me and Mr. Gabriel Pascal." This attempt to get changes out of Shaw was ticklish business, not for the faint of heart. Leslie Howard's daughter recalls that "the script writers walked on eggs when trying to cut or change any part of the dialogue." Anthony Asquith was awarded the first major encounter: he had the job of convincing Shaw to write a ballroom scene showing Eliza's triumph, a climax which never actually appeared on the stage. Asquith succeeded. But, predictably, the most effective concession-getter was Pascal himself. "I went to GBS," Pascal said, "and told him I needed several changes. He smiled and started his

Irish fight; and I started my Hungarian fight; and I think the Hungarian is more effective than the Irish because I won."

Although Shaw wrote, under pressure, much of the additional material for the film version of *Pygmalion,* the script of the film was certainly not totally his work. The first script was, in fact, not actually written by Shaw but by his former director, Cecil Lewis. Mr. Lewis recently wrote to me: "I wrote the original script of *Pygmalion* in Hollywood. It was later rewritten by W. P. Lipscomb and others." "There has been more tinkering with *Pygmalion,*" wrote Blanche Patch, "than with any other work of his." The final script did, however, have the approval of Shaw, and he even appeared on the screen in a spoken preview introducing the finished film to the audiences of the movie theatres.

As Shaw did not so completely control the script of *Pygmalion* as he did with both his previous and subsequent films, so he did not so completely control the production. But, being Shaw, he did insist on a strong advisory capacity. Pascal and I, he said, "are in business together. He doesn't move a step without my advice." Still photos of the production were sent to Shaw throughout the filming, and he managed to assert considerable influence over even minute details through his comments. "I showed him the still photos weekly," Pascal wrote, "and he immediately recognized with his critical eye the development of the characters by the players. He saw the slightest faults in their make-up or in their portrayal, or the slightest error in sets and decor, and he became my second artistic conscience." But Shaw was a far-away conscience to Pascal, and thus not a very troublesome one. Shaw visited the studio only to see the opening shots. "I don't propose to interfere in the direction of the picture," Shaw wrote to Pascal, "since I cannot, at my age, undertake it myself." Pascal, Asquith, and Howard were thus relatively free to be film makers.

Only an examination of the changes which *Pygmalion* underwent in its journey from stage to screen will show just how startling were the concessions that Pascal was able to wring from Shaw. Shaw's partnership with Gabriel Pascal moved him in his cinema practice far from his stated cinema theory. Pascal knew that if the motion picture *could* depart from the restrictions of the stage, the audience would demand that it do so. A work of art is expected to move about freely within its own limitations, not to assume the limitations of another medium. Pascal was out to adapt *Pygmalion* to the motion picture medium, not to repeat the filmed-play disasters of *How He Lied to Her Husband* and *Arms and the Man*. The medium of the motion picture itself controlled the demands which Pascal, Anthony Asquith, and Leslie Howard made upon Shaw.

The most obvious difference between the screen version and the play version of *Pygmalion* is the large amount of new material written especially for the screen. Shaw himself admitted that Pascal talked him into writing "all the new scenes that the screen makes possible and that are impossible in the theatre." These new scenes numbered fourteen, plus a written prologue. Seven of these new scenes were retained in some form by Shaw when, in 1941, he published a new Penguin edition of *Pygmalion* "technically possible only on the cinema screen or on stages furnished with exceptionally elaborate machinery." But, contrary to the contention of several commentators, the actual sound track version of *Pygmalion* is very different in dialogue and picturization from that published screen version. Indeed, the published screen version is closer to the text of the play than it is to what is presented in the actual movie. Only an examination of the movie itself shows just how extensive, and how in keeping with the demands of the movie medium, were the changes which Shaw made, or at least allowed, in the filming of his play.

The film begins with this message flashed upon the screen:

> Pygmalion was a mythological character who dabbled in sculpture. He made a statue of his ideal woman, Galatea. It was so beautiful that he prayed the gods to give it life. His wish was granted. Bernard Shaw, in his famous play, gives a modern interpretation of this theme.

This prologue not only explains the significance of the film's title for the benefit of the unsophisticated movie audience, but, introducing the romantic music which occurs again and again throughout the film, and speaking as it does of a "beautiful" and "ideal woman," it establishes the emphasis on the Higgins-Eliza relationship, a romanticization which continues throughout the film and which climaxes—in the most startling Shaw concession of all—in the romantic ending.

After this prologue, the film opens with a new, visual scene, which lasts for a full four minutes without significant dialogue, and which succeeds in establishing—in purely visual terms—the feeling of the locale. The first shot is a close-up of a violet. The camera pulls back to reveal Eliza holding her basket of flowers amid the hustle-bustle of a typical Covent Garden scene; she is surrounded by a colorful crowd engaged in inarticulate cockney chatter. Pickering approaches and listens, fascinated and amused, to the conversation about him. Then Professor Higgins is revealed, also listening interestedly. Suddenly thunder and lightning begin, and the scene cuts to a shot of milling opera-goers seeking shelter on the porch of a church next to the opera house down the street. The dialogue then proceeds with Freddy calling for a taxi, as in the play.

At the end of what was Act I, the movie adds a second new visual scene, this one lasting only twenty seconds. Yet in this short time the scene succeeds in communicating—again in purely visual terms—the atmosphere of Eliza's home neighborhood, just as the previous new scene established the atmosphere of her working locale. While Eliza and the taximan who has taken her home to Angel Court dispute over the fare (the dialogue of this new scene was included in the published screen version), the camera wanders about the narrow, dark court, probing up and down the street and alley, showing an obvious slum, with shots of garbage, dreary buildings, and an alley cat.

The third new sound track scene is, again, wholly visual. It is a forty-five-second pantomime scene of Eliza in her room, but it is entirely different from the pantomime scene which Shaw included in the printed movie version. That printed pantomime scene described, in stage directions, states of mind which would have been almost impossible to convey visually:

Eliza, chronically weary, but too excited to go to bed, sits, counting her new riches and dreaming and planning what to do with them. . . . This prodigal mood does not extinguish her gnawing sense of the need for economy suffi-

Leslie Howard as Higgins and Wendy Hiller as Eliza in the Gabriel Pascal production of *Pygmalion,* 1938.

ciently to prevent her from calculating that she can dream and plan in bed more cheaply and warmly than sitting up without a fire.

Instead, the sound track version shows Eliza dancing into her room, and then, to the accompaniment of charming lilting music, waltzing about, light and gay. She bustles about happily, stops to talk to her bird. She goes over to her mirror, stares at herself reflectively, then piles her hair on top of her head, duchess fashion, and makes aristocratic faces at herself in her mirror.

Act II of the play began just after Higgins has shown his elaborate phonetic equipment to Pickering. The movie creates a fourth new highly visual scene to let us in on the show. This thirty-five-second scene fades in on an extreme close-up of a lighted match. To the accompaniment of busy, buzzing music, the screen shows, in montage, a gas flame being lit, a flickering lamp spinning, a close-up of something that looks like radar to modern eyes. Higgins is seen in the foreground, pointing, explaining. Quick cuts throughout, then the camera moves to an extreme close shot of a human ear; the camera pulls back slowly to reveal that the ear is a cast model. Several quick shots of recording apparatus are then shown, making confusing chattering noises. Higgins speaks: "So you see, my dear Pickering, a perfect recording, amplified!" He then adds, "Well, tired of listening to sounds?" and the conversation continues as in the play.

The movie shows the preparations for Eliza's bath which took place off-stage in the play. The movie scene, which contains only nineteen lines of dialogue, is much more visual and much less verbal than the scene Shaw included in the published movie version, which includes sixty-five lines of dialogue. This fifth new movie scene lasts two minutes and is connected with the previous and subsequent scenes by cinematic

Eliza at home in Angel Court; Wendy Hiller in *Pygmalion,* 1938.

continuity. After being told that she has to take a bath, Eliza, screaming and protesting inarticulately all the while, is pushed out of Higgins's drawing room by Mrs. Pearce. Higgins interrupts Eliza's shouts, and the camera zooms in for an extreme close-up of his face as he says to her, almost threateningly: "I will make a duchess out of you!" Her screams and protests continue on the sound track as the scene is wiped off the screen like a bulls-eye shrinking into a dot, which then quickly opens up again as Eliza, now out in the hallway, pleads with Mrs. Pearce for mercy and insists upon the unnaturalness of bathing. The camera follows Mrs. Pearce as she goes to the bathroom, where in a quick montage sequence, we see shots of water faucets, of steaming water, a big jar being emptied into the tub, all accompanied by ominous music. Eliza appears at the door of the bathroom in a big bathrobe, obviously Higgins's. Mrs. Pearce says, "Now come along. Take that thing off." Eliza replies, "Oh I couldn't, Mrs. Pearce: I reely couldn't. I never done such a thing." Mrs. Pearce bares Eliza's shoulders, as Eliza lets out still an-

Leslie Howard and Wendy Hiller in *Pygmalion*, 1938.

other whoop, and the camera pans quickly to a shot of the mirror, covered with steam. Eliza screams harder than ever, evidently having just seen herself in the mirror. A towel quickly covers the mirror just as the camera settles on it. Eliza's screams are deafening as a quick montage sequence shows shots of Eliza covered with soap, a close-shot of the shower head, then the water suddenly bursting out, steaming, right into the camera. At this, Eliza lets out the worst screech of all and then several long screams, as the sound dissolves into the sound of piano music taking up the rhythm of the screams, and at the same time the visual scene dissolves into a shot of Pickering and Higgins, talking, as in the play, of Higgins's character with respect to women.

At the very end of Act II, just before the tea-party scene in Mrs. Higgins's drawing room, the printed movie version creates a scene which begins with narration: "There seems to be some curiosity as to what Higgins's lessons to Eliza were like. Well, here is a sample." The sample given, a conventional stage conversation scene, was not the one used in the actual film. Instead, an entirely new visual scene, the sixth sound track addition, was created as an example of the lessons; and it was moved to a place immediately *after* instead of immediately *before* Eliza's tea-party failure. The highly impressionistic scene drastically telescopes time, and uses some extreme technical tricks—motion, music, editing, light—to heighten tension, to break the ordinary tone of reality, to make us believe that Eliza's ordeal is an unusual one and might well produce unusual results. Here is that scene, which lasts for four minutes and fifty seconds, but which has only a few lines of dialogue:

Fade-in to close-shot of the back of Eliza's head, throbbing, as if she is crying. The camera pulls back and reveals Eliza lying on a sofa with her face buried, her whole body wracked with sobs. In the background we hear, and then see, Higgins and Pickering shouting at one another:

PICKERING. Let's call the whole thing off.

HIGGINS. Nonsense! I said I'd pass this gutter-snipe off as a duchess and pass her off as a duchess I will! [*Taking out a card*]. You see that? It's an invitation from the Transylvanian Embassy. I'm going to take her there!

PICKERING. You're mad!

HIGGINS. I tell you, Pick, that girl can do anything. [*Turning to Eliza*] Eliza!

Eliza! Stop snivelling, girl! Eliza, I'll give you another chance. Will you work? [*Close-shot of Eliza, who looks up and smiles*].

HIGGINS. Good! [*Close-shot of both their faces, framed together, slightly smiling, with a slight but unmistakable romantic suggestion*].

The scene dissolves into a long montage sequence, with Higgins's voice growing louder and sharper, accompanied by plodding and insistent music, as he demands, "NO! NO! NO!" He repeats, "NO! NO! NO!" and then, "Do it again! I've told you five hundred times! Once more!" Quick fades and cuts, showing much passage of time, and servants and teachers coming and going, coming and going. A tilted, dizzy camera cuts to Eliza, repeating Higgins's words to the accompaniment of a plunking xylophone, "How kind of you to let me come." Higgins pops several marbles into Eliza's mouth. Cut to Eliza in bed, reading *Etiquette*. Higgins comes in and orders her out of bed. Cut. Higgins and Eliza curtsy and then waltz. Pickering and Higgins dance with each other to instruct Eliza. Quick cuts and fades throughout this entire scene, much of it in shadow and in silhouette. Eliza responds to Higgins's questions with a string of honorary titles: She says, "Your holiness." He shouts, "An Archbishop, not the Pope!" She whines and cries. In several quick cuts, Eliza practices more titles. Several more quick cuts of Eliza talking and studying furiously. Higgins cries, "If I can do it with a splitting headache, you can do it." The cuts and fades grow quicker and quicker until all is unintelligible and spinning; the music screeches, faster and faster, until SMASH. The camera suddenly stops and Eliza conks Higgins on the head with an icebag. Dissolve. Higgins says: "Send for dressmakers, hair-dressers, make-up artists, manicurists, and all the rest of those parasites." And the pace begins again, as the "parasites" come and go, in innumerable quick shots, at one place the shots succeeding one another in a star-flash fade. Then a close-shot of a foot being pedicured; the camera moves up the leg to a full view of Eliza—miserable, in a mud pack; the camera keeps moving into a shot of Higgins, eating placidly. Fade-out.

Immediately after this highly visual, cinematic lesson scene, the elaborate Embassy Ball scene, which was merely an off-stage garden party

Wendy Hiller and Leslie Howard in *Pygmalion,* 1938.

in the play, begins. The actual movie scene, as we would expect, is much more visual than the scene Shaw included in the printed movie version. In this long ten-minute, forty-second scene, the seventh new sound track scene, Eliza's triumph is communicated to the viewer in visual terms, with the sparse dialogue always secondary. The arrival of the elegantly dressed Eliza and Pickering and Higgins at the Embassy, in the rain, and the awed reaction of the crowd, is much as described in the printed movie version. As the Duchess arrives at the Embassy, the crowd bows. Next, Higgins, Pickering, and Eliza enter the Embassy, and the movie exploits its possibilities for spectacle: beautiful costumes, lovely music, dancing, the camera moving in waltzing motion, mirror scenes, lovely rooms. Higgins is accosted by his Hungarian pupil, called Aristid Karpathy in the sound track version, Nepommuck in the printed movie version, and referred to as Nepean—although he doesn't actually appear—in the play version. After Karpathy moves off, Eliza joins Higgins and Pickering. She looks frightened; she mutters "Ready" under her breath, and they are announced. The three walk up the stairs amid crowds of people: then Higgins hides behind a post, watching the crowd surround Eliza. As Eliza wanders about, and is introduced to the elegant crowd, everyone gazes at her admiringly. Much social chit-chat is heard, and much questioning about the identity of Eliza. Quick cutting throughout indicates the passage of time. In the background, a woman says, "She has such a proud look. As though she belongs at Covent Garden." An imposing woman asks, "My child, my son would very much like to dance with you." The son adds, "If I may be allowed the honor." Higgins and Karpathy are seen separately taking in Eliza's triumph. Then Karpathy moves over to Eliza, and Higgins watches as they talk together. The camera shoots Eliza from a very low angle, thus making her look very imposing and regal. Eliza moves off, says to the hostess, perfectly, with the xylophone rhythm practiced in the lesson scene: "How kind of you to let me come." And the hostess responds with a gasp, overcome: "O my soul!" As Eliza turns to bow before the Duchess, the Duchess is heard to murmur, "Charming!" Higgins and Karpathy and the hostess then speculate about the identity of Eliza. Karpathy exults, as he did in the printed movie version, about her "air of divine right," and "those resolute eyes"; but in the film he adds the phrase, "those high cheek bones," especially appropriate to the very lovely Wendy Hiller. Finally Karpathy decides that Eliza must be a Hungarian princess. Pickering smiles happily. Higgins nods, satisfied. After several more elegant views and dynamic cuts, dazzling the viewer with all the spectacle, Eliza dances with a gentleman, and everyone backs up and makes room for

Facing page, above, Eliza is presented to the Duchess at the Embassy Ball; Wendy Hiller, Violet Vanbrugh, and Irene Browne in *Pygmalion,* 1938.

Below, Violet Vanbrugh as the Ambassador's Wife, Esme Percy as Aristid Karpathy, and Leslie Howard as Higgins in *Pygmalion,* 1938.

Eliza's triumph; Wendy Hiller in *Pygmalion,* 1938.

them. The camera moves back from Eliza and the crowd, giving a spectacular panoramic view of the whole lovely ballroom, with Eliza in triumph at the center, as the lilting waltz music swells. The scene fades out.

The eighth and the ninth new scenes were included in the printed movie version (but in a more verbal form) as well as in the actual film. In the movie they are both short (twenty-five seconds; and one minute, fifteen seconds) transitional scenes establishing continuity between the play's Act IV and Act V. Act IV of the play version of *Pygmalion* ended with Eliza down on her hands and knees on the hearthrug looking for the ring which Higgins has violently dashed into the fireplace. In the movie, Eliza finds the ring, then flings it down on the dessert stand, and goes upstairs in a tearing rage. We then see a mooning Freddy, in montage, hopelessly waiting at the closed door to the Wimpole Street home. Suddenly Eliza comes out of the house, and, startled, shouts at Freddy, "What are you doing here?" "Nothing," he answers. "As a matter of fact, I spend most of my nights here. It's the only place I feel really happy." After a little dialogue, as in the printed movie version, about her plans to jump into the river, Freddy tells Eliza: "I think you're the most wonderful, the loveliest . . ." and he kisses her on the cheek, sighing. He says sheepishly, "You let me kiss you!?" "Well, why not?" demands Eliza. "Why shouldn't I let you? Why shouldn't you be good enough for me? Kiss me again! Kiss me again!!" Freddy answers pleasantly, "All right." And he does. Their street scene is interrupted by a disapproving constable, who remarks, "This isn't Paris, you know!" Eliza walks away haughtily, as the scene fades out.

The next new movie scene, the tenth, is also a transitional scene. It lasts one minute, thirty seconds. It shows Eliza walking alone in Covent Garden, surrounded by a moody early morning haze. Nostalgic music from the ballroom is heard. A flower girl walks up to the fine lady Eliza and asks, in precisely the cockney dialect that Eliza had once used, "Buy a flower from a poor girl?" Eliza smiles, then, in a close-up, turns sad, and then turns angry. The play, we see in Appendix C, had narrated this scene in dramatic exposition much later in the story: In the play, Eliza told Pickering, "Last night, when I was wandering about, a girl spoke to me; and I tried to get back into the old way with her, but it was no use." (Appendix C compares all three versions—the play, the published screen version, and the actual film—of Act V of *Pygmalion*.)

The scene cuts to Higgins and Mrs. Pearce in the Wimpole Street apartment. This is the eleventh new scene; this one, fifty seconds long. When Mrs. Pearce gives Higgins his morning coffee, he asks tartly, "Didn't Eliza tell you to bring tea?" "She didn't wait to tell me," replies Mrs. Pearce matter-of-factly, "she's gone." "Gone!" Higgins explodes, as he tumbles out of bed. He paces over to the table and around and around it at increasing speed. Suddenly he shouts, "Where the devil is my engagement book? What are my appointments?" He throws the papers from the table all about the room. Calmly, Mrs. Pearce replies, "I don't know." Threateningly, Higgins mutters, "If she isn't here, confound her. . . ." And Mrs. Pearce interrupts rationally, "Then you'd better *find* her." Higgins bellows, inspired: "We'll put an ad in the newspaper!" After a cut to show the passage of a few moments, Higgins yells into the telephone, "What! You can't help us find her? What are the police for, in heaven's name?" He slams the telephone down and then turns savagely to Mrs. Pearce: "Oh I don't care *what* becomes of her. . . . Where the devil could she be?" The scene fades out.

The twelfth new scene, only twenty seconds long, follows immediately. It shows Higgins and Pickering running frantically across a busy street in Covent Garden, searching. A succession of quick, short shots shows the desperation of their pursuit as the staccato camera cuts alternately to a fountain, bustle on the street, flower girls, more bustle. Higgins goes up to one of the flower girls and demands, "Have you seen Eliza Doolittle?" "Nyo," she replies haughtily. Fade-out. The scene then fades in to Higgins and Pickering running up a flight of stairs. The camera follows them as they burst into Mrs. Higgins's drawing room, and the movie continues with Act V of the play, changed as indicated in Appendix C.

The thirteenth new movie scene is a one-minute interlude showing Higgins furiously stalking down the street after Eliza's departure from his mother's home. The scene is described on page 187 of Appendix C.

The final new scene is the most famous and most startling of all the changes which Pascal wrung from Shaw. This two-minute scene, described on page 188 of Appendix C, gives the film a romantic ending, in keeping with the increased romantic tone of the whole film. Appendix C shows that the play had ended ambiguously, with Higgins fully expecting Eliza to come back. But Shaw told us in an epilogue to the play that Eliza married Freddy. In the printed screen version, also described in Appendix C, Higgins declares that Eliza will marry Freddy, and the epilogue confirms this. In the actual movie, Eliza and Higgins are reunited, although still somewhat ambiguously, when Eliza appears at the Wimpole Street apartment and Higgins asks her, incurably Higgins-like, "Where the devil are my slippers, Eliza?" There is no epilogue to the

Above, Marie Lohr as Mrs. Higgins talks with Wendy Hiller as Eliza, Leslie Howard as Higgins, and Scott Sunderland as Colonel Pickering in *Pygmalion,* 1938.

Below, Wilfred Lawson as Doolittle, Wendy Hiller, Scott Sunderland, Leslie Howard, and Marie Lohr in *Pygmalion,* 1938.

actual film. The movie's new final scene, like most of the cinematic additions, was used, incidentally, by Alan Jay Lerner in *My Fair Lady*. The many similarities of text explain why that fabulously successful musical play and, later, musical film, were presented "in association with Gabriel Pascal" and why the Pascal Estate, like the Shaw Estate, receives one per cent of the *My Fair Lady* profits. Shaw certainly did not intend all along to imply in his film that Higgins and Eliza are to be permanently united. In the early stages of the filming, Shaw, as we have already seen, was fearful that a romantic ending might be imposed upon him. Instead, he intended to show on the screen scenes from the play's epilogue where Eliza and Freddy, now married, are described in their flower shop. Shaw wrote bluntly to Pascal: "I have to stick in the flower shop." Shaw described the shop as "half florist's, half greengrocer's and fruiterer's with a fine bunch of property grapes for Freddy to weigh for a lady customer." What kind of hypnotic powers Pascal, Asquith, and Howard used over Shaw to get him to leave out his flower shop and to approve the final ending of the film only the gods now can tell us. But Mrs. Pascal has reported that at *Pygmalion's* sneak preview, which the Pascals and the Shaws attended together, the ending of the film brought to Shaw's face "a faint smile about the white beard." And at the public premiere of the film a reporter who asked Shaw why he had allowed Higgins and Eliza to be reunited was put off by a quip and by a comment about how perfectly Shavian the whole film was. "It is too inconclusive," he later wrote, "to be worth making a fuss about."

These fourteen new scenes represent a considerable total quantity of new material. Shaw's insistence that a movie could simply reproduce a play as it had appeared on the stage had been modified by his later admission that events which for practical reasons had to take place offstage could effectively be represented on the screen. Indeed, this admission brought into the film of *Pygmalion* new visual scenes which occupied thirty-one and a half minutes, out of a total playing time of eighty-five minutes. These new visualizations in the screen version of *Pygmalion* thus account for 37 per cent of the film's entire playing time.

The professional film makers who created the actual film of *Pygma-*

lion from a script which Shaw worked on and approved saw to it that this was not a mere recorded play. Shaw's theory of the cinema was simply not followed. In addition to the fact that over one third of the film consisted of new material, many other changes prove the fact that this *Pygmalion* exploited many filmic possibilities which the stage, of course, could not offer.

The film contains a good deal of visual material accompanying the dialogue, the filmic counterpart to "stage business." The film exploits the visual possibilities of this "stage business," however, for many effects which the stage, far-away, at a constant distance, without visual dynamism, could never duplicate. The film combines elements of spectacle and movement, speed and surprise, and musical and lighting virtuosity to create a visual excitement which parallels the emotional and intellectual excitement at such climactic scenes as Eliza's lessons and Eliza's triumph at the Ball; but the film also creates a visual excitement throughout, at less climactic moments, as the camera races about, often blurring in its speed, as it tries to keep up with a restless Higgins who is often chasing after a fearful Eliza, a restless Higgins who is always pacing, always playing with objects in his hands, paper-weights, apples, vases. This motion is compounded over stage motion, for when Higgins moves, the camera moves to keep up with him, and the observer has the illusion that he himself is moving. Motion is even more dramatically felt through the technique of cutting, as the observer constantly changes the distance and angle of his vantage point.

The cinema's increased powers of visualization accompanying the dialogue are used in *Pygmalion* for increased humor as well as for increased dynamism. This use of visual humor is shown most obviously in the famous tea-party scene at the home of Mrs. Higgins, the scene which provides Eliza with her first test. The wonderfully prim artificiality of the situation is established at the very beginning, with a lingering close-up of Clara Eynsford Hill and Eliza shaking hands by daintily rubbing two of their fingers together. Throughout the scene, all of Eliza's remarks are greeted with close-shots of varying facial reactions to her shocking sentences, subtle reactions which the stage could not force us to see.

The scene is filled with long silent pauses while everyone frantically stirs his tea and we watch their faces. Thus, when the subject of weather comes up and Eliza adds two *new* lines—"The rain in Spain, they say, stays mainly in the plain," and "In Hampshire, Hereford, and Hartford, hurricanes hardly ever happen"—the camera slowly pans from face to bewildered face during an excruciatingly long pause, longer certainly than could have been maintained with interest on the stage. Similarly, when Eliza says, ". . . but my father he kept ladling gin down her throat till she came to so sudden that she bit the bowl off the spoon" we are treated to close-shots of both the exasperated Pickering and the shocked Vicar. Eliza's own later discomfiture is communicated by the close-shot of her puzzled face as she finds herself crippled with a cup in one hand and a plate in the other. After she finally gets rid of her plate, her frantic effort to succeed is shown by her imitating the whirlwind tea-stirring of the other guests, and by her holding out *all* her fingers, instead of just the little one, as she tries to drink. Finally, when Higgins signals Eliza that it is time to leave, she coolly replaces on the serving tray her half-eaten sandwich, as the camera catches the bulging eyes of Mrs. Eynsford Hill.

Much of the close-up visual humor is more fleeting than in the tea-party scene. Throughout the scene of Doolittle's first appearance, for example, he continually wheezes, as the others back away reeling from the smell, with expressions of utter asphyxiation on their faces. Mrs. Pearce at one time snatches a box of chocolates away from Higgins with the disapproving look of a den mother.

A third function is served by visual additions acting as an accompaniment to the dialogue: subtle editorial comments can be made by the position of the camera. It is an old cinematic trick to shoot a character from a high angle when he is dominated, to shoot him from a low angle when he is dominating. Thus, a very low camera and some dark shadows—a good exploitation of creative lighting as well as creative camera angle—make Doolittle very imposing, even frightening, when he says at his first appearance, "I come about a very serious matter, Governor." The most interesting camera-angle editorial comments are those which silently comment on the changing Higgins-Eliza relationship. When Higgins decides, "I shall make a duchess of this draggletailed guttersnipe," he stands over Eliza, as the camera shoots him from her angle, Higgins towering majestically high. When he tells her the conditions of her stay, "If you're naughty and idle you will sleep in the back kitchen among the black beetles . . .," he not only is shot from a low angle, but he even walks partway up the stairs so as to get still higher. And the ultimate step in camera angle as editorial commentator comes when Higgins says to Eliza, "If you refuse this offer you will be a most ungrateful and wicked girl," and he walks in front of her, blotting her completely out of view. The worm turns when finally, toward the end of the movie, Eliza asserts her newly found independence from Higgins. Then *she* is shot from a low angle, and she becomes the towering figure.

The framing power of the camera can make editorial comments as well as can its angle. Thus, early in the movie, as Higgins and Eliza haggle over the price of lessons, the camera suddenly shoots a close-up of the two of them, very close together, obviously framed into the shot. They are held there, framed together, with an unmistakable romantic suggestion.

Visual accompaniment in *Pygmalion* adds subtleties of character development, as well as visual excitement, humor, and editorial comment. The camera, of course, more efficiently and surely than any stage techniques, concentrates our minute attention on the character speaking, revealing subtleties in face or body as well as in word. But the camera can also concentrate our attention on the reaction of the character listening. Thus we are able to watch social experimenter Higgins becoming interested as Doolittle expounds his social philosophy regarding middle-class morality. And thus, in a more extended manner, during the whole of the scene in which Higgins ignores Eliza after her triumph at the Ball, the attention of the film viewer is concentrated on Eliza's reaction to the conversation, for *that* is what is essential to the theme, preparatory as it is to her rebellion and, consequently, to her finally coming to life as an independent soul. The scene begins with a shot of the inside of a door, which Eliza opens. She walks toward the camera very slowly, very dejectedly. The camera follows her as she turns on the lights. Higgins tells Pickering about his boredom with the whole affair, but the camera remains quite steadily focused on Eliza, as she listens and reacts to their conversation. The camera frames her face in a close-shot as Higgins says, "Thank God, it's all over," and we watch her shudder. The camera follows her as she gets Higgins's slippers and places them in front of him. We see her shudder again, and start to get angry, as Higgins says, "Now I can go to bed without dreading tomorrow." After Higgins leaves the room, the camera remains on Eliza during a long pantomime: she sits in the dark, the ball music swells in the background. The camera shoots Eliza's back, shaking with sobs; then it shoots a close-up of her face, weeping, and of her clenched fists. All of this is in place of the play version's and printed movie version's more obvious and exaggerated direction, which perhaps would have been necessary for communication of her reaction on the far-away stage: "Finally she gives way and flings herself furiously on the floor, raging."

Throughout the film version of *Pygmalion*, music, of course, as well as visuals, accompanies the dialogue. The cinema achieves a much greater unity of sound and sight than is possible in the theatre, not just because there are fewer sound limitations imposed upon the film maker, and because the music can be better regulated to enhance rather than drown out the dialogue, but because *all* of the sound is mechanically reproduced through the microphone and there is thus no jarring—as there is in the theatre—between real sound and mechanical sound. The music of Arthur Honegger throughout *Pygmalion* helps to set the background mood and to guide the emotional reaction of the viewer, whether romantic in the ballroom, or exciting in the laboratory scenes, or nostalgic in the repetition of the ballroom waltz when Eliza returns to Higgins.

The film version of *Pygmalion* departed from Shaw's theory of the cinema, and obeyed some of the demands of the motion picture medium, not only in the *addition* of visual material but in the economy that results from *omission* and by *replacement* of the verbal by the visual. Under the economy of the cinema, things which are shown do not have to be said. Thus, for example, as we can see by the lineouts in Appendix C, the parlormaid does not have to tell Mrs. Higgins that Henry is sending the police after Eliza because we saw and heard it for ourselves. Dramatic exposition can thus be replaced by direct representation.

Economy also results from the fact that the motion picture, unlike the stage, does not have to preserve conversational continuity. Where the stage has to move conversation from one topic to another, connected by some logical coherence, the motion picture can simply cut into that part of a conversation which it wants and then cut away. This cinematic economy is especially obvious near the beginning of the film *Pygmalion*, where much nonessential subject matter is cut out of the dialogue. Almost all of the Eynsford Hill family chatter is cut out of the film, because conversation does not have to be continuous while Eliza's presence and Higgins's eavesdropping are being established for the audience. In the crowd scenes, too, continuous but nonessential conversation is replaced by occasional remarks and a good deal of visualization.

The technical freedoms of the movie medium allow a similar economy in exits and entrances. Characters appear or disappear simply by a cut of the film: dialogue does not have to prepare for their entrance onto the stage or their exit from it. Thus all the printed movie version dialogue preparing for the exit of Eliza, Higgins, and Pickering from the Embassy Ball is omitted from the actual film version of *Pygmalion*. Pickering does not have to say to Eliza, as a kind of summary, final statement, as he did in the printed movie version, "You have won it ten times over," because we have *seen* her unmistakable triumph. Higgins does not have to say, "Let us get out of this. I have had enough of chattering to these fools," and Pickering does not have to add, "Eliza is tired; and I am hungry. Let us clear out and have supper somewhere." Instead of all this, with the economy of the cinema, when enough has been shown, the scene simply fades out—and, very dramatically, at a point of visual and musical climax.

The technique of the cinema allows other kinds of economical replacement, too. Because the time continuity of reality and of the stage can be broken by the editor's shears, series of actions can be telescoped in time and consequently increased in exitement, as in the highly cinematic lesson scene and ballroom scene, which, through editing, take up much less time and much less dialogue on the screen than they would in reality or on the stage. This economy is shown more simply in hundreds of places throughout the film, as when Higgins goes to the telephone to call the police, and the editor cuts away all the time-consuming details of the placing of the call.

The cinema's ability to destroy, similarly, the continuity of space also caused changes in *Pygmalion's* stage-to-screen journey. During the tea-party scene, Higgins does not have to exclaim out loud "Covent Garden!" when he realizes where Eliza and the Eynsford Hill's had previously met. Instead—and more naturally—in a close-shot which instantly bridges the space gap between Higgins and us, he whispers it to himself on top of the others' lines, while only we are watching him. Similarly, while Higgins and Pickering are talking about their profession in the first scene, all of Eliza's muttered complaints ("Let him mind his own business and leave a poor girl . . .") are spoken over their lines, with the camera moving us closest to those characters whom we are to hear most clearly at the moment.

Many of the minor omissions and replacements in the screen version of *Pygmalion* were due not to the intrinsic nature of the film medium but were due to external circumstances of the cinema industry. Lines and situations were changed because somewhere on the globe someone might have been offended: the film, as Shaw had pointed out, had to, for profit reasons, "go around the world unchallenged." Thus, for example, the language of *Pygmalion* on the screen is less explosive than the language of *Pygmalion* on the stage. All of Higgins's frequent damnings are deleted, and Freddy's "Damnation!" is changed to "O blast!" Mrs. Pearce's comment about Eliza not wanting to be a "dirty slut" is changed to "dirty girl," and Higgins does not call Eliza a "damned impudent little slut." Eliza does still use her "scarlet expletive," which had caused a major scandal when the play was first produced in London in 1914. But by 1938 the impact of "Not bloody likely" had so weakened that it no longer created a sensation, not even in the sensitive movies. *My Fair Lady,* incidentally, to get the desired impact from Eliza's social gaucherie found it necessary to substitute Eliza's "move your bloomin' arse," spoken at the Ascot races. The sexually scandalous, too, was deleted from the film: Doolittle never mentions that he isn't married, and so Eliza does not tell Mrs. Pearce, as she did in the play, "Her that turned me out was my sixth step-mother"; and so, also, as we see in Appendix C, all the lines referring to Doolittle's coming marriage are deleted from the final scenes.

The international nature of the motion picture also caused many specifically British references to be omitted or changed. References to Charing Cross, Ludgate Circus, Trafalgar Square, Hammersmith, Tottenham Court Road are all cut from the film version of *Pygmalion*. "Lisson Grove prudery" becomes "slum prudery." Similarly, "I'll take it down first in Bell's Visible Speech; then in broad Romie" becomes "I'll take it down in short hand." The Sarcastic Bystander tells Higgins he comes from "Anwell Hinsane Asylum" instead of simply from "Anwell." "Small talk" becomes "slang," and in one place, for the sake of identification, "dustman" becomes "garbage man"—and that is when Doolittle refers to Higgins's letter written to America.

The screen version of *Pygmalion* was also changed from the play to bring about, for the mass audience, a greater overall simplicity. Throughout the film, as is particularly noticeable in Appendix C, the structure is smoothed out and simplified, with pieces of conversations moved to other places in order to settle one issue at a time. The fabric is thus less complicated, with a substitution of simplicity for the play's interweaving of ideas and events. The discussion between Higgins and Mrs. Higgins about the motives for Eliza's having bolted is, for example, in the film completed *before*, instead of both before and after, the appearance of Doolittle.

Some of the most significant differences between the play and the film are caused by this cinematic tendency toward simplification. Several hundred lines of dialogue are cut, whole pages are lost, in an effort to narrow the story, to concentrate on the Eliza-Higgins relationship. Just as the additions tended to emphasize the Eliza-Higgins theme, so do the omissions. Doolittle's lines are the ones which are most severely cut, as we can see clearly in Appendix C. Not only details about Doolittle's background are lost, but also much of his Shavian philosophy about middle-class morality. As Doolittle's class consciousness is weakened, so is Higgins's. He does not say, for example, "Don't you know that a woman of that class looks a worn out drudge of fifty a year after she's married?" nor does he tell Eliza that as a common girl she has no possible future.

Light chatter that is nonessential to the basic Eliza-Higgins relationship, no matter how filled this dialogue is with Shavian paradox, is eliminated from the severely cut tea-party scene. And the subtleties of the Eliza-Higgins debate in the last act, again filled with Shavian paradox, are freely cut, as we can see in Appendix C.

As the social dimension of *Pygmalion* is weakened, the romantic Cinderella-like story is correspondingly strengthened. Even certain characteristics of both Higgins and Eliza are altered so as to make them more immediately attractive, more fitting as a romantic pair. Higgins is made less violent and harsh than he was in the play. He simply says to Eliza, "A woman who utters such depressing and disgusting sounds has no right to be anywhere"; he does not add, as he did in the play, "no right to live." He does not shout, "Give her orders: that's enough for her." His antiwoman and antimarriage speeches are omitted, and so is his devotion to his mother. Eliza, as a flower girl, is not quite so crude as in the play. The lines about her not knowing what to do with her handkerchief are cut, and so are those in which Mrs. Pearce makes clear the necessity of burning Eliza's hat. And Eliza, as a lady, is made even more attractive in the film because we have *seen* Freddy's devotion to her and, most significantly, her great triumph at the Ball. Later, Eliza's snobbery about attending her father's wedding is conveniently eliminated, as all reference to Doolittle's nonmarried state are cut. What remains, after a great deal of omission, is the clear and simple situation of a Galetea finally being fully created by her Pygmalion, finally asserting her own individual soul, and, becoming independent, being free to choose. She chooses Higgins.

In transferring *Pygmalion* to the screen, then, Shaw allowed, as he had earlier forbidden, "transpositions, interpolations, omissions, and alterations." The finished film, with much added and much left out and much changed from the play, opened at the Leicester Square Theatre in London on October 6, 1938. Ignoring the changes, Shaw wrote to Pascal: "You have had a tremendous triumph, on which I congratulate you and myself." Shaw was as happy with his new Eliza as he was with the triumphant new film. He told Wendy Hiller: "You've nearly wiped my old play off the map." The triumph soon spread from London to the rest of England. Mrs. Patrick Campbell wrote to Shaw:

From a friend I heard of the huge success of *Pygmalion* at the Odeon Theatre, Chesterfield, with a population of twenty-three thousand, and there were twenty-one thousand seats sold in the week. And I hear that the miners came in their rough clothes straight from the mine and enjoyed every word of your wit. And you on a percentage! You must be making more money than you know what to do with.

After working out some details with Loews, Inc., for the American distribution of *Pygmalion*, Pascal travelled to New York to witness a similar American triumph. "*Pygmalion* was a revolution from the first day in New York, understand me?" Pascal reported. "On the first day on Broadway it was two blocks the queue." In city after city, *Pygmalion* broke American box-office records. An astonished *Variety* piled up the adjectives—"big," "surprise," "strong," "hot," "smash"—as the film moved across America. *Variety* finally called *Pygmalion* "one of the wonders of post-depression Broadway" and "the Gibraltar of pictures." Pascal concluded:

America does not want little monkey stories, because they have plenty little monkeys there themselves. Everyone there is crazy for Bernard Shaw. His are not little monkey stories, you see? Understand me?

From Hollywood, Pascal wrote to Shaw: "You are a greater boxoffice star here than their Greta Garbo."

Pygmalion's success soon grew to international proportions, as it filled theatres in Canada, South Africa, Australia, and, finally, Continental Europe.

Although financial figures are a well-guarded motion picture industry secret, there is no doubt that *Pygmalion*, which at a modest $675,000 managed to keep within its preproduction budget, was a tremendous box office success. (The film even repeated its financial triumph when it was rereleased in 1944, and again in 1949.) Pascal and Shaw did, indeed, reap a rich harvest on *Pygmalion*, but Shaw contended that the film's financial success backfired:

> Suppose you have a film success and receive £20,000 for the first time in your life! That is what happens at best. Immediately you are taxed 19 s 6d in the pound not only on the £20,000 but on your ordinary earnings as well. That is, you collect money for the war and get a commission of sixpence in the pound, which does not pay for the overhead. In short, you are a ruined man, as I am at this moment, thanks to the colossal success of *Pygmalion*.

The box office success of *Pygmalion* was aided by the critics, who, as a full-page advertisement in *Variety* put it, "fan the blaze with plaudits everywhere." *The Motion Picture Review Digest* counted 112 reviews—111 favorable, and one mixed. Out of nine New York newspapers, eight critics placed *Pygmalion* on their lists of "The Year's Ten Best." Shaw won the Academy Award for the "best screen play of the year." (He later commented about the Oscar: "It's not *real* gold; it's just a sham.") W. P. Lipscomb, Cecil Lewis, and Ian Dalrymple won the Academy Award for the best "adaptation." The National Board of Review gave a special commendation to the performance of Wendy Hiller as Eliza.

What had the phenomenal critical and financial success of the film version of *Pygmalion* proved? What had been proved about Shaw's theory of the cinema? The play had been extensively adapted, both in accord with some important intrinsic demands of the medium and with the external circumstances of movie profit, when in this pull and tug between Shaw and Pascal it was moved from stage to screen. Shaw had certainly been proved wrong in his contention that a play could without adaptation be successfully moved to the cinema: a comparison between the play and the actual film proves that this successful Shaw-Pascal *Pygmalion* was certainly not merely a filmed play, as the disastrous *How He Lied to Her Husband* and *Arms and the Man* had been.

But was the *Pygmalion* film a distinctive art, a true motion picture? The answer is that the Shaw-Pascal film was neither a pure play nor a pure film; it was something in between. It was not a pure play—no successful film could ever be. It was not a pure film, for it was not, as cinema aestheticians demand, originally conceived and worked out in visual terms. It was neither pure play nor pure film; it was, instead, all that it hoped to be: a successfully adapted motion picture version of a Shaw play.

Although the play *Pygmalion* was presented successfully by Shaw and Pascal in the different medium of the motion picture, and was thus adapted, it did not become an entirely different work of art. The theme was simplified, made less paradoxical, less social, more romantic, but Shaw still claimed it as his own. The change in ending did not change the whole meaning and effect. Shaw had planted in his original play many textual hints that Galetea would be united with her Pygmalion once she became an independent creation, once he could remove the burdens that inequal society had placed on her manners and her soul, once Pygmalion could shout with joy, "By George, Eliza, I said I'd make a woman of you; and I have." Shaw had planted the original play full of dramatic conventions which focused on the Eliza-Higgins relationship, and which predicted that the relationship would be dramatically fulfilled; he only subverted our expectations after the play was over, in the epilogue, where he told us that Eliza was to marry Freddy. This subversion of the expected is, of course, a perfectly Shavian trick. But the play dramatically told us one thing; the epilogue, with a wry grin, told us another. The movie version gives us a simplified and romanticized story of the creation of a free human soul. Shaw insisted that what we saw on the screen *was* his play. When Shaw appeared on the screen in his spoken introduction to the film, he specifically endorsed the film as being true to *Pygmalion.*

We would expect to see, in the wake of the overwhelming success of the Shaw-Pascal *Pygmalion*, a new conscious development of Shaw's theory of the cinema. A successful movie adaptation of a play had to mean that certain changes in accord with the intrinsic and extrinsic demands of the new medium would be allowed. If a film is to be true to the theme and effect of the original play, it cannot be true to the original stage techniques. But Shaw had already, before *Pygmalion*, made up his mind that the techniques, language, and action of the motion picture and of the play were the same, and no amount of reality would change that. He never even acknowledged that he had made concessions to Pascal. He admitted that the *Pygmalion* film remained essentially true to the theme and effect of the play, but he did not admit that, in doing so, it had necessarily undergone important technical changes. He took full credit for the film as if it *were* merely a filmed play. Shaw cabled Louis B. Mayer of MGM, in response to congratulations on the success of *Pygmalion*:

Of course I'm pleased because I have had my own way in preparing the scenario of the film. Producers must understand that the art of telling a story is a knack you either have or don't have. Very few people have it. I am one of them.

Shaw told a neighbor that the reason the *Pygmalion* film was so much like the original was that he personally saw to it. When the neighbor told Shaw that many people thought it to be the best film ever made, Shaw replied: "It is."

The success of *Pygmalion* made Pascal as confident as it made Shaw. He took big ads in the trade papers to announce: "I promise to my friend Bernard Shaw, to my American and English distributors, and to all exhibitors that I will come up to the expectations they have in me as a Producer, and will try my best not to disappoint them after the kind reception *Pygmalion* had throughout the world." Pascal's life-work was now utterly clear: to continue to bring Shaw to the cinema. He became a naturalized Briton, bought a farm at Chalfont St. Peter, and settled down to stay.

Pascal was just as certain that *Pygmalion's* success was due to his film as Shaw was that the success was due to his play. With *Pygmalion*, Pascal announced, "I was feeling my way. Now I have the courage." And with this courage, Pascal decided to go-it-alone. He severed his relationships with Anthony Asquith and Leslie Howard; he decided to direct, as well as produce, the next Shaw film himself. But *which* Shaw film was to be the *next* Shaw film was not so easy a decision. Shaw discussed film plans with agents and writers, with financiers and with his

Greer Garson visits with Gabriel Pascal and Shaw.

favorite actors—and especially with his favorite actresses. Elisabeth Bergner was a Shaw choice for a *Saint Joan* film, but it was cancelled in a welter of controversy over what Shaw called a "Catholic censorship." Katherine Hepburn was considered for the role of Joan in another production. So was Greta Garbo. Plans for this film developed so far that a full screen play was prepared—113 pages of text plus 15 of epilogue, a script which now resides in the British Museum. Greer Garson was a special Shaw favorite. She had appeared on British television in 1937, a year before the *Pygmalion* film, in a version of *How He Lied to Her*

Husband, the first Shaw play to be televised. Now Miss Garson was a frequent Shaw visitor. Pascal headquarters soon announced that the next Shaw-Pascal film was to be *The Doctor's Dilemma*, with a cast of C. Aubrey Smith, Roland Young, Sir Cedric Hardwicke, and Greer Garson. The script was to be written by Ian Dalrymple, who had collaborated on the screen play for *Pygmalion*. Later, Pascal announced that a *Doctor's Dilemma* script had been completed by Howard Estabrook. But the announcements from Pascal headquarters flashed in regularly, contradicting one another like war dispatches: The next Shaw-Pascal film was to be *The Devil's Disciple*, to be filmed in Hollywood. The next Shaw-Pascal film was to be *Caesar and Cleopatra*; it was to be *Candida;* it was to be *The Millionairess*.

All of these projects fell through. The next Shaw-Pascal film was actually to be *Major Barbara*, "A Discussion in Three Acts."

Major Barbara

After the success of *Pygmalion* in the movies, the name of Bernard Shaw was no longer poison to the financiers. Gabriel Pascal found himself holding a financial trump card. Shaw, still glowing with the triumph of *Pygmalion,* expressed the fullest confidence in Pascal, whose producing firm, called General Films, was now allied solidly and publicly with the suddenly valuable Bernard Shaw. Pascal had the advantage not only of Shaw, but of a name almost equally valuable. Cinema critic C. A. Lejeune noted that any film producer in the world "would give his ears" for the new leading lady named Wendy Hiller. Pascal had *her,* too—on contract. The most important factor in the decision to follow *Pygmalion* with *Major Barbara* was Wendy Hiller's desire and availability to play the title role.

With the names of Bernard Shaw and Wendy Hiller waved before them, the financiers came running. Nicholas Davenport and J. Arthur Rank, in on the ground floor, again had a hand in the financing of the film. They were joined by financier C. M. Woolf. And Shaw himself was so enthusiastic about this new film that he even invested in it part of his 10 per cent (before taxes) royalty payment from *Pygmalion.*

The actual filming of *Major Barbara,* in spite of the ease with which Pascal collected the money, never did run smoothly. The war was the major villain. In September of 1940, Pascal cabled to a friend in America: "Everytime we get the camera and players set up and are ready to shoot, we must race for air raid shelters." During one week, air raids allowed only one partial day of filming. Eventually, as the film, originally scheduled for ten weeks' shooting, dragged on into double that time, the players and technicians began ignoring the air raid warnings. Even Shaw, when he was making his trailer which was to appear as his personal introduction to the completed film, refused to go into the shelter during an alarm. By Pascal's own count, Nazi planes dropped 125 bombs in the vicinity of the *Major Barbara* set. The company was often forced to travel more than 100 miles to get out of range of the constant airplane noises. Once, when the company returned to the East End of London to complete a scene which had been started there previously, the houses had disappeared.

War-caused personnel problems also delayed the filming. David Tree, playing Charles Lomax, was called up for duty in the army, but eventually was released so that filming could continue. Andrew Osborn, originally set to play the role of Adolphus Cusins, was drafted, and was replaced by Rex Harrison.

Troubles seemed only to increase the verve of Shaw. The victorious and confident Shaw descended upon General Films and almost cleared out Pascal's studio. He sat down to write *this* screen play himself. Just as Pascal had decided to direct this film without aid, so Shaw decided to write it without aid. In this second Shaw-Pascal film, Shaw alone received screen-play credit: "Scenario and Dialogue by Bernard Shaw." Shaw contributed not only the script for *Major Barbara* but—a bit more than during the filming of *Pygmalion*—his personal presence. Shaw made visits both to the Denham studios and to location filming. While watching the big Salvation Army meeting in Albert Hall, Shaw got so excited that he rushed onto the set, joining the extras in the singing and cheering crowd scene. "My apologies for interfering on Friday," he later wrote to Pascal. In a studio visit on September 12, 1940, Shaw—always interested in the verbal—complained about several language matters, especially the diction of Rex Harrison. Shaw jotted down this note to himself: "Cusins thinks that when an actor is unfortunate enough to have to speak

Robert Morley, Wendy Hiller, and Gabriel Pascal visit Shaw and his secretary, Blanche Patch, in Shaw's study during the filming of *Major Barbara.*

old-fashioned verse, he should be as colloquial as possible so as to make it sound like cup-and-saucer small talk. This of course only throws the verse away. When I write verse it must be deliberately declaimed as such—I mentioned this to Rex."

Shaw's completed *Major Barbara* script added nineteen new scenes to the material of the play. But many of these new scenes were very short and were heavily laden with dialogue left over from the play, dialogue simply placed into new, formerly off-stage settings. Most of the additions were not visually inventive. Few of them functioned in anything like the same cinematic way as had the new scenes in *Pygmalion.*

Shaw later published a *Major Barbara* "screen version" for Penguin Books. But, as with *Pygmalion,* the *Major Barbara* published screen version is actually much closer to the text of the play than to what is seen and heard in the film. Only six of the nineteen new cinema scenes were retained, in highly verbal form, in this Penguin edition, and two new scenes which did not appear on the screen at all were included in this published screen version. Always excited by the movies, Shaw explained in a note the reason for his new cinema scenes:

> The greater resources of the film, both financial and artistic, make it possible to take the spectators through the great Undershaft factory and industrial colony instead of putting them off with a spoken description; and the same is true of half a dozen other scenes for which there is neither time nor money in theatres as distinct from cinemas.

The film version of *Major Barbara* begins with a message from Shaw, flashed on the screen in his own handwriting:

> Friend, what you are about to see is not an idle tale of people who never existed or things which could never have happened. It is a parable. Do not be alarmed. You will not be bored by it. It is, I hope, both true and inspired. [Shaw included this previous sentence in his Preface to his original play.] Some of the people in it are real people, whom I have met and talked to. One of the others may be YOU. There will be a bit of you in all of them. We are all members one of another. If you do not enjoy every word of it, we shall both be equally disappointed. Well, friend, have I ever disappointed you? I hope that I have not.
>
> (Signed) Bernard Shaw

The opening scene of the film is a new ten-minute scene which Shaw called "Prologue" in the published screen version. This opening scene shows the meeting of Barbara, the rich Salvation Army major, and Adolphus Cusins, the impoverished Professor of Greek, at a Salvation

Facing page, Wendy Hiller, Rex Harrison, and Gabriel Pascal talk with Shaw on the set at Denham Studios during the filming of *Major Barbara.*

Rex Harrison, Robert Morley, Shaw, and Pascal on the Albert Hall set during the filming of *Major Barbara.*

Army street gathering, and Cusins's growing infatuation with Barbara—all of which took place before the rise of the curtain in the play. The scene is, as we would expect, more cinematic in the actual film than in the published screen version. We get to see some of the East End of London atmosphere as the camera probes about; we see by Cusins's reaction to the sermon of Barbara that he is interested in more than her preaching ability; we get some good, framed, romantic close-ups of Barbara and Cusins as they look into each other's eyes. The dialogue is not continuous: as Barbara and Cusins walk to a tram they don't have to chat

Facing page, above, Rex Harrison and Wendy Hiller talk with Pascal and Shaw in Undershaft's Office, on the set of *Major Barbara.*

Below, Rex Harrison and Gabriel Pascal during the filming of *Major Barbara.*

constantly, as they did in the published screen version; and, thanks to the editor's shears, we don't have to follow them every step of the way. The visual is substituted for the verbal: Where the printed version tells us in the dialogue that Wilton Crescent is "a fashionable address," the actual film shows us a close-shot of the two doorbells on Barbara's luxurious home, and the engraved words, "Visitors"; "Servants."

The second new scene, only 15 seconds long, shows visually and humorously the immediate *result* of the meeting of Barbara and Cusins which we had witnessed in the first scene. As Cusins had entered Barbara's fashionable Wilton Crescent home at the end of the previous scene, he exclaimed, surprised at the luxury, "Heaven help me!" The scene immediately jumps time and space, as it fades into the outside of a Salvation Army shelter. Barbara, in uniform, comes walking outside toward the camera. Then the viewer sees a huge drum coming through the door; the drum passes the camera to reveal Cusins, the cynic, now fully captured by Barbara. He is himself in a Salvation Army uniform, and is attached to the drum. As he pounds the drum with abandon, the scene fades out.

The third new scene (forty-five seconds), which follows immediately, indicates simply an indeterminate passage of time. The scene fades into a rainy, gloomy street outside the Salvation Army shelter. As Barbara and Cusins walk along the dreary street, Cusins remarks, "Remember the first time we walked about here—Major?" Barbara replies with a smile, "Yes, and you wanted to take me home in a taxi." "It takes the daughter of a millionaire," concludes Cusins, "to teach economies to a penniless Professor of Greek."

There is then a cut—it is obviously just a short time later, when Barbara and Cusins have reached their destination—to a new scene (twenty seconds) which serves as a transition to the beginning of the dialogue of the play. The setting, as at the beginning of the play, is the interior of the home of Barbara's mother, Lady Britomart. The film shows Barbara walk into the house, and Cusins walks in immediately after her. Morrison, the butler, comes to Cusins, and stops him: "Right this way, sir. Let me take your raincoat." Cusins replies, embarrassed, "Oh, excuse

Rex Harrison as Adolphus Cusins, Walter Hudd as Stephen Undershaft, Penelope Dudley-Ward as Sarah Undershaft, and Marie Lohr as Lady Britomart in the Gabriel Pascal production of *Major Barbara,* 1941.

me!" and, in his fluster, drops his wet raincoat down on the floor. Cusins and Barbara then walk into the drawing room. As they enter, Lady Britomart is saying to her son Stephen, "I shall need all your countenance and authority," and the dialogue continues as in Act I of the play, except for the elimination of all the expository dialogue between Lady Britomart and Stephen, dialogue which, in the play, had explained the relationship between Cusins and Barbara which we, in the film, had just seen for ourselves.

After a few lines of conversation, Lady Britomart says to the butler: "Morrison, go tell everyone to come to the drawing room at once." Morrison answers, "Certainly ma'am," and goes out. The film gives us here its fifth new scene (one minute, five seconds), as it includes the off-stage event of Morrison's encounter with the rest of the family, and, in so doing, adds a bit of humor. As Morrison leaves the drawing room, the scene cuts to the recreation room, where Sarah Undershaft, Barbara's sister, and Charles Lomax, Sarah's beau, are plinking at a piano and singing: "When a body meets a body, comin' through the Rye," and where Barbara and Cusins are reading. As Morrison enters the room, Charles goes into another song, with Sarah joining in, singing: "He has a message from her ladyship." Sarah says, "Come along Morrison, now, you must sing it." They all insist. Morrison clears his throat and sings: "Her ladyship requires your presence in the drawing room." They all cheer. The scene cuts to a shot of them all walking into the drawing room, where Barbara says, "Mother, are Cholly and Dolly to come in?" And the dialogue then continues as in the play.

The sixth new movie scene (one minute) serves, like the previous new scene, to break up the play's long unbroken conversation in Lady Britomart's drawing room. It shows the off-stage event of the home-coming of the head of the household: the long-absent Andrew Undershaft, "The Cannon King! The rival of Krupp and Skoda! The multi-millionaire!!"—as Cusins previously had so excitedly phrased it. Undershaft had separated from Lady Britomart, when Barbara was a little girl, because he had insisted upon continuing the strange tradition of passing the management of the Undershaft-Lazarus factory to a foundling. He has been summoned to his family by Lady Britomart in order to settle more money upon his daughters and to deal with the troublesome problem of son Stephen's profession. The film adds both humor and suspense by breaking away from the drawing room to the off-stage event of Undershaft's arrival at the Wilton Crescent home. In the play, Morrison simply announced Undershaft's arrival, and he walked in. In the film, Morrison comes in, announces Undershaft, and then walks down the stairs, with the camera following him, to the accompaniment of light but suspenseful music. The camera approaches the back of Undershaft. Then the scene cuts swiftly back to the drawing room for a few lines of expectant dialogue from the family. Then another quick cut, showing, as only the cinema can, simultaneous action. We see the back of Undershaft as he walks up the stairs. As he steps into the drawing room, the sound track music plays a fanfare, and everyone in the room jumps up and snaps to attention. At the moment that Morrison intones Undershaft's name, the camera shoots a close-shot of the glowing, grinning face of actor Robert Morley. We thus see Undershaft for the first time at a point of heightened dramatic interest. As Lady Britomart says, "Good evening, Andrew," the music becomes soft and gentle, and we are given a very favorable first impression of Undershaft. The dialogue then continues as in the play. After Undershaft wrongly identifies all the members of his family, the film adds a small bit which shows that this terrible figure is well remembered and well loved by his servant. Morrison appears at the door with a mug and Undershaft asks him, "What on earth is this, Morrison?" "Your hot lemon and ginger, sir," the servant replies. "You always have it at a quarter past nine." Undershaft grins: "Your memory seems to be a great deal better than mine." The dialogue of Act I then continues again.

The seventh new scene, lasting only thirty seconds, shows us a part of Barbara's home religious service which was merely referred to at the end of Act I of the play. The camera follows Barbara and her father as they move out of the drawing room to the nursery, where the service is already under way. As Barbara invites Undershaft to visit her Salvation Army shelter, we hear "Onward Christian Soldiers" coming from the nursery. They enter the room. We see Cusins at the organ, singing with gusto, aided by Sarah and Charles. Lady Britomart enters the room and lets herself down into a chair, with resignation. Barbara and Undershaft, in close-up, look into one another's eyes and smile, already in obvious close and tender sympathy with each other. The "Onward Christian Soldiers" music continues, but suddenly it is played by brass instruments instead of the organ. As the music continues, the scene changes. The eighth new scene (also thirty seconds long) is thus linked by music with the previous scene. The new scene serves as a smooth, nicely cinematic, transition between the play's Act I and Act II. It begins with a close-shot of a flag at the moment that the brass takes over the music from the organ. The camera pulls back a little from the flag and reveals

that it is a Salvation Army flag. The camera pulls back still further and reveals a parade, marching along to the tune of "Onward Christian Soldiers." Barbara is marching happily along at the front of the parade, with children running gaily beside her. The shot cuts to children waving from dingy windows as the parade marches along. The camera follows the parade as it marches into the shabby yard of the Limehouse Shelter of the Salvation Army. Vagrants are revealed sitting about, eating and talking. The viewer is thus introduced to the neighborhood of the shelter at which the action of Act II will take place. The dialogue, between a man and a woman in the yard, begins as in the play.

The ninth new scene, thirty-five seconds long, breaks up the long conversational scene in which Rummy Mitchens (Marie Ault) and Snobby Price (Emlyn Williams), pretending to be sinners, are revealed free-loading, with some cynicism, on the Salvation Army's charity. In the play, Bill Walker makes his entrance by simply bursting onto the stage. But in the film, the scene cuts to outside the shelter and shows us his approach. With our attention focused exclusively on Bill Walker (Robert Newton), we watch him walk to the fence and glower at the young Salvation Army aide, Jenny Hill (Deborah Kerr), as she runs down the shelter stairs into the yard. Bill kicks down the fence. A ragged, whore-like woman comes up to Bill and greets him, but he roughly shoves her aside, stalks into the yard, glares at Jenny, and accuses her, as in the play, of stealing his girl for the sake of the Salvation Army.

Later, the play's continual dialogue is similarly interrupted to show us, in the tenth new scene, only twenty seconds long, Undershaft's arrival outside the Salvation Army shelter. In the play, he simply walked onto the stage. In the film, we watch him arrive outside in a big black shiny Rolls-Royce, as the children of the neighborhood flock around fascinated at the unaccustomed sight. He speaks gently and kindly to a little girl

Facing page, above, Robert Morley as Undershaft and Wendy Hiller as Barbara in *Major Barbara,* 1941.

Below, Barbara interviews Bill Walker; Wendy Hiller and Robert Newton in *Major Barbara,* 1941.

who has fallen. Then the scene cuts back into the interior of the shelter for some conversation between Rummy and Peter Shirley, the old outcast; and then the scene cuts back again to the outside of the shelter. Peter is shown in a window looking down on the commotion caused by Undershaft's arrival. Barbara comes out to meet Undershaft, who is just finishing smoothing out the incident of the fallen little girl. Barbara picks up the girl, and greets her father. After a few lines of dialogue, Peter closes the window. The camera tracks in to a shot of the outside of the window; then suddenly the scene cuts to a shot of the inside of the window. Barbara and Undershaft, who are now—with good filmic economy—*inside* the shelter, walk up to Peter and talk as in the play.

The eleventh new scene, which takes place later in Act II, is a substantial one, five minutes long. It shows Bill Walker's challenge to wres-

Undershaft visits Barbara at the Salvation Army Shelter; Robert Morley and Wendy Hiller in *Major Barbara,* 1941.

tler Todger Fairmile, who is now a Salvation Army preacher. Its function, like most of the new scenes, is simply to show off-stage events. In the play, Bill only described the event to Barbara. In the published screen version, a scene similar to the one in the actual film, but more verbal, is presented in flash-back as Bill tells of it. But in the actual film, the whole scene, so as to show simultaneous action, is cut into the midst of the conversation in which Barbara is telling her father about the desperate financial plight of the Army. It begins with a shot of Bill running along a dock. A ship whistle is heard, as the camera pulls back and sweeps along, showing a panoramic view of the whole harbor neighborhood. Bill hears Salvation Army music, stops to scratch the back of his head, puzzled as to where it comes from. Then the scene cuts to a shot of a Salvation Army band, led by Todger and by Bill's former girl, Mog. Bill approaches and sees Todger and Mog. The scene then cuts to the inside of a public bar, evidently in the neighborhood. Bill enters, orders, lights a cigarette. The waiter brings his beer; Bill nervously guzzles it down in one gulp, then walks out of the bar. The camera follows Bill as he walks along the river, approaching again the Salvation Army gathering, his courage now bolstered. Bill and Todger begin verbal sparring, in dialogue similar to that of the printed movie version, until Todger forces Bill down on his knees to join the group in prayer.

The twelfth new scene is only ten seconds long. Just as the General (Dame Sybil Thorndyke) is entering the Salvation Army shelter, after Bill's soul has been worked on by both Barbara and by Todger Fairmile, the movie adds a two-sentence scene between Undershaft and Bill Walker. Undershaft gives his card to Bill and says quietly, "Mr. Walker, perhaps we can help each other. You'd better come and see me." "I don't want your charity," Bill replies indignantly. Undershaft says, "It's not charity I'm offering you, it's work." This scene sets up the reappearance of Bill Walker in the final scene at the Undershaft factory, and is part of what we shall see is added prominence given to Bill in the movie version.

Snobby Price's encounter with his mother is the thirteenth new scene, this one twenty-five seconds long. It creates good visual humor in a

Rex Harrison as Adolphus Cusins and Wendy Hiller as Barbara, with Dame Sybil Thorndyke as the General, in *Major Barbara,* 1941.

newly invented scene which shows the *result* of Snobby's false public confession of mother-beating. It serves as another interruption to the conversation of the play's Act II. Snobby's mother is shown, in a series of quick cuts, storming about the shelter with determination and fury. Finally she bounds into the room where all the characters are talking. She grabs Snobby by the collar, and then picks him up bodily and rolls him down the stairs, screeching at him all the while. After he scrambles to his feet and runs away terrified, she chases after him, screaming, "Who's been beatin' whose mother?!"

Off-stage events are brought into view for the sake of lively spectacle and touching contrast in the fourteenth new scene, forty-five seconds long. Just after the General accepts Undershaft's money, and hence plunges Barbara into despair as her ideal of the Army is crushed by its accepting money with blood on it, the movie shows Cusins organizing a wild—almost hysterical—parade to Albert Hall for the big Salvation Army meeting at which Undershaft's gift is to be announced. Cusins shouts to the Salvation Army workers outside the shelter, "Our shelter is saved!" He is answered by a chorus of cheers. He shouts again, "The Army's saved!" He is answered by a louder chorus of cheers. He shouts for a third time, "Everybody's saved!" He is answered by a still louder chorus of cheers. Everyone both inside and outside (except Barbara) shouts "Glory Hallelujah!" The band members grab their instruments; Cusins grabs the Salvation Army flag. He leads the way out the door, a parade forming behind him. After a cut back to the General, who invites Undershaft to march in the parade with them, and after some dialogue in which Barbara expresses despair, the scene cuts back—showing simultananeous action—to the forming parade. Jenny Hill shouts, "Glory Hallelujah!" as she flourishes her tambourine and marches away. The crowd answers Jenny's shout with a tremendous shout of "Glory Hallelujah!" Cusins commands, "Play up, there! Immenso Giubilo!!" The parade moves off, full of enthusiasm—the camera follows it down the street. The scene cuts back to a close-shot of Barbara, dejected, in great contrast to everyone else. Once more the scene cuts to excited, jubilant paraders marching away, singing and shouting. The camera catches Undershaft, who yells to Cusins, "My ducats and my daughter!" Cusins yells back, "Money and gunpowder!" The camera cuts back once more to Barbara, who groans, in close-up, "My God, why hast Thou forsaken me?" The scene continues, as in the play, with Bill Walker's taunts, and with his realization that Snobby Price has stolen his money, and with Barbara's attempts to give some hope to outcast Peter Shirley. The dialogue for the rest of the scene is similar to that at the end of Act II of the play. As Barbara and Peter walk off together into the darkness, the music swells to an emotional climax. The camera now remains stationary, and watches them grow smaller and indistinct. Before the scene fades out, the camera lingers on the solemn and depressing scene of a slum street, a scene accompanied with sorrowful music. Then a very slow fade-out.

Three transition scenes in a row are added to the movie at this point, between the dialogue of the play's Act II and Act III. The printed movie version adds still another transition scene, a conversation between Barbara and Peter "outside an unpretentious eating house."

Shaw decided to include in his screen play the spectacular Salvation Army meeting which takes place off-stage in the play. This same scene was also represented, in shorter form, in the printed screen version. For this fifteenth new movie scene, lasting four minutes, fifteen seconds, Shaw changes the site from the Assembly Hall in the Mile End Road to the more spectacular Albert Hall. He also changes the dialogue so that the number of people at the meeting is increased from 1,000 to 5,000. The scene opens in great contrast to the previous sorrowful slum scene with its slow fade-out: A sudden, startling burst of gay band music is heard as a low camera looks up to a towering, majestic figure—the leader of the combined Salvation Army bands. A fast-moving, sweeping camera moves back to take in all the excitement of the packed Albert Hall. Silence falls as the leader of the band prepares to speak. The leader intones, "Let us pray," and everyone in the huge congregation immediately either bows or kneels. The camera, now suddenly still, soon begins to pull back slowly, showing the entire soundless Hall. In a medium-shot, the leader, after a pause, says, "Amen." And immediately, he announces, "The General!" The entire congregation jumps up cheering; the camera pulls back again for another panoramic view of the excited Hall. The film scene continues, as in the printed movie version, with the General's speech announcing that the Salvation Army has been saved by an anonymous benefactor, and with the conversation, now in the cloakroom, in which Undershaft invites Cusins to come to his flat for a chat.

The sixteenth new movie scene follows immediately. It is a highly visual one-minute, forty-five second picturization of Barbara, despondent, alone on the quiet wharf, in striking contrast with the previous boisterous Albert Hall meeting. In the printed movie version, without this interplay of contrasts, the scene of Barbara on the wharf appears before, instead of after, the Albert Hall scene. Unlike the scene in the printed movie version, the actual film scene is almost entirely without dialogue. It begins, accompanied by somber music, with a dark, moody shot of

Barbara alone on a deserted wharf by the riverside. The scene cuts to a watchman smoking a pipe on the sidewalk far above Barbara. A neon sign in the background blinks on and off insistently: "Bodger's Whiskey." The scene cuts back to Barbara, who crosses slowly to the edge of the water and gazes into it. As we watch Barbara, we see the watchman in the background start down toward her. After she throws her bonnet into the river, the watchman speaks a few tentative words to her, as in the printed movie version. But, in the film, the visual can replace the verbal: there the watchman does not have to say to Barbara, as he did in the printed movie version, "I saw you throw your bonnet into the river," because we saw it too. Barbara asks, "Do you think you could find me a taxi to take me home?" The watchman replies, "Taxi? What you want, by the looks of you, is an ambulance." Barbara smiles wanly, replies softly, "Ambulance?" And she faints into the arms of the watchman. The scene fades out very slowly as Barbara falls.

The seventeenth new scene, which follows immediately, is a six-minute, five-second representation of a conversation between Undershaft and Cusins. In sharp contrast with the previous somber scene on the wharf, this new scene opens on a close-shot of a tray full of sparkling liquor, with gay laughter heard in the background. The camera pulls back to reveal Cusins and Undershaft comfortably chatting, in Undershaft's flat. As the scene progresses, Cusins gets drunk on vodka and "temperance burgundy," while Undershaft offers him both Barbara and a job in the munitions factory. The actual sound track scene is highly verbal, except that Cusins does not make several references, as he does in the printed movie version, to the fact that he is getting drunk, for we can see perfectly well that he is getting drunk. This scene and the previous one at Albert Hall are examples of the actual representation of material that had to be woven into the play as dramatic exposition. The movie then continues with the beginning of the play's Act III, but in the dining room at Wilton Crescent, instead of in the drawing room.

The eighteenth new scene, one minute, forty-five seconds long, is added in the midst of the greatly altered Act III of the play. It serves as a transition between the final Wilton Crescent scene and the tour of the

Undershaft-Lazarus factory. The published screen version adds a conversational scene about motor cars while the characters wait in the entrance hall for the cars which are to take them to the factory. Instead, with the economy of the film, the editor simply cuts from a shot of Undershaft and Stephen talking to a shot of the outside of their house. The door of the house opens; they all come out and get into two cars, and drive off. The camera shoots a new scene from the interior of Undershaft's car. As Cusins, who is driving, turns to look into the back seat, the camera shows what he sees, Undershaft and Barbara in conversation. Their talk is freely adapted from a conversation which, in the play and in the published screen version, had taken place earlier, at the Wilton Crescent home. Several deletions take away some of the intensity of Barbara's bitterness toward her father over the loss of Bill Walker—for it is important in the simpler film that the audience not dislike Undershaft, who is a much more straightforward, kind, simple character in the sound track version than in the other versions. Some additions give an added importance to Bill Walker, foreshadow his reappearance and salvation, and make Barbara's sudden consolation a bit more believable than it was in the play. As an example of stage-to-screen dialogue change, I have included here the entire new scene, with the deletions from the play ~~lined out~~ and the additions in CAPITALS:

UNDERSHAFT. ~~Never mind~~, my dear. ~~He thinks~~ I have made you unhappy. ~~Have~~ HAVEN'T I?

BARBARA. ~~Do you think I can be happy in this vulgar silly dress? I! who have worn the uniform.~~ Do you understand what you have done to me? Yesterday I had a man's soul in my hand. I set him in the way of life with his face to salvation. But when we took your money he turned back AGAIN to drunkenness and derision. [*With intense conviction*]. I will never forgive you that. NEVER. ~~If I had a child, and you destroyed its body with your explosives—if you murdered Dolly with your horrible guns I could forgive you if my forgiveness would open the gates of heaven to you. But to take a human soul from me and turn it into the soul of a wolf! that is worse than any murder.~~

UNDERSHAFT. Does my daughter despair so easily? Can you strike a man to the heart and leave no mark on him? [*BARBARA PERKS UP AT THIS*] YOU FORGET, MY DEAR, HE GAVE UP HIS HARD-EARNED

POUND TO SAVE HIS SOUL. DO YOU KNOW WHAT A POUND MEANS TO SUCH A MAN? IT'S YOUR FAITH THAT'S FAILING —NOT HIS. WILL HE EVER STRIKE A WOMAN AGAIN AS HE STRUCK JENNY HILL? YOU'VE SENT HIM ON THE ROAD TO HIS SALVATION. IT MAY NOT BE *YOUR* ROAD, BUT *HE* WON'T TURN FROM IT.

BARBARA [*her face lighting up*] Oh, YES, you are right: he can never be lost now: where was my faith?

CUSINS. Oh, clever clever devil!

BARBARA. You may be a devil; but God speaks through you sometimes. [*She takes her father's hands and kisses them*] You have given me back my happiness: I CAN feel it deep down now, though my spirit is troubled.

UNDERSHAFT. You have learnt something, MY DEAR. That always feels at first as if you had lost something. [*A CRESCENDO OF MUSIC EMPHASIZES THE IMPORTANCE OF UNDERSHAFT'S LAST SENTENCE. THE CAMERA MOVES FROM THE INTERIOR OF THE CAR, WITH NO BREAK IN CONTINUITY, TO THE OUTSIDE OF THE TWO MOVING CARS. FADE-OUT*].

The most cinematic scene in the film now begins: the scene at the great Undershaft factory. This is the nineteenth and last additional scene; it continues to the end of the film. Although, as we have seen, the greater resources of the cinema, according to Shaw, "make it possible to take the spectators through the great Undershaft factory and industrial colony instead of putting them off with a spoken description," Shaw did include, in the printed movie version, a great deal of spoken description and even an Arturo Toscanini concert, and—as in the play—much Shavian philosophy and Shavian paradox. The sound track version, however, is very different from both the play and the printed screen version. It is highly visual, with no concert, very little paradox, no spoken description, and with only the barest of necessary exposition of "The Gospel of St. Andrew Undershaft." Of the 1,143 lines of dialogue in the printed movie version of this scene, only 210 lines, many of them in changed sequence, are heard in the actual film. At the beginning of this scene—which takes place in several different settings within the factory establishment—the movie shows a full five minutes and forty-five seconds of visual action, with no significant dialogue whatever.

The new scene—the whole scene with all its parts lasting sixteen minutes and thirty seconds—opens with a close-shot of a huge sign: "Undershaft and Lazarus." Then the camera pulls back and shows huge, beautiful, modern buildings. In a montage scene, full of fast cutting, we see shots of heavy equipment, and then a panoramic shot of the entire huge plant. This is all accompanied by busy, excited music. We see a close-shot of Barbara, goggle-eyed. As the camera rushes about the plant, Cusins walks into view; then the whole group walks into view. Workmen stand aside for them. Majestic music begins. More shots of heavy equipment—and huge ingots. Barbara and Cusins are shown, alternately, in close-shot, startled and frightened. More huge ingots. The visitors shield their eyes. A workman rings a signal bell which echoes throughout the plant. A sign is shown: "Beware of hot ingots." A close-shot of an ingot moving up a ramp. Several shots of busy, happy workers. Another close-shot of an ingot. A huge roar in the background. They all shield themselves from the light and the heat. Over the roar, Cusins shouts, "The raw material of destruction." Undershaft shouts in reply, "Or *con*struction. How about railway lines?" More quick montage is flashed on the screen: equipment, machines, a close-shot of a gigantic shovel-like machine. Sparks fly. The visitors cower. In the background, Undershaft shouts, "One gets used to the danger—moulding steel." Then shots of boiling metal in cauldrons, followed by quick cuts to towering ramps, workers, fire. Undershaft shouts again, "Have you found anything discreditable?" Stephen answers sheepishly, "No." In the midst of a montage sequence showing a huge furnace and more machines, the camera shows a series of close-shots of the faces of the visitors, as their expressions slowly soften and change to admiration. Even Barbara manages a smile. In the background, Undershaft declares, "Dare you make war on war? Here are the means!" Suddenly the music explodes as the camera shoots close-shots of bombs. Cusins stares transfixed. A close-shot of Barbara's face shows her horror as she sees the expression on Cusins's face. Undershaft tauntingly says to Cusins, "Do you want it?" Cusins replies, "You have me in a horrible dilemma. I want Barbara." "Like most young men," says Undershaft, "you greatly exaggerate the difference between one young woman and another." Barbara cuts into the conversation, "Quite true, Dolly." Fade-out, indicating a passage of time and space between this site and the next one.

Fade-in to reveal an exhausted Lady Britomart, in another factory building, surrounded by the other, equally exhausted characters, and by a mad conglomeration of machinery and buildings. She complains to her husband: "I refuse to walk another step through all these sheds and pipes and boilers. They mean nothing to me. I have never asked you to come and look at the kitchen range and the scullery sink. Why is that roof making a noise like a whale with asthma?" Undershaft replies in the paternalistic tone he always uses with his wife, "It is breathing, my love. Come and see." They walk to a huge pile of something. "This is ridiculous," complains Lady Britomart. "Is it snow, or salt, or what?" Cusins answers, "Nitrates to make explosives." "Or sulphates to fertilize your fields," replies Undershaft. "If you prefer the explosive way, that's your affair, not mine. Come, Euripides, you think that nitrates are good for nothing but death. Now I'll show you the sort of life they produce." Fade-out, again indicating a passage of time.

Fade-in to a moving car entering a modern, clean village. In montage, the camera shows several shots of open fields and lovely, free sky. "This is where my workers live," announces Undershaft. "They own everything, and I own nothing." Lomax comments, "Cooperative type, eh?" "Exactly, Mr. Lomax," replies Undershaft. "It makes it very difficult for them to leave my employment. But then they do not want to leave it." "Why?" asks Lady Britomart. "Because they cannot better themselves, my love," replies Undershaft. "Slavery, I call it!" she answers. "You would, my dear," replies Undershaft sweetly. Fade-out on another shot of the lovely little village.

Fade-in on several shots of happy, healthy children playing. A close-shot shows Barbara's face, impressed. The visitors walk to one of the houses, and are welcomed by a mother with a little child. Fade-out.

Fade-in to a shot showing several churches. Hymn singing is heard. "This is the result of our belief in religious freedom," announces Undershaft. "Its official name is The Meeting Place of All the Religions. But the men call it Piety Square." As they walk along a path, Stephen asks, "Are you sure that all this pampering is really good for the men's characters?" "My dear boy," Undershaft replies, "when you are organizing civilization you have to make up your mind whether trouble and anxiety are good things or not. If you decide that they are, then, I take it, you simply don't organize civilization; and there you are. However, our characters are safe here. A sufficient dose of anxiety is always provided by the fact that we may all be blown to smithereens at any moment." A sudden crash of music concludes Undershaft's speech. Fade-out.

Fade-in to several shots of a lovely park. Barbara is sitting on a bench, watching Cusins approach. "Well?" she asks. "Not a ray of hope!" declares Cusins as he sits down next to Barbara. "Everything is perfect! Wonderful! Real! It only needs a cathedral to be a heavenly city instead of a hellish one." They get up and walk along, joining the others of the family as they all stroll happily along the walk. The dialogue then continues, but much more sparsely than in the printed screen version, as Lady Britomart exults in her possession of all this, and as Cusins explains why he, as a foundling, is eligible for the Undershaft inheritance.

The site changes again, to Undershaft's office, where, in dialogue similar to that of the play and the printed screen version, Undershaft and Cusins talk about the terms of Cusins's employment. Fade-out.

Fade-in on another new setting, outside a modern office building. Barbara is waiting, looking out over the bustling scene before her. A caravan of materials passes by, and in the group of workers, the camera shows Bill Walker. Barbara shouts to him, and Bill shouts back, "Hello there, Judy! Your father's given me a job! Three pounds ten a week." Barbara exults in Bill's good news. Bill calls back as he moves away, "How's that for salvation, eh?" As Bill and the other workers disappear down the street, Cusins approaches Barbara. He tells her that he has accepted her father's job offer. In a conversation much sparser than that in the other two versions, Barbara explains her decision to accept Cusins and then justifies her father's philosophy. When Lady Britomart joins them, Barbara runs up to her, shouting "Mama!" Lady Britomart asks, "Well, Barbara: What do you want?" Barbara replies, "I want a house in the village to live in with Dolly." The sound track then adds a tremendous crescendo of music, as Barbara and Cusins run exultingly down the stairs. The music builds to the romantic theme of the film, as Barbara and Cusins mingle with all the happy workmen. Undershaft stands majestically far above them, on the top of the stairs, waving. Bill joins Barbara and Cusins, and the three of them walk along gaily, arm in arm, right into the camera, as the scene fades out. And "The End," the credits, and "A Gabriel Pascal Production" are flashed upon the screen.

This final scene is, of course, extremely important to both the theme and effect of the film. It must convince the viewer, intellectually and emotionally, that the might and power controlled by Undershaft can lead to a social reorganization in which poverty and injustice are eliminated. Pascal unleashes here the power of the cinema--he uses, as is obvious in the description above, cutting and camera motion and sound, the dynamism of the cinema, to create a visual and aural impression. After building to an intense peak of excitement, he slows the pace and tension so as to exploit the contrast of the peace and joy of nature, of domestic happiness, of religious tranquillity. At the very end, he quickens the pace to conclude with a smashing affirmative statement of human solidarity: Barbara, Cusins, and Bill Walker—the heiress, the intellectual, the workman—joined in happiness as the Superman stands supreme, overseeing all. In this final scene the medium of the motion picture is pushed toward its potential.

Shaw told his public why he wrote new scenes, and except for the sudden inspiration of the finale, Pascal, in *Major Barbara*, was satisfied with that simple function: to bring in off-stage events. Subtracting the time spent on nonvisual straightforward talk, the nineteen new *Major Barbara* scenes, bringing in off-stage events, lasted thirty-one and a half minutes, coincidentally exactly the same length of time as the new visual scenes in *Pygmalion*. But *Major Barbara* was 121 minutes long; so where the film version of *Pygmalion* had included new visual scenes comprising 37 per cent of the film's entire playing time, the film version of *Major Barbara* included new somewhat-visual material comprising 26 per cent of the film's entire playing time. Little is accomplished by most of these new scenes—only a bit of relief from the long conversations, through the presentation of some spectacle or simultaneous action, and occasionally some little humor or suspense or contrast or heightening of interest. The direction is generally dull and matter-of-fact, with the characters talking, relatively unedited, in front of an inactive camera. Pascal's direction and Shaw's writing were both more stagelike than the direction and writing in *Pygmalion. Major Barbara* was a movement back toward Shaw's theory of the motion picture as a filmed play.

All of the new material in the film version of *Major Barbara* is not, of course, in the form of whole new scenes. As in *Pygmalion,* some of the old dialogue is accompanied by effective visualization. The power of the cinema to tamper with time is, for example, exploited in the scene in the Salvation Army shelter when Undershaft prepares to sign the fifty thousand pound check (raised in the inflation of the motion picture from the five thousand pounds of the play) that will save the Army and will betray Barbara. The suspenseful preparation is prolonged, by editing, beyond the length of time that it could occupy in either real life or on the stage: the camera takes extra time to show, one after another, in close-shots, the faces of the eager, tense observers. Editorial comments are made by camera placement, most interestingly when Undershaft climbs high into a pulpit of the Salvation Army as he expounds to Cusins his religion of money and gunpowder, freedom and power.

A good deal of material—indeed, several pages—was removed from *Major Barbara* on its stage-to-screen journey. Act III is the most heavily cut, primarily because much of its dialogue was replaced by the visual. The movie no longer has to communicate in dramatic exposition the events of the night before. In the play, Cusins had to tell about his drinking with Undershaft. He doesn't have to talk about it in detail in the movie because we saw it. In the play, Barbara has to say to Cusins, "Now tell me what happened at the meeting?" And then he does. In the film, Cusins's narration about the meeting is cut, for we ourselves saw it all. After Undershaft arrives on the scene, the play's Act III has several pages of witty Shavian dialogue concerning son Stephen and his future. In keeping with the filmic tendency toward simplification of issues and of minor characters, most of this conversation is omitted in the movie, and thus many of the complicated details about the Undershaft foundling tradition are lost, along with some good Shavian jabs at modern education and at respectable people's assurance that they know all about morality. All of the description in dialogue of the Undershaft factory is cut, for we are soon actually to see it.

This film, like all others, had to "go round the world unchallenged," and so Cusins is not an indifferent "collector of religions," and so Shaw's satirical gibes against the Church of England are eliminated. All references to the Jewishness of Lazarus, Undershaft's partner, are omitted. Snobby Price's disbelief in the devil is cut; and "Selp me Gawd" becomes "Selp me"; "Gawd elp im!" becomes "Eaven elp im!" The whole structure of Cusins's speech explaining his parents' illegal marriage is changed so that he won't end with "I was born and bred a bastard."

The omissions in *Major Barbara* narrow the story and simplify the characters, just as did the omissions in *Pygmalion*. Much of Lady Britomart's ridicule of Charles Lomax is eliminated as unnecessary to the basic plot, weakening but not essentially changing the characters of each. Most of the Cusins comments about Greek and Paganism, and a good deal of his quotation of Homer, Euripides, and Aristophanes, are also deleted in the movement toward simplification. More importantly, much of the Shavian social attack on contemporary England is lost in the weakening of the roles of the foolish and ineffective upper-class Stephen Undershaft and of the protesting social-outcast Peter Shirley. Although Undershaft remains Shaw's persuasive Superman, his central position in the play is weakened and his ambiguous character is simplified. His defense of his cannon business and the first presentation of his money and gunpowder philosophy are deleted from the Act I scene in Lady Britomart's drawing room. Several pages of dialogue are cut from the Cusins-Undershaft conversation in the Salvation Army shelter, and thus much of Undershaft's philosophy of power and a good deal of Shavian paradox is lost. Bill Walker, on the other hand, is emphasized in the movie. He is presented as the primary example of man victimized by poverty. In the preface to the play, Shaw spoke of the "doom" of Bill

Walker, but in the movie Bill is saved by Undershaft's beneficent socialization. What remains, after a good deal of omission and addition, is a clear, uncomplicated and unparadoxical story of the conversion of Barbara to her father's belief in the utter morality of a power which is strong enough to reorganize society so as to eliminate the one real evil—poverty. Although simplified, the social focus remains primary.

The Shaw-Pascal *Major Barbara* was essentially true to the theme of the original play. Shaw wrote the screen play, and Pascal transferred it to the screen with only moderate adaptations. It was certainly less a film than *Pygmalion* had been. *Major Barbara* remained more a literary than a pictorial art; it did not utilize the potentialities of the movie makers' unique tools of camera, microphone, and editor's shears. To the degree that it remained true to the technique of the original play, the movie was less true to the artistic effect of the play; for, not fitting the medium, the movie turned out to be pictorially dull where the original had been verbally exciting.

The Shaw-Pascal *Major Barbara* was not ready for its world premiere until March 20, 1941, sixteen months after the filming began. The first showing, away from London bombs, was a notable social occasion. The lavish premiere was held in Nassau, sponsored by the Duke and Duchess of Windsor, and publicity-conscious Pascal gathered together the reporters as he arrived at the theatre in the company of Miss Katherine Hepburn.

Major Barbara, which finally cost over $1,000,000, compared with *Pygmalion*'s $675,000, was a disappointment both financially and critically. *Variety* did not exult as it had done when reporting the box-office success of *Pygmalion.* Instead, it used words ranging from "doing well," to "okay," to "light," to "low gear," to "dull and dismal." *Variety's* National Box-office Survey finally concluded that "Major Barbara is only good to thin." J. Arthur Rank's biographer contends that the slow box-office for *Major Barbara* prevented the film from grossing in England an amount even equal to its cost. "It was Shaw," he contends, "who was the chief sufferer. . . . he lost about £20,000." Tax complications made Shaw's losses on *Major Barbara* even higher.

The critics were as lukewarm toward *Major Barbara* as the box-office was. *The Film Daily's* poll of 548 film critics put *Major Barbara* in 22nd place. The Academy Awards noticed it not at all. Although most of the critics found things to admire in the movie—especially Wendy Hiller and Robert Newton—nearly all of them complained of the film's comparatively static, talky, noncinematic quality. "Despite some brilliant qualities," concluded *The New Statesman* in a typical review, "we rarely forget that *Major Barbara* was written for a room with three walls." "Although Gabriel Pascal has given an excellent production . . . to *Major Barbara*," concluded *The Commonweal* in a frequently stated comparison, "he was not so successful in cinematizing this Shaw item as he was with *Pygmalion*."

Shaw claimed the movie version of *Major Barbara* as his own. He again appeared on the screen—as he had with *Pygmalion*—in a good self-advertising introduction to his film. But this eight-minute short, made for America, was—to Shaw's fury—held up for several months by United Artists, the American distributor, because they feared the political repercussions of Shaw's straightforward invitation to Americans to come help the English win the war.

Although all of Shaw's public statements praised the *Major Barbara* film, apparently not even Shaw was as totally happy with this film as he had been with *Pygmalion*. He admitted in an unpublished letter dated April 14, 1941, that some reason must be found for the mediocre reception of the film. He admitted not that the movie version—his own screen play, or Pascal's direction—may not have fit the medium; he admitted only that the movie was "badly cast."

There is no evidence that the comparative failure of *Major Barbara* caused Shaw to have any doubts about his cinema theories. Indeed, when he came to publish his "screen version" of *Major Barbara*, he thought in terms of the original play, not in terms of the actual working screen play. When, a few months after the release of *Major Barbara*, Shaw came to write a scenario for *Arms and the Man* for Pascal, he wrote a screen play that brings in some off-stage action, but which was otherwise the same as the play. Shaw was reverting more and more to his old cinema theory. The previously unpublished text of Shaw's original 1941 very stagey screen play for the unproduced *Arms and the Man* is included in this book as Appendix D. An unreconstructed Shaw noted on this 1941 film script:

> No changes of location are needed in the 3rd Act beyond the usual close-up, mediums, and full-shots. It is a mistake to interrupt the play by changes of scene *after the audience has become interested in the characters and story.*

For the next three years, an undaunted Pascal—now, as he put it, "cinematically wedded to Shaw"—surged back and forth across the Atlantic issuing public announcements and buying trade publication advertisements trumpeting his future ventures with Bernard Shaw. The next Shaw-Pascal film was, at one time or another, promised to be: *Saint Joan* (with Greta Garbo; but the British Ministry of Information is said to have demurred at the idea of a film in wartime showing the English burning a French patriot); *The Devil's Disciple*; *Arms and the Man* (with Ginger Rogers. And with Clark Gable. Then with Rex Harrison. Then with Paul Muni); *Candida* (with Katherine Cornell. Then with Greer Garson); *Captain Brassbound's Conversion* (with Alfred Lunt and Lynn Fontanne); *The Millionairess* (with Katherine Hepburn); *The Shewing Up of Blanco Posnet.*

Finally, in mid-1944, the news started cropping up, with varying degrees of confirmation, that Pascal was to film Shaw's *Caesar and Cleopatra*. That was to be the final authorized Shaw film; that was to be, in more ways than one, the end.

Caesar and Cleopatra

GABRIEL PASCAL, producer and director, started filming Bernard Shaw's *Caesar and Cleopatra* on June 12, 1944—just six days after D-Day. The choice of this play was not an easy one. Shaw, for one, was not enthusiastic about the prospect of *Caesar and Cleopatra* on film. He had previously complained, in an unpublished letter: "As the play is not a play at all, but a history (quite a dead thing), and, compared with *Pygmalion*, would cost a frightful lot of money, I am not very sanguine about the practicability for the screen." But Pascal liked the play, especially its possibilities for spectacle, and *he* was not worried about whether it would cost a frightful lot of money. J. Arthur Rank, no longer just a rich flour miller, but now one of the most significant names in the British film industry, was ready to put money and the name of "The Rank Organisation" behind the Shaw-Pascal *Caesar and Cleopatra*. Rank looked to the opportunity of establishing British films—with the combination of *Caesar and Cleopatra* and Sir Laurence Olivier's elaborate *Henry V*—as a potent and prestigious force on the world market. The availability of Vivien Leigh to play the role of Cleopatra was the climactic factor in the final choice of this Shavian history play.

Once the choice was made, Shaw pitched in with full cooperation. He personally chose Claude Rains as Caesar. Shaw himself set to work, unaided, on the screen play. Now that Shaw was an old hand at film writing, he had total confidence in his picture-making abilities. As he and Pascal worked on *Caesar and Cleopatra,* they were virtually alone and free. The old pressures for extensive adaptation were gone. "There was not a script writer left in the studio," Shaw wrote. When Pascal wanted a new sequence, "he very simply asked me for it and got it."

Shaw not only wrote the required new sequences, but he regularly watched over the film as it was being made. In addition, once a week Pascal conferred formally with Shaw, showing him still photographs of the growing production. No detail of the film-making was too trivial for Shaw's attention and active cooperation. Miss Marjorie Deans, Pascal's scenario editor, has salvaged, in her book *Meeting at the Sphinx,* some of the once-voluminous Shaw-Pascal correspondence, most of which, according to Mrs. Pascal, has subsequently been lost and stolen. Here, as a sample of the scope and nature of Shaw's cooperation on the production of *Caesar and Cleopatra,* is an exchange of letters concerning the make-up and costuming of Britannus:

Shaw, Vivien Leigh, and Gabriel Pascal during the filming of *Caesar and Cleopatra.*

G.B.S. *to* G.P. 1/7/44

Britannus is so hopelessly wrong that he will hold up all the scenes in which he appears until he is redressed. I enclose a suggestion of what he should look like. At present he is a handsome young military man instead of an elderly academic literary secretary, very unlike all the others. He must have an academic gown.

G.P. *to* G.B.S. 8/7/44

Britannus: since I received your sketch, I have discarded his original costume, which I never liked very much, and have had a long gown made for him; and he will have a kind of shepherd's plaid, which I hope to get next week. I am sending you herewith a photograph of the gown, with a completely different belt, which I hope you will like very much. His wig I have had remade with red hair, as you suggest, and a new moustache, turning down. It is not yet completely to my satisfaction, but they are making a new one which will be nearer to your design.

G.B.S *to* G.P. 9/7/44

Britannus must be mainly in blue: the shepherd's plaid is only for the

Shaw, Vivien Leigh, and Gabriel Pascal during the filming of *Caesar and Cleopatra.*

tunic. That is why the blue overall should be an academic *gown,* opening all down the front. They have plenty of such things in Oxford still.

G.P. *to* G.B.S. 23/7/44

I made a new costume, a new wig, and a new moustache for Britannus, and am sending you herewith photos of his costume and make-up. The costume is now a lovely corn-flower blue, and the shepherd's plaid hood is checked in pinkish-white and a natural brown, woven in Scotland.

G.B.S. *to* G.P. 26/7/44

Dear Gabriel,

Britannus's costume is all right now; but the moustache is hopeless. He must have Dundreary whiskers—yellow whiskers. In great haste,

G.B.S.

(This letter was accompanied by a water-colour sketch of Britannus's head.)

G.B.S. *to* G.P. 28/7/44

My dear Gabriel,

In the sketch of Britannus I rushed off to you I painted his eyebrows black. They should, of course, be yellow. The wig, moustache, and whiskers can all be made on a frame which he can put on like a helmet: it cannot be stuck on with spirit gum. The colour should be auburn or downright yellow.

Academic gowns and hopeless moustaches—and constant Shaw nagging—were not Gabriel Pascal's only problems. Pascal never got along with Claude Rains, and for a good part of the filming they refused to speak to each other. When Pascal learned that Vivien Leigh was expecting a baby, he had to rearrange the shooting schedule so that all her scenes could be shot first. Then she suffered a miscarriage, and her scenes were postponed for six weeks, throwing the schedule off once more. Because of the war, equipment and skilled craftsmen were scarce or unobtainable. The rocket bombing of London began a few days after the start of the filming. One bomb exploded next to the Pharos set. Pascal wrote to Shaw about another bomb: "The French windows in my sitting-room were blown completely in and the ceiling in my bedroom was cracked completely, so I am having the same gay start on the picture as I had with *Major Barbara* during the blitz." The German bombings lasted for eight

Shaw entertains Pascal with a Roman helmet used as a prop in *Caesar and Cleopatra.*

weeks, but the English sun refused to shine for several months. The delay in the filming of outdoor shots began to be financially intolerable. Eventually—in desperation and with a Hollywoodian bravado—the company moved from England to Egypt, carrying with it huge chunks of a Sphinx for assembly on the Egyptian sands just outside Cairo. Not the least of the production's difficulties, according to Miss Deans, was the loss of 330 papier-mache shields, held together by a tasty glue, which were eaten by the Egyptian natives.

Shaw sent this photograph of himself, Pascal, and French composer Georges Auric to his friend Molly Tompkins.

Shaw and Pascal, unpressured by defenders of movie technique and thus free to indulge Shaw's theory of the cinema, created, as they worked so closely on the production of *Caesar and Cleopatra*, by far the least cinematic of all the three Shaw-Pascal films. Shaw specifically warned Pascal not to "change the play into an exhibition of camera conjuring." Shaw did create new scenes, as before, to show events which took place off-stage in the play and to smooth out the gaps between the acts. But these new scenes, 16 of them, occupied only 13 minutes, 30 seconds, out of a total playing time of 128 minutes. Thus, where new visual scenes in the screen version of *Pygmalion* had accounted for 37 per cent of the film, and in *Major Barbara* new visual material had accounted for 26 per cent of the film, all of the new scenes in *Caesar and Cleopatra* accounted for only 11 per cent of the film's entire playing time. Most of these new scenes were lavishly spectacular. They did little except provide a lovely backdrop for the talk. Working for the first time with Technicolor and with a huge budget and with a historical setting, Shaw and Pascal substituted sheer spectacle for the more dynamic and functional cinematic methods which had crept into their two previous films.

Caesar and Cleopatra has had two different beginnings. In some editions, the play version opened with a gambling scene among Egyptian soldiers on the Syrian border of Egypt. In this scene, a conversation between Belzanor (the Captain of the Queen's Guard), a Persian soldier, and Bel Affris (a messenger), delivered the necessary exposition: the conversation tells of the Roman invasion of Egypt, the complicated political background of that invasion, and the disappearance of Queen Cleopatra. In other editions of the play, the Belzanor-Persian-Bel Affris scene was called "An Alternative to the Prologue." In this case, the "Prologue" was an expository monologue delivered to the modern audience by the god Ra, "an august personage with a hawk's head." The film begins with a shortened version of the Belzanor-Persian-Bel Affris scene, which soon fades into the first new movie scene. The new scene is wholly visual, one minute long, and serves many functions: it is important as spectacle, it establishes the mysteriously shimmering mood of the early part of the film, it performs an expository function by showing the presence of Roman soldiers in Egypt, and it even, by showing something of Caesar's relations with his dog and his men, helps to establish immediately the unexpected kindly character of Caesar. Although Shaw published no "screen version" of *Caesar and Cleopatra*, I am able to quote, thanks to Mrs. Pascal, the mimeographed final shooting script, with both its dialogue and its Shavian descriptions of the spectacular visuals shown in the actual film. Shaw tells us that, while writing this film, he was conscious of himself playing with the whole world—perhaps a bit like Caesar and the other Shavian Supermen:

Pages 120 and 121, Claude Rains as Caesar and Vivien Leigh as Cleopatra on the sands of Egypt in the Gabriel Pascal production of *Caesar and Cleopatra,* 1945.

Dissolve: Through the violent blast of the Roman bucinator, to Sphinx and Roman Camp in the Desert. Night. Medium-Close Shot: The Roman Bucinator. He is blowing a blast on his bucina which is coiled round his body, its brazen bell shaped like the head of a howling wolf. The camera tracks past him and past a camp fire which sends up a column of smoke. In the background we see a large tent, obviously the camp forge. The shadows of the blacksmith and his workers, and a horse which is being shoed, are seen in silhouette through the canvas against the flickering flames of the forge; the sound of hammering is heard in counterpoint against the musical background. The camera continues its movement and passes in front of a pool with palm trees reflected in its surface. Horses are tethered on the bank of the pool. On the far side we look down a vista of tents with camp fires burning here and there among them. In the distance soldiers are grouped around the largest of these camp fires. Their voices reach us distantly singing an old Roman refrain. Continuing its tracking movement, the camera now shows a square tent with ornamental fringe and insignia, larger and more important than the rest. This is the General's tent, with one or two staff tents beyond. From the General's tent there comes the figure of a man who puts aside the tent flap and stands a moment in the doorway looking out into the night. A white wolf-hound runs to greet his master, who drops the flap and goes forward, moving in the same direction as the camera which continues tracking with him, showing him pass a couple of Roman sentries who come to attention as he goes by. A group of soldiers coming in the opposite direction carrying a heavy load (perhaps of canvas and tent props) are obviously startled by this unexpected meeting with their General, and prepare to drop their load ready to salute him; but the man signals to them to go on their way. They look after him adoringly. The man goes out past camera, passing a forest of shields and spears planted upright in the sand.

The scene then dissolves into a shot of the eerie moonlit desert at night, and on into the play scene where Caesar hails the Sphinx and compares it with himself.

The second new scene is just a quick cut, five seconds long, bringing into view the marching Legions of Caesar at the moment when Cleopatra, huddled in the paws of the Sphinx, hears the sound of the Roman war trumpet and whimpers, trembling, "What was that?" The third new scene, fifteen seconds long, also shows the approaching Legions, this time as Cleopatra, by now taught queenliness by her "old gentleman," decides to wear her crown to greet the terrible, conquering Caesar.

In his final shooting script, Shaw included two different endings for the play's Act I, allowing Pascal to take his choice. In the play, when the frightened Cleopatra hears the soldiers' shout of "Hail, Caesar!" she realizes that her own old gentleman is the conquerer of the world, and, with a great sob of relief, she falls into his arms. In the rejected shooting script ending, the same scene is described in exuberant detail. Shaw takes advantage, too, of his opportunity to dictate the music to composer Georges Auric: "Cleopatra turns in the direction towards which the swords are pointing, and finds Caesar on the throne, his hitherto severe expression changed by a smile of extraordinary charm and kindliness. Fascinated and enlightened, she throws herself into Caesar's lap, flinging her arms around his neck. All the wood and brass in the orchestra let fly with every note in the chromatic scale fortissimo! Meanwhile the strings put on their mutes; and the screen goes black." The actual film ending shows Cleopatra falling more simply into Caesar's arms, and then shows Caesar's discomfiture: "Caesar appears a little astonished at finding himself with a woman in his arms. He does not know what to do with her. He tries to maintain his dignity. He looks sidelong at the officers." A close-shot shows the captain trying to repress a grin; and then Caesar looks at the inert figure of Cleopatra and he too begins to smile: "He shrugs apologetically at the officers, yet there is a hint of masculine triumph."

Shaw decided to indicate the passing of this first night through an elaborate musical accompaniment to the actual movement of the moon across the sky: "The instruments drop out one by one, the extreme discords first, then the 13ths, 11ths, 9ths, down to the diminishing 7ths, on which the muted strings join in with Schubertian sweetness, and modulates back to the nocturne of the Sphinx in the desert. Simultaneously the blacked-out screen lightens into the desert scene with the moon in the east. The moon, accompanied by the nocturne music, passes across the screen to the west to indicate the passing of the night. The music is broken twice by a syncopated throb and flash of summer lightning. Towards the end of the transit the moon fades; the sky brightens into dawning sunlight; and the oboe cuts in with a pastoral descant." Happily, Pascal refused to use this unrealistic, stagelike trick. Instead, he cut directly to the Roman occupation of Egypt.

The occupation is the fourth new movie scene. It is a highly visual scene, lasting two minutes, forty seconds. Pascal had intended to show the occupation in pantomime, but when he asked Shaw for a few lines of dialogue to be spoken by some Egyptian bystanders, Shaw volunteered an entire new scene. Here is how Shaw described what is actually shown on the screen:

> Noise outside: first the Roman trumpets; then the Alexandrian mob flying in terror, expressed by hurried music, culminating in the appearance on the screen of the street with the people running away in all directions, hiding where they can or crowding against the houses to leave the road clear for a column of Roman soldiers marching with a discipline which contrasts strongly with the disorder of the crowd. The Centurion, cudgel in hand, marches beside the files. The buglers and drummers are at the head of the column. Quick march. Meanwhile, the crowd as it flies shouts inarticulately while it is in motion.

Out of the flying crowd, a woman is heard screaming hysterically: "The Romans! The Romans! They're coming! They're coming!!" The Centurion barks to his troops the command of "Halt!" He calls his troops to attention as a drum roll echoes throughout the street. He addresses his troops in stentorian style: "We wait here for our second-in-command, Rufio. This city is Alexandria. Remember that: Al-ex-andria, the capital of Egypt. You've got to behave yourselves here. Be stiffish with the men; but you may fraternize with the women." The troops respond with cheers and laughter. The Centurion commands: "Silence! Silence I tell you!" A flourish then sounds across the street. "*That* is Rufio," announces the Centurion, and he continues, "Attention! Half turn, left!" The command is repeated by a lieutenant, as Rufio walks into view. He addresses the Centurion: "See that building? That's the Royal Palace. Caesar's in there. I'm going now to join him. Keep a platoon of picked men within call.

Vivien Leigh as Cleopatra and Claude Rains as Caesar in Gabriel Pascal's *Caesar and Cleopatra,* 1945.

They may be wanted. Picked men, you understand." "Yes, sir!" responds the Centurion. The scene then cuts to a group of Egyptians watching the occupation, and Shaw manages here to spirit in a few lines of dialogue which had been cut from the Belzanor-Persian-Bel Affris Prologue. "What are these Romans?" one of the Egyptians complains with bravado. "Peasants, brought up to scare crows; sons of smiths and millers and tanners." "Are we not nobles?" responds another Egyptian. He continues, "We are consecrated to arms, descended from the gods!" "The gods are not always good to their poor relations," suggests another. The camera swings off them as they look to the background, where Rufio and the soldiers are moving toward the Palace. "Let us wait and take sides with the winner," suggests the noble Egyptian. "Ptolemy!" shouts a guardsman. "Cleopatra!" shouts another. "Cleopatra *or* Ptolemy," insinuates a third. The next shot is a close-up of the boy Ptolemy, cut onto the screen immediately upon the pronunciation of his name by the third bystander. The film then proceeds with the material from Act II of the play, as Ptolemy, prompted by Pothinus, begins his rehearsed speech.

A little ten-second scene, the fifth new one, is added in the midst of the long dialogue scene in the Egyptian Council Chamber in Act II, where Caesar and the Egyptians talk politics. In this new scene, a Roman tax officer whispers to Caesar and shows him on a papyrus the amount of taxes available in Alexandria. Caesar then knows how much to demand from Pothinus: 16,000 talents (another case of movie inflation—in the play, Caesar demanded 1,600 talents). This scene could obviously not have taken place on the stage, for the humor comes from the whispered information which *we* hear but which the Egyptian bystanders do not.

In the film, the long Council Chamber scene is broken up into two separate days. Four consecutive new scenes show the time-break. At a humorous high point in the conversation, when Cleopatra says, "You are very sentimental, Caesar; but you are clever; and if you do as I tell you, you will soon learn how to govern," the scene cuts away to the next scene. The sixth new scene, thirty-five seconds long, effectively increases the tension by showing some of the political unrest that is taking place on the streets of Alexandria on that very night: A hostile night-time mob gathers outside the Library, threatens a Roman sentinel, and shouts, "Egypt for the Egyptians!" The crowd cheers wildly when they discover their leaders, Pothinus and Lucius Septimius, entering the Library. The seventh new scene is a moody one-minute, twenty-five-second pantomime, showing what Caesar is doing at that same time. The setting is the King's Room in the Palace. Caesar sits, busily working at documents on a table, his face lit by an oil lamp. Caesar finally leans back, stretches, gets up, and walks to a window meditatively. Britannus offers him a flask of barley-water, and the music changes to a lullaby as Britannus slowly dims the oil lamp. The color is lovely and eerie: "The room is now lit," says the shooting script, "by a cold, early morning light."

That same lullaby forms a transition to the next scene, two minutes, fifteen seconds long, in Cleopatra's bedroom. According to Miss Marjorie Deans, Shaw and Pascal originally planned this to be the only new scene in the film. It adds a good deal to the physical beauty of the film; it also plays a little with suggestions of romantic attachment between Caesar and Cleopatra—and then, Shavian-like, pulls them back again. Here is how the final shooting script describes this delightful addition to the Shaw canon. Each camera shot is consecutively numbered:

200. Cleopatra's "Bedroom." Day. Medium-Close Shot: Cleopatra.

The lullaby music continues over the dissolve. The camera tracks in through the window, as though moving in on a sunbeam, to show Cleopatra fast asleep in bed. We hold her long enough to let the audience take in her immediate surroundings. Then the lullaby is interrupted by a brilliant reveille from the Roman military trumpets under the windows outside. This finishes the music. Rudely awakened, Cleopatra raises herself on one elbow, rubbing her eyes.

CLEOPATRA [*calling*] Ftatateeta! Ftatateeta!

The camera, which has drawn back to hold Cleopatra's new position, continues its backward movement to show Ftatateeta entering from behind camera and coming forward to stand beside her mistress. She has not put on her official robe; and her powerful and handsome body is seen apparently naked, except for a rich sash or sumptuous belt which serves also as an apron. She carries bath towels on her arm. Her attitude is as commanding as ever.

FTATATEETA. Get up, child. You must be bathed this morning.

CLEOPATRA [*dismayed*] No! I had my month's bath the day before yesterday.

FTATATEETA. In future you must have a bath every day.

CLEOPATRA. No, no: I should die of it.

FTATATEETA. You must. Your life is changed. You are still my child; but to all others you are now a grown woman and a queen.

200A. Medium-Close Shot: Cleopatra.

Her face begins to assume its new look of childish arrogance and conceit as she looks round the magnificent bedchamber. She sits up and clasps her arms round her knees.

CLEOPATRA [*to herself, with satisfaction*] Yes, I am a Queen. [*She considers the situation, intrigued, and then turns eagerly towards Ftatateeta*] Ftata, what will Caesar do with me? [*Ftatateeta sits down into picture*].

200B. Medium-Close Shot: Ftatateeta.

Ftatateeta looks back at her young mistress with an expression that is half rueful, half-admiring.

FTATATEETA. Ask rather what you will do with him. My child, you have charmed him. You are safe; you are powerful. I will guide you until you learn to guide yourself. Fear nothing.

200C. Medium-Close Shot: Cleopatra.

She begins to laugh.

CLEOPATRA. Who could fear Caesar? He is not great and terrible. He is only an elderly gentleman, rather wrinkled and sad-looking, but very kind.

200D. Medium-Close Shot: The Two, Favouring Ftatateeta.

FTATATEETA. He is a magician; and magicians can change their shapes as they please. Everything about him is magical. He would not sleep in the golden chamber; he made his soldiers bring a bare stretcher from the camp and put it in his study. [*Ftatateeta rises*].

200E. Medium-Close Shot: Cleopatra and Ftatateeta.

Ftatateeta kneels by the pillow behind Cleopatra, twisting her hair into a knot on the top of her head ready for the bath.

FTATATEETA. Even then he did not sleep in it, for he sat up working like a slave all night. Yet everyone obeys him as if he were a god. I think he is a god in disguise; for he has changed your nature, has he not?

CLEOPATRA. Oh, yes, he has. That is true, Ftatateeta. Before he came, I was afraid of you more than of anyone else on earth; and now I am not afraid of you at all! [*Cleopatra leans away from Ftatateeta and picks up a mirror*].

200F. Close-Shot: Cleopatra in the Mirror.

Cleopatra speaks to her reflection in the mirror.

CLEOPATRA. Tell me what I must do to begin with now that I am really a Queen! [*Ftatateeta's hand comes in and takes the mirror away*].

200G. Medium-Shot: Ftatateeta and Cleopatra.

Holding the mirror in one hand, Ftatateeta pulls back the coverlet with the other.

FTATATEETA [*unyielding*] You must begin by having a bath every day. [*Cleopatra lies still, pouting*]. [*Putting down the mirror*] Come, child, and get it over. You will soon get used to it and love it. [*Ftatateeta gives Cleopatra a playful pat and holds up a long bath robe. Cleopatra gets up, shuddering*].

CLEOPATRA. Never, It is too dreadful. [*Ftatateeta helps her on with the robe and leads the way to the bathroom, followed by Cleopatra*].

CLEOPATRA. If I must be washed again so soon, it must be a scented bath, Ftatateeta. Have you scented it?

FTATATEETA. No: Caesar hates perfumes. [*Cleopatra, delaying before she gets into the bath, has picked up a stick of rouge from a tray held by one of the ladies, and is looking at herself in a mirror held by another one, preparing to make up her lips*].

FTATATEETA. And if you redden your lips, he will not kiss them. [*Cleopatra drops the lipstick almost guiltily. She turns away from the camera, drops her robe, and steps down into the pool*].

200H. Medium-Close Shot: Ftatateeta.
Her eyes follow her young mistress.

FTATATEETA. He must indeed be a god: for only a god could be so unlike a man.
Dissolve.

In order to pick up the conversation of the play version where it broke off in the midst of Act II, the film script has to create another new scene (thirty seconds), the ninth film version interpolation. Without creating any new dialogue, Shaw gets Cleopatra back into Caesar's company, so they can continue their conversation. Now that her bath is over, Cleopatra is seen approaching Caesar in the King's Room:

201. The Council Chamber. Day. Medium-Long Shot: Cleopatra and Ftatateeta (shooting from the direction of the throne toward the Queen's Apartments).
Cleopatra, now most regally dressed, comes through the entrance from the Queen's Apartments, followed by Ftatateeta. Camera pans with them as they cross the room to the doorway to the King's Room. The entrance is guarded by two Roman sentries, solemn, phlegmatic fellows. They would like to bar Cleopatra, but she draws herself up haughtily and passes through, signaling to Ftatateeta to remain outside. Ftatateeta is horrified at Cleopatra's going in alone, but the sentries, having seen the Queen's gesture, take a delight in keeping Ftatateeta out.

202. The King's Room. Day. Medium-Shot: Caesar and Britannus, Cleopatra at Door in Background.
Caesar is seated at his desk, his back partly turned to the door so that he does not see Cleopatra. Britannus is standing beside Caesar facing the door. Seeing Cleopatra, he straightens up in amazement. Cleopatra hesitates a moment, and then tiptoes forward from the doorway to stand behind Caesar's chair. Camera tracks in toward the desk as she does so. She leans round and takes away the plan he is studying. Caesar's eyes follow the plan till they come to rest on Cleopatra. Camera now holds the two in Medium-Close Shot.

A gift for Caesar. Vivien Leigh as Cleopatra is helped out of her carpet by Claude Rains as Caesar and by Basil Sydney as Rufio in *Caesar and Cleopatra*, 1945.

Caesar and Cleopatra then continue their conversation as in Act II of the play version: although the time is now a day later, and the place is the King's Room instead of the Council Chamber.

After Cleopatra and Caesar complete their conversation, the film gives us the tenth new scene, twenty seconds long. It shows, in simultaneous action, more civil strife. Just before a soldier comes in to report, "There is an army come to Alexandria, calling itself the Roman Army," we see those troops commanded by Achillas, cheered by the crowd as they march by. An anti-Roman crowd then attacks the Tax Receipts Office. The "S.P.Q.R." sign is torn down, and as it falls, one of the young Egyptians tramples it.

The eleventh new scene is a twenty-second visual connection between Act II and Act III. Shaw's job is to move the action from inside the Palace to the quay in front of the Palace. We see Cleopatra rush toward one of the corridor arches so that she can watch Caesar's boat depart for the lighthouse. We see what she sees. Into Cleopatra's view moves a sentinel, walking along the quay; then the scene cuts to that sentinel. Apollodorus hails him, and the dialogue continues as at the beginning of Act III.

The twelfth new scene, like the previous one, is a twenty-second visual connection, this time between the two sites of Act III. The purpose of the scene is to move the action from the quay to the Pharos and its lighthouse. In the play, the site is changed by a simple "Meanwhile. . . ." But in the movie, we watch Apollodorus, in a beautiful pictorial shot of the harbor and his picturesque boat, move away, singing, toward the lighthouse, with Cleopatra wrapped in the blanket. Apollodorus looks toward the lighthouse. We see what he sees. And then the scene cuts from a shot of the distant lighthouse to the platform on the lighthouse itself, where Rufio and Caesar sit munching dates.

The thirteenth new scene is a five-second quick cut to show simultaneous action. Between Apollodorus's jump into the sea and Caesar's following him, the film increases tension by showing the approach of the attacking Egyptian troops.

The fourteenth new scene is intended simply to inform the viewer of the six-month time gap between Act III and Act IV. This was a particularly troublesome spot for Pascal, who desperately wanted a new scene from Shaw. On July 23, 1944, Pascal wrote to Shaw:

> Incidentally, when I come to the Music Room sequence, reading from the play and the script, I always have the feeling that a very short new scene would be useful to bridge the time gap of six months since the foregoing scene on the Pharos. You start Act IV with the following statement: "Cleopatra's sousing in the east harbour of Alexandria was in October 48 B.C. In March 47 she is passing the afternoon in her boudoir in the palace." It is this interval that I want to cover smoothly on the screen, instead of leaving the audience in ignorance of the time-situation until Cleopatra tells Pothinus: "These six months we have been besieged in the palace by my subjects."

To this, Shaw replied coldly: "I think there must be a definite break in the continuity after the lighthouse scene; but I will study it and see what can be done with the help of your suggestions." Pascal tried again and again, but he could not arouse Shaw's enthusiasm for a new transition scene. Pascal sent Shaw several suggestions, but none of them met with his approval. Finally, a whole year later, Shaw wrote a playful Barber Shop scene which managed to sneak in the needed bit of time information. But the difficulties which plagued the entire production of *Caesar and Cleopatra* were particularly hard on this new scene. Studio space was no longer available; so the Barbar Shop set was built outdoors, in a corner of the huge Denham lot where several crowd scenes were shot during the summer of 1945. But the sun continually refused to shine—until the key character, Basil Sydney as Rufio, was no longer available.

Here is the entire text of the unshot Barber Shop scene, another delightful addition to the Shaw canon, not included in either the shooting script or the sound track. It is included here through the kindness of Miss Marjorie Deans:

A barber's shop in Alexandria. The barber is operating on a customer wrapped in the usual surplice. He has almost finished with him, and is holding two bronze mirrors (looking-glasses have not yet been invented) so that the customer can see the back of his head.

BARBER. How is that, Excellency?

CUSTOMER. Perfect.

BARBER [*putting aside the mirrors*] Brilliantine?

CUSTOMER. Yes: plenty of it. But not the perfumed sort.

BARBER [*applying the wash and brushing it in*] I understand, Excellency. A royal major domo must be neutral. If you have the same scent as a courtier he thinks you have stolen it from him.

CUSTOMER. True. I meet nobody but courtiers: you meet all sorts. These Romans now. What do you make of them?

BARBER. To a barber, Excellency, all men are alike. Romans, Greeks, Egyptians, Jews wear the same robe in my chair and say the same things. Fair or dark, the same scissors cuts them all. What can you say of any man but that he is a man?

CUSTOMER. But these Romans are barbarians: they burn our library, one of the seven wonders of the world. They are magicians: they dig wells in the salt sand and draw fresh water from them. Their biggest and heaviest men swim like dolphins and carry the Queen on their backs.

BARBER. That might be the Queen's magic. She rides on Caesar's back now, on land as on the sea. She has made him king here these six months. [*The substance of this exchange was preserved in the transition scene that finally was included in the sound track version*].

CUSTOMER. Do not believe it. He has made her Queen.

BARBER. One good turn deserves another. But I know nothing about women: I am not a lady's hairdresser.

CUSTOMER. And all Romans are alike to you?

BARBER. All men are alike to me.

CUSTOMER. You would not say that if you knew Caesar and his henchman Rufio.

BARBER. Ah, I forgot Rufio. You are right, Excellency: no other man alive has such whiskers. My one professional ambition is to shave them off and make him look like a human being. [*Rufio strides in*].

RUFIO. You are engaged. How soon will you be free?

BARBER. Your worship's name was the last word in our mouths. Three minutes, general: not a moment more.

CUSTOMER. Don't you recognize me in this gown?

RUFIO. What! The royal major domo! I crave your pardon: I have seen you only in your court splendour.

CUSTOMER [*to the barber*] Finish up quickly. Do not keep the general waiting.

RUFIO. Take it easy: I am in no hurry.

CUSTOMER. You are a busy man, general: always in a hurry. [*to the barber, rising*] There: that's enough. [*He throws off his gown and stands in his breeches and singlet until the barber fetches his official coat and arrays him in his courtly magnificence. Rufio throws himself into the vacated chair*].

RUFIO. Now you look like yourself, major. [*The barber approaches him with the surplice*] No gown for me. Take it away.

BARBER. But, general, the cut whiskers will be all over your clothes.

RUFIO. Cut a single hair of my whiskers and I will cut your thumbs off. Let my whiskers alone. Attend to my hair.

BARBER [*disappointed, pitifully*] Oh, general, I had set my heart on your whiskers.

RUFIO. You would. Your Queen says they remind her of a lousy bird's nest. I have to banquet with her and with Caesar this afternoon. Make them look glossy and smell nice.

CUSTOMER. I must take my leave, general. I also have to be on duty at the banquet. Au revoir.

RUFIO [*offhandedly*] Good afternoon.

The customer goes out, giving a coin to the barber as he passes.

BARBER [*half voice*] A thousand thanks, Excellency. [*He bows the customer out and returns to the chair*]. Nobody in Alexandria under sixty lets hair grow on his face, general. Can I not persuade you to have them off?

RUFIO. Have them off! What should I look like without them? My authority is in them. I should look like that bumptious noodle who has just left us. Do as I tell you and look sharp about it.

The barber, with a sigh, resigns himself to his task. The scene fades out.

As a substitute for this abandoned Barber Shop scene, Miss Deans explains that Pascal "fell back on Shaw's alternative suggestion" for leading into Act IV: a thirty-second scene "which shows the old musician and the harpist girl approaching the Palace." According to Shaw's shooting script description, the harpist girl (a very young Jean Simmons) is seated "on a handsome Bactrian camel, half-caged in red curtains." The old musician is seated on "a well-caparisoned ass." As the two ride toward the palace, they pass Egyptian citizens, who are heard talking:

FIRST CITIZEN. The Romans are magicians. For six months, a mere handful of them have held the palace against the whole of Egypt's armed forces.

SECOND CITIZEN. And look at their escape from the Pharos. Who but a magician could swim like a dolphin at Caesar's age, carrying the Queen on his back?

THIRD CITIZEN. That might be the Queen's magic. She rides on Caesar's back, on land now, as on the sea.

Laughter of citizens, fading into laughter of Cleopatra's ladies.

The next two new film scenes, the fifteenth and the sixteenth of the interpolations, are transition scenes between Act IV and Act V. The shortest of these, only twenty seconds long, is a wholly visual scene which shows—the play version neglected to show it or explain it—how Caesar was able to get *out* of the besieged Palace in order to join his troops:

Shooting from the quayside we see a crowd of Egyptians attacking the Palace Gate. Suddenly the gates swing open, and before they have time to think what happens, a centurion and phalanx of Caesar's guard appear and spread out in a solid wall of shields in V formation, the apex being Caesar, a few paces behind them. The "wall" spreads out right and left of the steps, firmly and inexorably. The Egyptians scarcely make any fight; they are too astonished. They press back and back as Caesar's guard comes down the steps. Caesar follows them a few steps behind. Dissolve.

The other new transition scene is the most cinematic of the interpolated scenes. It is an elaborate one-minute, forty-second montage, which shows the Roman victory mentioned in the play's Act V. This scene is not described in Shaw's shooting script; it is Pascal's invention. In the sound track version it is made up of quickly edited shots of battles, victorious Romans, fleeing Egyptians, fast riding across the desert, and, finally, a mystical series of shots showing Caesar alone in the desert with the Sphinx. As Caesar approaches the Sphinx, to the accompaniment of weird, haunting music, he prayerfully echoes his earlier speech: "For I am he of whose genius you are the symbol: part brute, part woman, and part god." A hollow voice, apparently from the Sphinx, answers droningly: "Hail, Caesar!"

The final scene is importantly changed from the play. A fifty-second addition changes the tone of the play's ending and slyly looks forward to the *next* play, *Antony and Cleopatra*. The end of the play version has a melancholy tone, as Cleopatra tells Apollodorus that she hopes Caesar will not return, but "I can't help crying, all the same." Instead, in the shooting script and the sound track versions:

She waves her handkerchief to Caesar, vigourously; but very quickly the waving becomes perfunctory. Her head turns involuntarily to the direction of the open sea and her eyes seek the far, far distance. The same shining look comes in her eyes that we have seen before whenever her thoughts have turned to Mark Antony. Under her breath she murmurs, "Mark Antony!" The screen is then filled with Cleopatra's radiant face, "and a little smile of anticipation." The scene fades out and THE END appears on the screen.

These sixteen new scenes filled up the spaces between acts and locations. They showed us a little of what the play left out. They were all lovely to look at. But obviously they did very little cinematically. Like the rest of *Caesar and Cleopatra*, the pictures were a background against which Shaw's lines were spoken. Instead of using the potentialities of the medium, the film placed the characters, talking, into the midst of spectacle.

The play had introduced several settings of exotic and elaborate nature. Grasping at this opportunity in the absence of a dynamic cinematic screen play, Pascal outdid himself—and the financiers—in turning these exotic settings, in the Technicolored film, into something lavishly, spectacularly, pictorial. Some of the critics even suggested later that the real star of the film was set designer Oliver Messel. The shooting script describes, for example, what the screen shows as the action moves from the Sphinx in the desert to the extraordinarily elaborate interior of Cleopatra's Throne Room:

Interior of Memphis Throne Room and Colonnade.

55. Tracking-Shot.

As we dissolve, the camera is tracking forward, and we see a flickering light which appears for a moment behind the eyes of the Sphinx before its image fades away. The light defines itself as the flame of a torch which is held in the hand of a huge Nubian slave standing on guard in front of a massive doorway. The camera is tracking swiftly towards this doorway through a colonnade of pillars and statuary. The slave peers ahead of him fearfully. As the camera stops, holding him in Medium-Long Shot, his face suddenly registers extreme terror. He throws down the lighted torch, turns and runs headlong through the doorway, shutting it behind him.

Crowds of extras come to watch Caesar and his troops leave Egypt; Cecil Parker as Britannus, Claude Rains as Caesar, and Basil Sydney as Rufio in *Caesar and Cleopatra,* 1945.

56. Long-Shot: Caesar and Cleopatra.
The camera is shooting down the colonnade, through the open end of which we see the desert and the tiny figure of the Sphinx on the horizon. Caesar and Cleopatra are approaching through the moonlight. She is still leading him by the hand. They enter the colonnade.

57. Medium-Shot: Caesar and Cleopatra.
The camera tracks alongside Caesar and Cleopatra as they walk through the colonnade, passing in and out of the weird shadows thrown by the pillars and statues.

Caesar is amused, interested, excited, peering keenly about at the strange architecture and the statuary between the pillars of the colonnade, figures of men with wings and hawks' heads and vast black marble cats; but Cleopatra hurries him along impatiently, looking around her for the sentries, obviously puzzled by their absence. The camera stops and pans round to show them reach the door at the end of the colonnade. Caesar picks up the lighted torch thrown down by the Nubian slave, and is examining the architecture of the roof while Cleopatra, finding the door ajar, pushes at it ineffectually. Seeing this, Caesar goes to her assistance.

57A. Medium-Close Shot: Caesar and Cleopatra.
Cleopatra is trying to open the door. Caesar comes in beside her and starts to push it open.

57B. Medium-Shot: Caesar and Cleopatra.
As the door starts to open, they go forward.
The Memphis Throne Room. Night. Set Note.
This is a huge columned hall, having the air of a deserted Temple rather than of a Palace. Its atmosphere is mystic and austere. At the far end, facing the doorway to the colonnade, is a throne on a raised dais. There is a door behind the throne. On either side of the dais is a standing candelabra. Right of the throne is a columned archway leading to the interior of the palace. In the centre of the right hand wall is a huge statue of a bird.

Here is the description, from the shooting script, of what we see on the screen as Cleopatra's music room in the Palace of Alexandria, the scene which opened Act IV of the play:

This is a room in Pompeian style with at least two doors—left and right from Cleopatra's divan. The walls are covered with delicate murals. Slender pillars surround the walls, Greek with Pompeian detail in the Capitals. There is a decorative pool in the centre. Above the pool the room is open to the sky. At one end is a raised platform with steps, on which is the resting-couch used by Cleopatra. Over this is a canopy to shelter her from the rays of the sun.

The spectacular soon engulfed most of the other characteristics of the film. Pascal even hired an astronomer to reproduce the exact location of the stars in the Egyptian sky at the time of Cleopatra. Far from helping the film, all this extreme historical accuracy merely blurred the fun of Shaw's play. Shaw's vision of ancient Egypt was, of course, extremely personal, full of paradox and anachronism. He got his fun by showing us that the people and situations of Caesar's day are exactly like the people and situations of our own day. Pascal, instead, showed the viewer an exotic and very explicitly Egyptian Egypt. The cost of the film skyrocketed, as Pascal's extravagance was added to the cost of the many production difficulties. Shaw was proved right in his early prediction that *Caesar and Cleopatra* would cost an inordinate amount of money. The first budget estimate for the film had been 250,000 pounds. By the

Cecil Parker as Britannus, Raymond Lovell as Lucius Septimus, Stewart Granger as Apollodorus, Basil Sydney as Rufio, and Claude Rains as Caesar confront Vivien Leigh as Cleopatra in *Caesar and Cleopatra,* 1945.

time the budget had come before J. Arthur Rank for final approval, the figure was 550,000 pounds. And now still more money was needed. "What does it matter?" Pascal is said to have asked. "Mr. Rank can sell a few more bags of flour." An associate of J. Arthur Rank recently described a scene at The Rank Organisation:

I walked into Rank's office one day to find Pascal on his knees, with the embarrassed Arthur Rank backing against the wall. Rank appealed to me for my opinion whether he should yield to Pascal's appeal that he could go to a higher figure. I advised against it. The film eventually cost about 1,250,000 pounds.

As the cost of the spectacular film mounted, even Shaw began to utter disenchanted sounds. "Pascal shocks me," Shaw wrote, "by his utter indifference to the cost."

Of course some parts of the film showed a real cinematic quality—and not just a static spectacle. The power of the close-up is cleverly used when the entire screen is filled with Caesar's nose as he tells the frightened Cleopatra, "It is a Roman nose!" Time is extended for suspense when the Nubian slave's threatened decapitation of Ftatateeta is prolonged into seven separate camera shots. Camera angle is occasionally used editorially: When Caesar is approaching the Sphinx the camera shoots down at him, making him, as the shooting script notes, "small and insignificant." By contrast, later the terrified Cleopatra looks up at Caesar and, as the script notes, "from Cleopatra's angle we see the magnificent head of Caesar." The visual occasionally replaces the verbal: Pictures of the Egyptian attack against the Pharos replace Apollodorus's verbal description of it; we see the ships burning in the harbor of Alexandria, so Rufio does not have to tell us about it; we watch the Egyptians drying up the harbor, so Rufio does not have to describe it; instead of Bel Affris's verbal praise of the effectiveness of the Roman Legions, we see them operating as they occupy Alexandria, as they escort Caesar from the besieged Palace, as they conquer the Egyptian forces in battle. But this is very little filmic inventiveness, very little exploitation of unique powers, in a very long movie.

Not much was cut from *Caesar and Cleopatra* during its stage-to-screen journey. As in the previous Shaw films, however, some simplification did take place. Once a decision was made to simplify the political and military situation in *Caesar and Cleopatra*, several small deletions and alterations and transpositions necessarily followed. Place names were omitted: in the actual film no mention is made of Syria, or Lake Mareotis, or Numidia. And persons' names were omitted too: no mention is made of Berenice, the sister of Cleopatra and Ptolemy; or of Cato; or of Juba of Numidia. "Vercingetorix" is changed to "the King of the Gauls," and Mithridates of Pergamos is not called "the great son of Eupator." Reference to political events is simplified: no mention is made of "the lawful debt due to Rome by Egypt, contracted by the King's deceased father to the Triumvirate," or to Cleopatra's father having cut off her sister's head and then slaying the sister's husband. Only the barest of reference is made to Pompey. "Pompey's party and the army of occupation" becomes simply "our enemies." "Our Rhodian galleys" becomes "our galleys."

As in *Pygmalion* and *Major Barbara*, minor characters were made less important than they were in the play. The elaborate plans of Belzanor, Bel Affris, and the Persian, characters originally created for dramatic exposition, are cut as unnecessary to the essential plot. The introduction of Ftatateeta into the Prologue is dropped as unnecessary. Her character is thus slightly weakened by the omission of her exhibition of courage and strength before the threats of Belzanor and the Persian. The role of Apollodorus is slightly lightened by the omission of much of his talk about art, and by the omission of most of his more elaborate gallantry. The movie creates much less fun and satire and anachronism around the person of the extremely British Britannus.

Neither the character of Cleopatra nor the character of Caesar was changed when *Caesar and Cleopatra* moved from stage to screen. Cleopatra lost almost nothing of her dialogue. As in the play, she is presented as a young girl who, in becoming a Queen, becomes a woman. The few lines which Caesar lost worked toward slight simplification of his character. Caesar remains the wonderfully Shavian paradox of the world-conquerer who acts like a modern man, like Cleopatra's "old gentleman," defying all heroic stereotypes; but some of his philosophical asides and verbal paradoxes are omitted, and so are some of the more mystical parts of his character. Physically, Caesar is made, according to Cleopatra's comments, "wrinkly" instead of "thin and stringy"—a change obviously made the better to fit the person of Claude Rains. The movie avoided, as did the play, any serious romantic suggestion between Caesar and Cleopatra, and it did not, as one might suspect a movie would, create any romance between two such likely candidates as Vivien Leigh as Cleopatra and Stewart Granger as Apollodoris. The only small gift given to the romanticists was the suggestion in the final scene that Cleopatra is waiting anxiously for Mark Antony to arrive to take the place of Caesar.

Shaw had his way in the filming of *Caesar and Cleopatra.* Little was added to the play except visual spectacle, and very little was cut from the play. And yet Shaw recognized that something was wrong. Shortly before the film was completed, Shaw was obviously not pleased with the way the film was going. "If he had his way," wrote Shaw's friend Stephen Winsten, "he would have scrapped it completely, for it seemed to him that Pascal had turned it into a dull, prosaic, illustrated history." Obviously, what was wrong was not script writer Shaw, but director Pascal, even though in this film Shaw's theory of the cinema had prevailed. When the film was finally completed, Shaw refused to appear personally in a preview, as he had with *Pygmalion* and with *Major Barbara*: "There is enough talk already in the film without me," he said. "One Sphinx is enough."

The press, too, sounded an uneasy note as *Caesar and Cleopatra* neared completion. As the release date was postponed again and again, the newspapers began to resound with attacks against the lavish cost of the film. Expenses obviously mounted daily. Pascal was constantly lectured, in articles and editorials, about the imprudence and dangers of squandering huge sums of money during wartime. Even Parliament entered the fray when one M.P. demanded that the government place restrictions on the rising costs of *Caesar and Cleopatra.* But J. Arthur Rank kept paying more and more. The film, indeed, became the most expensive ever made in Great Britain.

Finally *Caesar and Cleopatra* was ready for its premiere. The film opened on December 13, 1945—a year and a half after filming began. Pascal called out the press to a colorful, lavish opening attended by film stars and assorted celebrities. The London newspapers reported the biggest traffic congestion since V-J Day. And *The Times* of London announced in its Court Circular: "Queen Mary, attended by the Hon. Margaret Wyndham and Major the Hon. John Coke, was present at the first showing of the film *Caesar and Cleopatra* at the Odeon Theatre, Marble Arch, this evening."

The prerelease publicity and a huge advertising campaign paid off at first, with the film doing in London what *Variety* called "solid biz." But business died away as the British critics attacked the film mercilessly.

By the time *Caesar and Cleopatra* was ready to open in New York, J. Arthur Rank was desperately trying to save some of his huge investment. He asked a hand-picked member of his staff, William J. Heineman, to personally supervise the United States sales and distribution of the film. The pitch-men went all out to turn *Caesar and Cleopatra* into an American success. The ads screamed: "The Motion Picture Event of the Century," and "The motion picture that will establish itself as the greatest spectacle in the history of the industry!"

A new advertising pitch was tried for the American audience. *The New York Times* ads announced "A Sensational Spectacle of Seductive Beauty," and the ads billed "Vivien Leigh as the sinuous siren of enticement—*Cleopatra*!" The ads invited the viewer to

> SEE mighty Caesar seize the spoils of victory from Cleopatra herself . . . SEE the pleasure-mad revelry of pagan Rome, alluring, voluptuous Egypt . . . SEE the spectacular barges where wine flowed like water, joy was unconfined . . . A Temptation in Technicolor!"

Under the influence of less severe American reviews and the flashy ads, *Caesar and Cleopatra* opened across America to what *Variety* called "generally good business." The London *Times* passed on the good news: "The English film version of Mr. Bernard Shaw's *Caesar and Cleopatra* has been well received by audiences in the United States." But soon the hard-sell publicity campaign backfired, and business fell away. A Portland, Oregon, theatre manager explained what had happened:

Sometimes ballyhoo induces a lot of people to spend their money on a picture they think they're going to like—and when they've seen it they come out sore as the devil. It's the way a lot of our patrons felt after seeing *Caesar and Cleopatra.*

Variety soon announced just how bad the *Caesar and Cleopatra* losses were:

Britain's first major Technicolor spec, *Caesar and Cleopatra,* will lose its producer, J. Arthur Rank, approximately $3,000,000. That was learned this week in the U.S. with the tallying up by the picture's distributor here, United Artists, of estimated American gross. Pic, UA reported, will get approximately $2,500,000 in this market.

But *Variety* had been optimistic. Rank's loss was greater than $3,000,000. The American gross for *Caesar and Cleopatra,* according to the vice president of United Artists Corporation, was, even fifteen years after its release, only $1,885,847.72, which is not "approximately $2,500,000."

A J. Arthur Rank associate summed up the international financial records of the three Shaw-Pascal films: "I can say without fear of contradiction that *Pygmalion* was *very* profitable, *Major Barbara* adequately profitable, and *Caesar and Cleopatra* a disastrous loss." Although *Pygmalion* was always a more popular play than either *Major Barbara* or *Caesar and Cleopatra,* that fact alone hardly explains the vastly different reception given these three films. The quality of the movies themselves must have been an important factor in their reception.

Caesar and Cleopatra's critical reception was almost as disastrous as its box-office reception. The British critics were particularly hard on it. Richard Winnington of the *News Chronicle* called it "a dismal ordeal," complaining that the film "has stuck with desperate literalness to the lines of this Bernard Shaw play." Similarly, the critic for *The Spectator* complained of the "failure to utilize the camera with imagination." The London *Times,* finding it "hollow at the heart," accused Pascal of being "content to call in spectacle to fulfill the function of creature imagination." Although the American critics were kinder to the film, it failed to appear anywhere in any of their "best picture" ratings. The Americans generally praised the spectacle of the film, and most of the performances, but, like the British, complained of its basically "uncinematic" quality. The comments of the reviewer for *The Commonweal* are representative:

> As a spectacle, *Caesar and Cleopatra* merits high praise; but as a movie, it is dull. . . . Regardless of the heights GBS may have reached as a playwright, this film shows that motion picture writing is not one of his talents. The success of *Pygmalion* in movies was due, among other things, to the play's being rewritten for cinema.

Shaw's partnership with Gabriel Pascal had ended, with *Caesar and Cleopatra,* much less auspiciously than it had begun, with *Pygmalion.* Although Pascal was later, after Shaw's death, to produce *Androcles and the Lion* in Hollywood, the Shaw-Pascal partnership was now at an end, and so was Shaw's movie career. Shaw knew of the failure of *Caesar and Cleopatra.* Publicly, he refused to comment on the film, saying only, "It would be like asking a priest to talk out of confession." But privately, according to a Rank associate, Shaw said to Pascal: "You know, Gabby, that was a very bad film." Shaw still could not see that his failure to rework his play for the new medium of the motion picture was at fault. Never, even now at the end of his career, did Shaw change his theory of the cinema. He told Stephen Winsten: "You have seen the columns of invective poured on the final thing. There, again, they wanted nothing less than perfection and would not make allowance for an imperfect medium." Not only was the medium of the motion picture imperfect, but Shaw was quite sure that Pascal was, too. Shaw's doctor reports that he once told Shaw that the film of *Caesar and Cleopatra* had much less fire and sparkle than the play. Shaw agreed, and blamed Pascal: "Those foreigners have no sense of humor." As for Gabriel Pascal, he contended that the bad reviews of *Caesar and Cleopatra* were retaliation against Shaw for his many jabs at journalists. "It is all," argued Pascal, "part of a plot of critics to kill the picture."

If Shaw recognized the failure of *Caesar and Cleopatra,* and if J. Arthur Rank lost money by it, it was Gabby Pascal who suffered the most. The whirlwind who, in 1935, had pulled off the greatest *coup* in cinema history was told by J. Arthur Rank, in 1946, that he was not his idea of a director. Rank had a contract with Pascal for another picture;

but he bought up the contract and permanently severed his association with the expensive Gabriel Pascal. Worst of all, for his lavish wartime expenditure on *Caesar and Cleopatra*, Pascal was officially censured by the General Council of the Association of Cine-Technicians; and he was forbidden by them to function again, except under severe restrictions, on the floor of any British studio. In disgrace, Pascal left England for Hollywood.

Thirty-two years passed between the time of Shaw's contention that the silent cinema was more momentous than printing and the time of the failure of *Caesar and Cleopatra.* In all those years, Shaw himself was obviously fascinated, as if by a serpent's eye, by pictures which move and tell a story. He established a firm cinema theory, and supported it by a cinema practice. Of his three late films, *Pygmalion* departed most from Shaw's theory that the cinema was not a separate art from the drama: it was the film he least controlled; it was made the most cinematic; and it was the greatest financial and artistic success. *Major Barbara* departed moderately from Shaw's theoretical demands: he was largely responsible for it; it was moderately cinematic; and it was only moderately unsuccessful. *Caesar and Cleopatra* had the fewest alterations from the stage play: it was the film which Shaw more closely controlled; it was the least cinematic; and it was a financial and artistic disaster. The conclusion seems inescapable that Shaw, fascinated as he was by the movies, was a good movie writer to the degree that he departed from his own philosophy of the cinema, to the degree, that is, that his cinema practice contradicted his cinema theory.

AFTERWORD

FROM HIS exile in Hollywood, the unconquerable Gabriel Pascal fought to raise money for the next Shaw-Pascal film. All the titles that had come up for consideration before now were examined anew. Most of them Pascal announced were scheduled for immediate filming. The newspapers carried contradictory announcements that Pascal was about to film *The Doctor's Dilemma, The Devil's Disciple, The Shewing Up of Blanco Posnet, The Applecart, Saint Joan.* Pascal negotiated with producer Mary Pickford; he sold Deborah Kerr's contract to Metro-Goldwyn-Mayer and demanded that she star in his next film; he sought Gracie Fields for *Mrs. Warren's Profession*; he planned a *Candida* in Hollywood, a *Man and Superman* in Spain, an *Androcles and the Lion* in Rome. As the smoke began to clear, Pascal seemed particularly anxious to film *Androcles.* Ever since he had seen the Max Reinhardt production of *Androcles and the Lion* in Vienna in 1926, Pascal had talked of his devotion to the play and of his desire to film it. After trying Rome, he tried to finance the film in Mexico City. Shaw wanted Cantinflas to play Androcles, and Diego Rivera to design the film. But nothing went right in Mexico, and Cantinflas couldn't even speak English, so Pascal turned rather hopelessly to Hollywood. Eventually, RKO, in spite of the insults Shaw had heaped upon them, agreed to finance *Androcles* in Hollywood, to be produced by Pascal and directed by Chester Erskine.

Shaw wasn't happy with RKO and was obviously tired of the whole troublesome movie business. In June of 1950, just a few months before his death, Shaw advised Pascal to give up the idea of bringing Shaw to the cinema. Start a new career, Shaw advised him: "Look for a young Shaw; for though Shaws do not grow on gooseberry bushes there are as many good fish in the sea as ever came out of it. Anyhow, you must live in your own generation, not in mine." In October, Shaw's housekeeper telephoned to Pascal's wife: "Mr. Shaw," she said, "is asking for Mr. Pascal. He is dying." Valerie Pascal cabled her husband; but Pascal arrived just too late to see the Master.

The *Androcles* film continued—without the watchful ministrations of Shaw. With RKO's money behind him, Pascal went to town: he hired Robert Newton, who had been a hit in *Major Barbara*; he emptied the British studios of Maurice Evans, Reginald Gardiner, Alan Mowbray, Elsa Lanchester. He hired Jean Simmons, who had grown into a popular star since her tiny role in *Caesar and Cleopatra.* And—incredibly to everyone—he hired Victor Mature, then at the peak of his sword-and-sandal-epic career in Hollywood. The wars within the huge Hollywood studio will never be known. But by the time the film was released it had been turned into a Victor Mature-Jean Simmons love story, set against the orgies of Pagan Rome. Pascal said he was pleased with the finished product, "an important improvement over the original play." But the critics snapped that Pascal "had thrown Shaw to the lions of RKO." *The New Republic* spoke for most everyone when it called *Androcles and the Lion* "a public travesty of Shaw's work." Pascal never made another movie.

Gabriel Pascal turned to the stage. He was anxious to produce a musical version of his *Pygmalion* film for Broadway. Stubborn as always, he contacted Richard Rodgers and Oscar Hammerstein, and later he pleaded and negotiated unsuccessfully with Frank Loesser, Cole Porter, Leonard Bernstein, Gian-Carlo Menotti. Finally Lawrence Langner of The Theatre Guild suggested that Pascal talk to the team of Alan Jay Lerner and Frederick Loewe. Everyone knows the ending of *that* story. Although Pascal died before *My Fair Lady* was finally produced, a good proportion of the world's population—and perhaps The Pascal Estate most of all—is eternally grateful that the colorful, irrepressible, legendary Gabriel Pascal turned away from the motion picture after the death of Bernard Shaw and the disaster of *Androcles*.

The subsequent story of Shaw on the screen is generally not a happy one. When Shaw films flop, they do it big. In 1957, Otto Preminger tried to film Shaw's *Saint Joan*. The reviews of the resultant pageantlike, severely shortened movie are classics of critical invective: "An awkward, obtunded, and torpid bastardization of a great play" said *The New Yorker*. Everyone agreed—even Preminger's much-heralded new young star, Jean Seberg, who fled to the New Wave comforts of France. Hecht-Hill-Lancaster filmed *The Devil's Disciple* in 1959, changing directors in midstream and changing the play into a romantic melodrama which *Films in Review* called "a filmic abortion of Shaw's play." Two German Shaw films were not shown in this country: an *Arms and the Man* was made in 1958 and a *Mrs. Warren's Profession* was made in 1959. The only other Shaw films to date were two stylish, Technicolor movies, reasonably true to Shaw and reasonably true to the cinema. Both *The Doctor's Dilemma* in 1958 and *The Millionairess* in 1961 were successful film adaptations, and both were directed by Anthony Asquith, who had so clearly shown the way in *Pygmalion*.

What was the way that Asquith showed? What, finally, does the story of Shaw and the Cinema tell us about filmic adaptations of stage plays? The story of this book tells us more clearly what a film adaptation does not do than what it does. Clearly the failure of Shaw's theory of the cinema is an object lesson: a successful film does not merely record a play. The success of *Pygmalion* tells us something of what a successful adaptation does: the powers of the camera, editor's shears, and microphone are used so as to blend the verbal with a visual counterpart. Dynamism, excitement, humor, editorial comment, heightened characterization, verbal economy, a new time and space all result from the use of the filmic medium, and can all be made to function in the new whole which the movie is to become. What Asquith showed is that the director must decide what effect he wants and then know the cinema well enough to know how to achieve that effect in the *new* medium. In someone as verbal as Shaw, that will often mean that the director will want to achieve the effects of the language. To present the language in the most effective way possible does not mean simply setting up the camera and shooting the conversation. That produces, not the original effect of the language, but—in the new medium—a boredom: in a study of "Psychology of Film Experience," Hugo Mauerhofer reports that psychological investigation proves what experience shows, that "static scenes which are acceptable to members of book and theatre audiences are found excessively dull by those same individuals when they are an audience at the cinema." And making language effective on the screen does not mean zooming the camera around and dizzily distracting from the language, or burying the words in tons or acres of fancy scenery. It means what Asquith himself has called "an indissoluble marriage of words and pictures," it means emphasizing neither words nor pictures at the expense of the other. In primarily pictorial scenes, Asquith uses the cinema to acquire the precise visual effect desired; in primarily verbal scenes, Asquith uses the cinema to enhance the words, to blend, to complement. He says: "I try to make the visual flow and emphasis correspond to the rhythm and sense of the dialogue." Anthony Asquith explains how he did it in *Pygmalion:*

> The heart of a Shaw scene is nearly always a verbal one. . . . I prefer, therefore, to do such scenes in one continuous take. At the same time I try to achieve the different emphasis of long-shot, medium-shot and close-up by devising movements for the actors and the camera which will give me these gradations at the right moment, without having to interrupt the scene with a cut. It is what I might call a legato technique.
>
> Sometimes into these scenes I interject a staccato chord, as it were, by a sudden cut into a big close-up. Sometimes a scene which has started smoothly and flowingly leads naturally into a quick machinegun fire of individual close-ups. This would happen when the pace of the dialogue quickens and long paragraphs are broken up into short sentences.

Everyone who saw *Pygmalion* was struck by its "cinematic" quality even in its verbal scenes. That means that a skillful director was in charge, that he let the pictures speak and let the words speak, that Asquith cares about a blending of words and pictures into a new medium of expression, that he uses the powers of the unique tools of the cinema. Asquith sees the paradox of adaptation: to keep a play-made-into-film the same in matter, it must be skillfully changed in manner.

Film aestheticians, of course, write much about what a film can do *qua* film. The serpent's eye, as it did in Shaw's day, continues to fascinate. But its victim, if you like to call him so, is not only the viewer but the authors and critics who studiously stare back into its vastness. As they stare, they do learn something about the reasons for that fascination, and how to increase it and exploit it for memorable artistic creation. These cinema aestheticians talk often to themselves and often in cant, but they often teach us something about this exciting art. Much of what we have inductively discovered here about filmic adaptations of Shaw's plays confirms what we read in Vardac, Nicoll, Kracaver, Langer, Panofsky, Arnheim, Pudovkin, Adler and so many others. But this has been a book about Shaw and not a book about the aesthetics of the cinema—Shaw's theory was too unsophisticated for that. The cinema aestheticians look far beyond Shaw. Now they look, rightly so, to Fellini and to Resnais and to Antonioni and to Bergman. If these men can continue to force the cinema forward, building upon the work of the Griffiths and the Chaplins and the Eisensteins and the Flahertys and the Asquiths and even the Pascals—and learning from the mistakes of the Shaws—then maybe the cinema will yet become an invention much more momentous than printing.

APPENDIX A

Motion Pictures Made From The Works of Shaw

1921: *Roman Boxera* [*Cashel Byron's Profession*] (Czechoslovakian)

PRODUCER: Weteb Studios
DIRECTOR: Vaclav Binovec
SCREEN PLAY: Suzanne Marwille
CAST: Frank . . . . Frank Rose-Ruzicka
Marta . . . . Suzanne Marwille
Theodor . . . . V. Ch. Vladimirov
and: Ada Karlovsky, Alois Charvat, Joe Jahelka, J. Fiser, Vaclav Rapp
SETTINGS: Frantisek Josef Leopold
CAMERAMAN: Josef Kokeisl

1927: Cathedral scene from *Saint Joan* (British)

PRODUCER: Vivian Van Dam for Phonofilms
DIRECTOR: Widgey Newman
SCREEN PLAY: Bernard Shaw
CAST: Saint Joan . . . . Sybil Thorndike

1931: *How He Lied to Her Husband* (British)

PRODUCER: John Maxwell for British International Pictures
DIRECTOR: Cecil Lewis
SCREEN PLAY: Bernard Shaw
CAST: Her Lover . . . . Robert Harris
Her Husband . . . . Edmund Gwenn
Herself . . . . Vera Lennox
COSTUMES AND SETTINGS: Gladys Calthrop
CAMERAMAN: John J. Cox
EDITOR: S. Simmonds
DISTRIBUTED BY: In England: Wardour
In America: Bluebird
FIRST SHOWING: London: Carlton Theatre, January 10, 1931
Malvern Festival: August, 1931

1932: *Arms and the Man* (British)

PRODUCER: John Maxwell for British International Pictures
DIRECTOR: Cecil Lewis
SCREEN PLAY: Bernard Shaw
CAST: Major Paul Petkoff . . . . . . Frederick Lloyd
Major Sergius Saranoff . . . . Maurice Colebourne
Capt. Bluntschli . . . . Barry Jones
Major Plechanoff . . . . Charlton Morton
Nicola . . . . Wallace Evennett
Catherine Petkoff . . . . . . Margaret Scudamore
Louka . . . . Angela Baddeley
Raina Petkoff . . . . Anne Grey
COSTUMES AND SETTINGS: John Mead
DISTRIBUTED BY: Wardour
FIRST SHOWING: Malvern Festival: August 4, 1932
London: Regal, Marble Arch, September 24, 1932

1935: *Pygmalion* (German)

PRODUCER: Eberhard Klagemann for Klagemann-Film der Tobis-Rota
DIRECTOR: Erich Engel
ORIGINAL STORY: Bernard Shaw, translated to German by Siegfried Trebitsch
SCREEN PLAY: Heinrich Oberlander and Walter Wassermann
CAST: Eliza Doolittle . . . . Jenny Jugo
Professor Higgins. . . . . . . Gustaf Grundgens
Colonel Pickering . . . . . . Anton Edthofer
Alfred Doolittle . . . . Eugen Klopfer
DISTRIBUTED BY: Rota-Film

1937: *Pygmalion* (Dutch)

PRODUCER: Dr. Ludwig Berger for Filmex Company of Amsterdam
DIRECTOR: Dr. Ludwig Berger
SCREEN PLAY: Dr. Ludwig Berger
CAST: Eliza Doolittle . . . . Lily Bouwmeester
Professor Higgins. . . . . . . Johan de Meester
Colonel Pickering . . . . . . Edward Verkade
Alfred Doolittle . . . . Matthieu van Eysden
DISTRIBUTED BY: Filmex, Amsterdam

1938: *Pygmalion* (British)

PRODUCER: Gabriel Pascal

DIRECTORS: Anthony Asquith and Leslie Howard
SCREEN PLAY: Bernard Shaw, W. P. Lipscomb, Cecil Lewis
CAST: Henry Higgins . . . . Leslie Howard
Eliza Doolittle . . . . Wendy Hiller
Alfred Doolittle . . . . Wilfred Lawson
Mrs. Higgins . . . . Marie Lohr
Colonel Pickering . . . . Scott Sunderland
Freddy Eynsford-Hill . . . . . . David Tree
Mrs. Eynsford-Hill . . . . Everley Gregg
Miss Eynsford-Hill . . . . Lueen MacGrath
Mrs. Pearce . . . . Jean Cadell
Parlourmaid . . . . Eileen Beldon
Extra characters added to film:
Taximan . . . . Frank Atkinson
Vicar . . . . O. B. Clarence
Count Aristid Karpathy . . . . Esme Percy
Ambassadress . . . . Violet Vanbrugh
Ysabel . . . . Iris Hoey
Perfide . . . . Viola Tree
Duchess . . . . Irene Browne
Old Lady . . . . Kate Cutler
A Lady . . . . Cathleen Nesbitt
Constable . . . . Cecil Trouncer
Second Constable . . . . Stephen Murray
COSTUMES: Professor Czettell, Worth and Schiaparelli
SETTINGS: Laurence Irving
CAMERAMAN: Harry Stradling
EDITOR: David Lean
MUSIC: Arthur Honegger
DISTRIBUTED BY: In England: General Film Distributors
In America: Loew's, Inc.
FIRST SHOWING: London: Leicester Square Theatre, October 6, 1938
New York: Astor Theatre, December 7, 1938

1941: *Major Barbara* (British)

PRODUCER: Gabriel Pascal
DIRECTOR: Gabriel Pascal
SCREEN PLAY: Bernard Shaw
CAST: Major Barbara . . . . Wendy Hiller
Adolphus Cusins . . . . Rex Harrison
Undershaft . . . . Robert Morley
Bill Walker . . . . Robert Newton
Snobby Price . . . . Emlyn Williams
The General . . . . Sybil Thorndyke

Jenny Hill . . . . Deborah Kerr
Charles Lomax . . . . David Tree
Sarah Undershaft . . . . . . Penelope Dudley-Ward
Lady Britomart . . . . Marie Lohr
Stephen Undershaft . . . . . Walter Hudd
Rummy Mitchens . . . . . . Marie Ault
Peter Shirley . . . . Donald Calthrop
Mog Habbijam . . . . Cathleen Cordell
Todger Fairmile . . . . Torin Thatcher
Morrison . . . . Miles Malleson
James . . . . Felix Aylmer
Policeman . . . . Stanley Holloway
Ling . . . . S. I. Hsiung
Mrs. Price . . . . Kathleen Harrison

COSTUMES: Cecil Beaton
SETTINGS: Vincent Korda, John Bryan
CAMERAMAN: Ronald Neame
EDITOR: Charles Frend
MUSIC: William Walton; conducted by Muir Mathieson
DISTRIBUTED BY: In England: General Film Distributors
In America: United Artists
FIRST SHOWING: London: Odeon Theatre, April 7, 1941
New York: Astor Theatre, May 13, 1941

1945: *Caesar and Cleopatra* (British)

PRODUCER: Gabriel Pascal for the Rank Organisation
DIRECTOR: Gabriel Pascal
SCREEN PLAY: Bernard Shaw
CAST: Caesar . . . . Claude Rains
Cleopatra . . . . Vivien Leigh
Ftatateeta . . . . Flora Robson
Pothinus . . . . Francis L. Sullivan
Rufio . . . . Basil Sydney
Britannus . . . . Cecil Parker
Apollodorus . . . . Stewart Granger
Lucius Septimus . . . . Raymond Lovell
Achillas . . . . Anthony Eustrel
Theodotus . . . . Ernest Thesiger
Ptolemy . . . . Anthony Harvey
Nubian Slave . . . . Robert Adams
Lady Attendants . . . . . . Harda Swanhilde
Olga Edwardes
1st Centurion . . . . Michael Rennie
Major-domo . . . . Esme Percy

Belzanor	Stanley Holloway
Persian	Alan Wheatley
Bel Affris	Leon Genn
Wounded Centurion	James McKechnie
Sentinel	John Bryning
Boatman	Anthony Holles
1st Porter	Charles Victor
2nd Porter	Ronald Shiner
1st Sentinel	John Laurie
2nd Sentinel	Charles Rolfe
1st Nobleman	Felix Alymer
2nd Nobleman	Ivor Barnard
1st Guardsman	Valentine Dyall
2nd Guardsman	Charles Deane

COSTUMES AND SETTINGS: Oliver Messel
CAMERAMAN: F. A. Young. Photographed in Technicolor
EDITOR: Frederick Wilson
MUSIC: Georges Auric; conducted by Muir Mathieson
DISTRIBUTED BY: In England: General Film Distributors
In America: United Artists
FIRST SHOWING: London: Odeon Theatre, December 13, 1945
New York: Astor Theatre, September 5, 1946

1953: *Androcles and the Lion* (American)

PRODUCER: Gabriel Pascal for R.K.O. Pictures
DIRECTOR: Chester Erskine
SCREEN PLAY: Chester Erskine and Ken Englund

CAST:	
The Emperor	Maurice Evans
The Captain	Victor Mature
Androcles	Alan Young
The Lion	Jackie
Lentulus	Reginald Gardiner
Metellus	Lowell Gilmore
Ferrovius	Robert Newton
Spintho	Noel Willman
Centurion	Jim Backus
The Editor	Alan Mowbray
The Menagerie Keeper	Gene Lockhart
Megaera	Elsa Lanchester
Lavinia	Jean Simmons
Cato	John Hoyt

COSTUMES: Emile Santiago
SETTINGS: Albert S. D'Agostino, Charles F. Pike
CAMERAMAN: Harry Stradling

EDITOR: Roland Gross
MUSIC: Constantin Bakaleinikoff
DISTRIBUTED BY: RKO Radio Pictures
FIRST SHOWING: London: Rialto Cinema, October 16, 1953
New York: Capital Theatre, January 14, 1953

1957: *Saint Joan* (American)

PRODUCER: Otto Preminger
DIRECTOR: Otto Preminger
SCREEN PLAY: Graham Greene
CAST: Saint Joan . . . . Jean Seberg
The Dauphin . . . . Richard Widmark
Dunois . . . . Richard Todd
Cauchon . . . . Anton Walbrook
The Earl of Warwick . . . . . John Gielgud
The Inquisitor . . . . Felix Aylmer
John de Stogumber . . . . . . Harry Andrews
de Courcelles . . . . Barry Jones
Archbishop of Rheims . . . . . Finlay Currie
Master Executioner . . . . . . Bernard Miles
Captain La Hire . . . . Patrick Barr
Bro. Martin Ladvenu . . . . . Kenneth Haigh
Robert de Beaudricourt . . . . Archie Duncan
English Soldier . . . . Victor Maddern
Lord Chamberlain . . . . . . Francis de Wolff
Duchess de la Tremoville . . . Margot Grahame
Bluebeard . . . . David Oxley
The Steward . . . . Sydney Bromley
PRODUCTION DESIGN: Roger Furse
ART DIRECTOR: Raymond Simm
CAMERAMAN: Georges Perinal
EDITOR: Helga Cranston
MUSIC: Mischa Spoliansky
DISTRIBUTED BY: United Artists
FIRST SHOWING: Paris: Opera, May 11, 1957
London: Leicester Square Theatre, June 19, 1957
New York: Victoria Theatre, June 26, 1957

1958: *The Doctor's Dilemma* (British)

PRODUCER: Anatole de Grunwald. A Comet Production
DIRECTOR: Anthony Asquith
SCREEN PLAY: Anatole de Grunwald

CAST: Mrs. Dubedat . . . . Leslie Caron
Louis Dubedat . . . . Dirk Bogarde
Sir Ralph . . . . Robert Morley
Cutler Walpole . . . . Alastair Sim
Sir Colenso Ridgeon . . . . . John Robinson
Sir Patrick Cullen . . . . Felix Aylmer
Dr. Blenkinsop . . . . Michael Gwynn
Emmy . . . . Maureen Delany
Newspaper Man . . . . Colin Gordon
Mr. Lanchester . . . . Terence Alexander
COSTUMES: Cecil Beaton
SETTINGS: Paul Sheriff
CAMERAMAN: Robert Krasker. Photographed in Metrocolor
EDITOR: Gordon Hales
MUSIC: Joseph Kosma
DISTRIBUTED BY: MGM
FIRST SHOWING: New York: 52nd St. Trans-Lux, December 17, 1958
London: Warner Cinema, April 23, 1959

1958: *Helden* [Arms and the Man] (German)

PRODUCER: H. R. Sokal and P. Goldbaum for the Bavaria-Filmkunst
DIRECTOR: Franz Peter Wirth
SCREEN PLAY: Johanna Sibelius and Eberhard Keindorff
CAST: Bluntschli . . . . O. W. Fischer
Raina. . . . . Liselotte Pulver
Louka . . . . Ellen Schwiers
Sergius . . . . Jan Hendricks
Katharina . . . . Ljuba Welitsch
Petkoff . . . . Kurt Kasznar
Nicola . . . . Manfred Inger
COSTUMES: Herbert Ploberger
SETTINGS: Hermann Warm, Bruno Monden
CAMERAMAN: Klaus von Rautenfeld. Photographed in Agfacolor
EDITOR: Claus von Boro
MUSIC: Franz Grothe
DISTRIBUTED BY: Bavaria-Filmverleih

1959: *Frau Warrens Gewarbe* [Mrs. Warren's Profession] (German)

PRODUCER: Heinz-Gunter Sass for Real-Film G.M.B.H.
DIRECTOR: Akos von Rathony
SCREEN PLAY: Eberhard Keindorff, Johanna Sibelius after an adaptation of the original stageplay by Anatole de Grunwald
CAST: Frau Warren . . . . Lilli Palmer

Sir George Crofts . . . . . . O. E. Hasse
Vivie . . . . Johanna Matz
Frank Gardner . . . . Helmut Lohner
Samuel Gardner . . . . Rudolf Vogel
Pread . . . . E. F. Furbringer
Mutter Warren . . . . Elisabeth Flickenschild
Liz . . . . Erni Mangold
Lulu . . . . Marlene Riphahn
Manon . . . . Christiane Nielsen
Mary . . . . Ann Savo

COSTUMES: Paul Seltenhammer
SETTINGS: Herbert Kirchhoff and Albrecht Becker
CAMERAMAN: Albert Benitz
EDITOR: Alice Ludwig-Rasch
MUSIC: Siegfried Franz
DISTRIBUTED BY: Europa Filmverleih

1959: *The Devil's Disciple* (American)

PRODUCER: Harold Hecht for Brynsprod, S.A., and Hecht-Hill-Lancaster Films, Ltd.
DIRECTOR: Guy Hamilton
SCREEN PLAY: John Dighton and Roland Kibbee
CAST: Rev. Anthony Anderson . . . . Burt Lancaster
Richard Dudgeon . . . . . . Kirk Douglas
General Burgoyne . . . . . . Sir Laurence Olivier
Judith Anderson . . . . Janette Scott
Mrs. Dudgeon . . . . Eva Le Gallienne
Major Swindon . . . . Harry Andrews
Lawyer Hawkins . . . . Basil Sydney
British Sergeant . . . . George Rose
Christopher Dudgeon . . . . . Neil McCallum
Rev. Malndeck Parshotter . . . Mervyn Johns
William . . . . David Horne
Essie . . . . Jenny Jones

COSTUMES: Mary Grant
SETTINGS: Edward Carrere, Terence Verity
CAMERAMAN: Jack Hildyard
EDITOR: Alan Osbiston
MUSIC: Richard R. Bennett
DISTRIBUTED BY: United Artists
FIRST SHOWING: London: Leicester Square Theatre, September 2, 1959
New York: Astor Theatre and Trans-Lux Normandie, August 20, 1959

1961: *The Millionairess* (British)

PRODUCER: Pierre Roube for Dimitri de Grunwald
DIRECTOR: Anthony Asquith
SCREEN PLAY: Wolf Mankowitz
CAST: Epifania . . . . Sophia Loren
Dr. Kabir . . . . Peter Sellers
Sagamore . . . . Alastair Sim
Joe . . . . Vittorio De Sica
Adrian . . . . Dennis Price
Alastair . . . . Gary Raymond
Fish Curer . . . . Alfie Bass
Mrs. Joe . . . . Miriam Karlin
Professor . . . . Noel Purcell
Polly . . . . Virginia Vernon
First Secretary . . . . Basil Hoskins
Nurse . . . . Diana Coupland
COSTUMES: Pierre Balmain
SETTINGS: Harry White
CAMERAMAN: Jack Hildyard. Photographed in Cinemascope and De Luxe Color
EDITOR: Anthony Harvey
MUSIC: Georges van Parys
DISTRIBUTED BY: 20th Century Fox
FIRST SHOWING: London: Carlton Cinema, October 20, 1960
New York: Paramount Theatre, February 9, 1961

APPENDIX B

Opening Scenes For Film Version Of *The Devil's Disciple* By Bernard Shaw

These previously unpublished scenes were written by Bernard Shaw for a projected, but never produced, film version of *The Devil's Disciple,* which was to have been produced by Gabriel Pascal. The original, signed by Shaw, is in the personal files of Miss Marjorie Deans, London.

St. James's Palace. London. 1777. The interior of one of the Royal Apartments. King George III is fussing about and gabbling. The Prime Minister, Lord North, is in attendance.

GEORGE III. Eh? What, what? A fuss about the Colonies? Is it kind of you, North, to bother me about such things? Haven't I enough to attend to?

LORD NORTH. Unfortunately, Your Majesty, the New England States have a considerable estimate of their own importance.

GEORGE III. What, what? Stuff and nonsense! States! What do you mean by States? Colonies are not States: they are parts of my State. Crumbs of it. Crumbs. What do you mean by New England? Where is it? Is it an island? Is it Robinson Crusoe's island? I never heard of it.

North patiently unfolds a map on the table, a table already crowded with documents. As he does this:

LORD NORTH. Your Majesty, New England is a substantial part of North America. Lord Germain believes that the New England States are the pith of the matter.

GEORGE III. What, what? North America. Columbus's discovery. Let me see. Let me see. America is important you know, North, quite important. Let me see. [*Looking at map*] That's a devilish big place, you know, North: devilish big. I had no idea it was so big.

LORD NORTH. Very big, sir: and all this side of it is in rebellion.

GEORGE III. What, what! Rebellion. Gone Jacobite! Has that drunken blackguard the Pretender broken out again?

LORD NORTH. They never heard of the Pretender, sir. They are dissatisfied.

GEORGE III. Damn their impudence! What about!

LORD NORTH. Taxes. And restrictions on their trade. They are actually fighting us: it is most serious. Sir John Burgoyne has been instructed to march south from Quebec along the line of the Hudson River: while Sir William Howe will be ordered to proceed north from New York City, to effect a junction.

GEORGE III. What, what? Burgoyne. That's a clever chap; but I don't like him. I feel that he is always laughing in his sleeve at me. Quite right to send him to America: quite right.

LORD NORTH. The two Generals are to act together. When they join, the rebels will be cut off and outnumbered. Their victory will be a certainty. Burgoyne is already on the march. Lord Germain has in hand a special despatch for Howe.

GEORGE III. Take care he sends that despatch. Germain is a lazy, idle, good-for-nothing dog. Never does today what he can put off till tomorrow. But it doesn't matter. Burgoyne can deal with any colonial mob single-handed. Let me hear no more of it [*Lord North shrugs his shoulders and rolls up the map hopelessly*].

Lord Germain's room in Whitehall. Day. Lord Germain and his Secretary. Lord Germain is dressed for the road, and is in a state of agitation, striding about the room.

LORD GERMAIN. Not ready yet! But you know I go into the country on a Friday.

SECRETARY. The fair copy will be in order for signature in about an hour, my Lord.

LORD GERMAIN. Won't do at all, I want to get down to the country. Have it for me when I return on Tuesday—er—Wednesday [*He pauses for a moment by a map of America on the wall*].

LORD GERMAIN. Whereabouts is Johnny?

SECRETARY [*pointing*] General Burgoyne is there.

LORD GERMAIN. Oh, *there!* Well, he can stay there until I come back to town. That place is thousands of miles away from New Amsterdam.

SECRETARY. New York now, my Lord.

LORD GERMAIN. My grandfather always called it New Amsterdam. Can't get it out of my head, somehow. Doesn't matter, does it? Anyhow, I'm off [*Exit Lord Germain, whistling "Lillibulero"*].

APPENDIX C

From Play To Screen Play To Sound Track: A Textual Comparison Of Three Versions Of Act V Of Shaw's *Pygmalion*

Play version: *Pygmalion*. Vol. XIV: *Ayot St. Lawrence Edition of The Collected Works of Bernard Shaw.* New York: Wm. H. Wise and Company, 1930.

Printed screen version: *Pygmalion*. Baltimore: Penguin Books, 1951.

Sound track version: *Pygmalion*. Produced by Gabriel Pascal, 1938.

In the following script of Act V of *Pygmalion,* the basic text is the Penguin Books printed screen version, which differs only slightly from the play version. These few differences are explained between double brackets. The extensive differences betwen the printed screen version and the sound track version are indicated as follows:

A. Type in CAPITALS indicates material not included in the printed screen version and the play version, but added in the sound track version.

B. ~~Line-outs~~ indicate material included in the printed screen version and the play version, but deleted in the sound track version.

C. Transpositions are clearly described as such.

Mrs Higgins's drawing room. She is at her writing-table as before. ~~*The parlormaid comes in.*~~

~~THE PARLORMAID [*at the door*] Mr Henry, maam, is downstairs with Colonel Pickering.~~

~~MRS HIGGINS. Well, shew them up.~~

~~THE PARLORMAID. They're using the telephone, maam. Telephoning to the police, I think.~~

~~MRS HIGGINS. What!~~

~~THE PARLORMAID [*coming further in and lowering her voice*] Mr Henry is in a state, maam. I thought I'd better tell you.~~

~~MRS HIGGINS. If you had told me that Mr Henry was not in a state it would have been more surprising. Tell them to come up when they've finished with the police. I suppose he's lost something.~~

~~THE PARLORMAID. Yes, maam [*going*].~~

~~MRS HIGGINS. Go upstairs and tell Miss Doolittle that Mr Henry and the Colonel are here. Ask her not to come down til I send for her.~~

~~THE PARLORMAID. Yes, maam.~~

Higgins bursts in. He is, ~~as the parlormaid has said~~, in a state.

HIGGINS. ~~Look here,~~ I SAY, mother; here's a confounded thing!

MRS HIGGINS. ~~Yes, dear.~~ Good morning, MY DEAR. [*He checks his impatience and kisses her, ~~whilst the parlormaid goes out~~*]. What is it?

HIGGINS. Eliza's bolted.

MRS HIGGINS [*calmly continuing her writing*] GOOD MORNING, COLONEL PICKERING. ~~You must have frightened her.~~

PICKERING. GOOD MORNING.

HIGGINS. ~~Frightened her! nonsense! She was left last night, as usual, to turn out the lights and all that; and instead of going to bed she changed her clothes and went right off: her bed wasn't slept in. She came in a cab for her things before seven this morning; and that fool Mrs Pearce let her have them without telling me a word about it. What am I to do?~~ [*FRANTICALLY*]: ELIZA'S BOLTED! WHAT AM I TO DO?

MRS HIGGINS. Do without, I'm afraid, Henry. The girl has a perfect right to leave if she chooses.

~~HIGGINS [*wandering distractedly across the room*] But I can't find anything. I don't know what appointments I've got. I'm [*Pickering comes in. Mrs Higgins puts down her pen and turns away from the writing table*].~~

~~PICKERING [*shaking hands*] Good morning, Mrs Higgins. Has Henry told you? [*He sits down on the ottoman*].~~

~~HIGGINS. What does that ass of an inspector say? Have you offered a reward?~~

~~MRS HIGGINS [*rising in indignant amazement*] You don't mean to say you have set the police after Eliza?~~

~~HIGGINS. Of course. What are the police for? What else could we do? [*He sits in the Elizabethan chair*].~~

~~PICKERING. The inspector made a lot of difficulties. I really think he suspected us of some improper purpose.~~

~~MRS HIGGINS. Well, of course he did. What right have you to go to the police and give the girl's name as if she were a thief, or a lost umbrella, or something? Really! [*She sits down again, deeply vexed*]~~.

~~HIGGINS. But we want to find her.~~

PICKERING. SOMETHING MIGHT HAVE HAPPENED TO HER. We can't let her go like this, ~~you know, Mrs Higgins.~~ HIGGINS, what ~~were~~ ARE we to do?

MRS HIGGINS. You have no more sense, either of you, than two children. ~~Why~~ –YOU MUST HAVE FRIGHTENED THE POOR GIRL.

[[Insert no. 1 comes in here in the sound track version. The transposed lines appear on pages 95–96 of the printed movie version, pages 171–172 in this appendix.]]

The parlormaid comes in and breaks off the conversation.

THE PARLORMAID. Mr. Henry: a gentleman wants to see you very particular. ~~He's been sent on from Wimpole Street.~~

HIGGINS. Oh, bother! I can't see anyone ANYBODY now. ~~Who is it?~~

THE PARLORMAID. HE'S BEEN SENT ON FROM WIMPOLE STREET.

HIGGINS. WHO IS IT?

THE PARLORMAID. A Mr Doolittle, sir.

~~PICKERING~~. HIGGINS. [*PUNCTUATING THE WORD BY CRESCENDOING ON THE PIANO*] Doolittle! ~~Do you mean the~~ A dustman?

THE PARLORMAID. Dustman! Oh, no, sir: a gentleman.

HIGGINS [*springing up excitedly*] By George, Pick, it's some relative of hers that she's gone to. Somebody we know nothing about. ~~[*To the parlormaid*] Send him up, quick.~~

~~THE PARLORMAID. Yes, sir. [*She goes*]~~.

HIGGINS [*eagerly, going to his mother*] Genteel relatives! Now we shall hear something. [*He sits down in the Chippendale chair*].

~~MRS HIGGINS. Do you know any of her people?~~

~~PICKERING. Only her father: the fellow we told you about.~~

~~THE PARLORMAID [*announcing*] Mr Doolittle. [*She withdraws*]~~.

Doolittle enters. He is resplendently dressed as for a fashionable wedding, and might, in fact, be the bridegroom. [[In the play version, the latter sentence reads: "He is brilliantly dressed in a new fashionable frock-coat, with white waistcoat and gray trousers."]] *A flower in his buttonhole, a dazzling silk hat, and patent leather shoes complete the effect. He is too concerned with the business he has come on to notice Mrs Higgins. He walks straight to Higgins, and accosts him with vehement reproach.*

HIGGINS. DOOLITTLE! HA, HA, HA: WHAT THE DICKENS HAS HAPPENED TO YOU?

DOOLITTLE [*indicating his own person*] ~~See here!~~ HENRY HIGGINS, Do you see this? You done this.

HIGGINS. Done what, man?

DOOLITTLE. ~~This, I tell you. Look at it.~~ Look at this hat. Look at this coat.

~~PICKERING. Has Eliza been buying you clothes?~~

~~DOOLITTLE. Eliza! Not she.~~ [[The phrase: "Not half!" was included in the play version.]] ~~Why would she buy me clothes?~~

MRS HIGGINS. Good morning, Mr Doolittle. Won't you ~~sit down?~~ COME IN?

DOOLITTLE [*taken aback as he becomes conscious that he has forgotten his hostess*] ~~Asking your pardon, maam.~~ [*He approaches her and shakes her proffered hand*]. Thank you, MAAM. [*He sits down on the ottoman, on Pickering's right*]. ~~I am that full of what has happened to me that I can't think of anything else.~~

~~HIGGINS. What the dickens has happened to you?~~

~~DOOLITTLE. I shouldn't mind if it had only happened to me: anything might happen to anybody and nobody to blame but Providence, as you might say. But this is something that you done to me: yes, you, Enry Iggins.~~ [[In the play version, Doolittle does not drop his "H's."]]

[[These lines, which we will call insert no. 2, come in here in the play version and in the printed movie version, but are moved in the sound track version to the place noted on page 171 in this appendix.]]

HIGGINS. THE POINT IS, Have you found Eliza? [[In the play version, this sentence reads: "Have you found Eliza? That's the point."]]

DOOLITTLE. Have you lost her?

HIGGINS. Yes.

DOOLITTLE. BLIMEY! You have all the luck, you have. NO, I ain't found her; but she'll find me quick enough now after what you done to me.

MRS HIGGINS. ~~But~~ what has my son done to you, ~~Mr Doolittle?~~

DOOLITTLE. ~~Done to me!~~ HE'S Ruined me. Destroyed my happiness. Tied me up and delivered me into the hands of middle class morality.

HIGGINS [*rising intolerantly and standing over Doolittle*] You're raving. You're drunk. You're mad. I gave you five pounds. After that I had two conversations with you, at half-a-crown an hour. I've never seen you since.

DOOLITTLE. Oh! MAD AM I? Drunk am I? ~~Mad am I?~~ Tell me this. Did you or did you not write a letter to an old blighter in America that ~~was giving five millions to found Moral Reform Societies all over the world, and that wanted you to invent a universal language for him?~~

~~HIGGINS. What! Ezra D. Wannafeller! He's dead. [*He sits down again carelessly*].~~

~~DOOLITTLE. Yes: he's dead; and I'm done for. Now did you or did you not write a letter to him to say that~~ the most original moralist at present in England, ~~to the best of your knowledge,~~ was Alfred Doolittle, a common ~~dustman?~~ GARBAGE MAN?

HIGGINS. Oh, ~~after your first visit~~ [[The play version reads: ". . . last visit"]] I remember making some silly joke of the kind.

DOOLITTLE. Ah! you may well call it a silly joke. It put the lid on me right enough. [*HE TOUCHES HIS HAT*]. Just give him the chance he wanted to ~~shew~~ SHOW that Americans is not like us: that they reckonize and respect merit in every class of life, however humble. [*CLOSE-UP OF MRS HIGGINS, GRINNING*] Them words is in his blooming will, in which, ~~Henry Higgins, thanks to your silly joking,~~ he leaves me ~~a share in his Pre-digested Cheese Trust worth four thousand~~ THREE THOUSAND POUNDS [[The play version reads: ". . . three thousand a year".]] a year on condition that I lecture for his THE Wannafeller Moral Reform ~~World~~ League as often as they ask me up to six times a year [*CLOSE-UP OF HIGGINS AND MRS HIGGINS, WHO GRIN AT EACH OTHER*].

~~HIGGINS. The devil he does! Whew! [*Brightening suddenly*] What a lark!~~

~~PICKERING. A safe thing for you, Doolittle. They won't ask you twice.~~

~~DOOLITTLE. It ain't the lecturing I mind. I'll lecture them blue in the face, I will, and not turn a hair. It's making a gentleman of me that I object to. Who asked him to make a gentleman of me? I was happy. I was free. I touched pretty nigh everybody for money when I wanted it, same as I touched you, Enry Iggins. Now I am worrited; tied neck and heels; and everybody touches me for money. It's a fine thing for you, says my solicitor. Is it? says I. You mean it's a good thing for you, I says. When I was a poor man and had a solicitor once when they found a pram in the dust cart, he got me off, and got shut of me and got me shut of him as quick as he could. Same with the doctors: used to shove me out of the hospital before I could hardly stand on my legs, and nothing to pay. Now they finds out that I'm~~

~~not a healthy man and can't live unless they looks after me twice a day. In the house I'm not let to do a hand's turn for myself: somebody else must do it and touch me for it. A year ago I hadn't a relative in the world except two or three that wouldn't speak to me. Now I've fifty, and not a decent week's wages among the lot of them. I have to live for others and not for myself: that~~ [[An obvious misprint in the printed movie version. The play version reads "that's."]] ~~middle class morality. You talk of losing Eliza. Don't you be anxious: I bet she's on my doorstep by this: she that could support herself easy by selling flowers if I wasn't respectable. And the next one to touch me will be you, Enry Iggins. I'll have to learn to speak middle class language from you, instead of speaking proper English. That's where you'll come in; and I daresay that's what you done it for.~~

~~MRS HIGGINS. But, my dear Mr Doolittle, you need not suffer all this if you are really in earnest. Nobody can force you to accept this bequest. You can repudiate it. Isn't that so, Colonel Pickering?~~

~~PICKERING. I believe so.~~

~~DOOLITTLE [*softening his manner in deference to her sex*] That's the tragedy of it, maam. It's easy to say chuck it; but I haven't the nerve. Which of us has? We're all intimidated. Intimidated, maam: that's what we are. What is there for me if I chuck it but the workhouse in my old age? I have to dye my hair already to keep my job as a dustman. If I was one of the deserving poor, and had put by a bit, I could chuck it; but then why should I, acause the deserving poor might as well be millionaires for all the happiness they ever has. They don't know what happiness is. But I, as one of the undeserving poor, have nothing between me and the pauper's uniform but this here blasted four thousand a year that shoves me into the middle class. (Excuse the expression, maam; you'd use it yourself if you had my provocation.) They've got you every way you turn: it's a choice between the Skilly of the workhouse and the Char Bydis of the middle class; and I haven't the nerve for the workhouse. Intimidated: that's what I am. Broke. Bought up. Happier men than me will call for my dust, and touch me for their tip; and I'll look on helpless, and envy them. And that's what your son has brought me to. [*He is overcome by emotion*].~~

MRS HIGGINS. ~~Well, I'm very glad you're not going to do anything foolish, Mr Doolittle. For~~ WELL, this solves the problem of Eliza's future. You can provide for her now.

DOOLITTLE [*with melancholy resignation*] Yes, maam: I'm expected to provide for ~~everyone~~ EVERYBODY now, out of ~~four~~ THREE thousand a year.

HIGGINS [*jumping up*] ~~Nonsense!~~ He can't provide for her. ~~He shan't provide~~

~~for her.~~ She doesn't belong to him. I paid him five pounds for her. Doolittle: YOU'RE either ~~you're~~ an honest man or YOU'RE a rogue.

DOOLITTLE [*tolerantly*] A little of both, Henry, like the rest of us: a little of both.

[[Insert no. 2 comes in here in the sound track version. The transposed lines appear on page 92 of the printed movie version, page 168 in this appendix.]]

HIGGINS [*THREATENINGLY*]. NOW YOU LISTEN TO ME. . . .

MRS HIGGINS [*INTERRUPTING*]. WILL YOU WAIT HERE FOR A MOMENT, MR DOOLITTLE? [*SHE TAKES HIGGINS INTO ANOTHER ROOM AND CLOSES THE DOOR BEHIND THEM, THE CAMERA FOLLOWING THEM. SHE TURNS TO HIGGINS*] HENRY, I HAVE A SURPRISE FOR YOU. DO YOU WANT TO KNOW WHERE ELIZA IS?

HIGGINS. YES, WHERE IS SHE?

~~HIGGINS. Well, you took that money for the girl; and you have no right to take her as well.~~

~~MRS HIGGINS. Henry: don't be absurd. If you want to know where Eliza is, she is upstairs.~~

~~HIGGINS [*amazed*] Upstairs!!! Then I shall jolly soon fetch her downstairs. [*He makes resolutely for the door*].~~

~~MRS HIGGINS [*rising and following him*] Be quiet, Henry. Sit down.~~

~~HIGGINS. I~~

~~MRS HIGGINS. Sit down, dear; and listen to me.~~

~~HIGGINS. Oh very well, very well, very well. [*He throws himself ungraciously on the ottoman, with his face towards the windows*]. But I think you might have told us this half an hour ago.~~

~~MRS HIGGINS. Eliza came to me this morning.~~ [[In the play version, the following sentence occurs here: "She passed the night partly walking about in a rage, partly trying to throw herself into the river, and being afraid to, and partly in the Carlton Hotel."]] ~~She told me of the brutal way you two treated her.~~

~~HIGGINS [*bounding up again*] What!~~

[[These lines, which we will call insert no. 1, come in here in the play version and the printed movie version, but are moved in the sound track version to the place noted on page 167 in this appendix.]]

PICKERING [*rising also*] ~~My dear Mrs Higgins, she's been telling you stories.~~

~~We didn't treat her brutally.~~ FRIGHTENED HER! We hardly said a word to her; ~~and we parted on particularly good terms.~~ [*Turning on Higgins*] Higgins: did you bully her after I went to bed?

HIGGINS. CERTAINLY NOT! Just the other way about. She threw my slippers in my face. ~~She behaved in the most outrageous way.~~ I never gave her the slightest provocation. THE MOMENT I ENTERED THE ROOM, the slippers came bang into my face ~~the moment I entered the room~~ before I had uttered a word. And she used THE MOST perfectly awful language. [*HE PUNCTUATES HIS SENTENCE BY BANGING ON THE PIANO*].

~~PICKERING [astonished] But why? What did we do to her?~~

~~MRS HIGGINS. I think I know pretty well what you did. The girl is naturally rather affectionate, I think. Isn't she, Mr Doolittle?~~

~~DOOLITTLE. Very tender-hearted, maam. Takes after me.~~

MRS HIGGINS. ~~Just so. She had become attached to you both. She worked very hard for you, Henry. I don't think you quite realize what anything in the nature of brain work means to a girl of her class.~~ [[In the play version, the phrase reads: ". . . to a girl like that."]] ~~Well, it seems that when the great day of trial came, and she did~~ I CAN'T SAY I'M SURPRISED. AND YOU MEAN TO TELL ME THAT AFTER ALL HER HARD WORK AND AFTER DOING this wonderful thing for you without making a ONE single mistake, you two sat there and ~~never~~ HARDLY said a word to her, ~~but talked together of how glad you were that it was all over and how you had been bored with the whole thing. And then you were surprised because~~ AND SHE ONLY ~~she~~ threw your slippers at you! *I* should have thrown the fire-irons at you.

~~HIGGINS. We said nothing except that we were tired and wanted to go to bed. Did we, Pick?~~

~~PICKERING [*shrugging his shoulders*] That was all.~~

~~MRS HIGGINS [*ironically*] Quite sure?~~

~~PICKERING. Absolutely. Really that was all.~~

MRS HIGGINS. You didn't thank her, or pet her, or admire her, ~~or tell her how splendid she'd been.~~

HIGGINS [*impatiently*] ~~But she knew all about that.~~ We didn't make speeches to her, if that's what you mean.

~~PICKERING [*conscience stricken*] Perhaps we were a little inconsiderate. Is she very angry?~~

MRS HIGGINS [~~*returning to her place at the writing-table*~~] ~~Well, I'm afraid she~~

~~won't go back to Wimpole Street, especially now that Mr Doolittle is able to keep up the position you have thrust on her; but~~ she says she is ~~quite~~ willing to meet you on friendly terms and to let bygones be bygones.

HIGGINS [*furious*] Is she, ~~by George? Ho!~~ [*HE TURNS TO PICKERING FOR CONFIRMATION OF HIS FURY*]. PICKERING! WHERE IS SHE? [*HE TURNS BACK TO HIS MOTHER*].

MRS HIGGINS. ~~If you~~ NOW promise to behave yourself, Henry, ~~I'll ask her to come down. If not, go home; for you have taken up quite enough of my time~~.

~~HIGGINS. Oh, all right. Very well, Pick: you behave yourself. Let us put on our best Sunday manners for this creature that we picked out of the mud. [*He flings himself sulkily into the Elizabethan chair*]~~.

~~DOOLITTLE [*remonstrating*] Now, now, Enry Iggins! Have some consideration for my feelings as a middle class man~~.

~~MRS HIGGINS. Remember your promise, Henry. [*She presses the bell-button on the writing-table*]. Mr. Doolittle: will you be so good as to step out on the balcony for a moment. I don't want Eliza to have the shock of your news until she has made it up with these two gentlemen. Would you mind?~~

~~DOOLITTLE. As you wish, lady. Anything to help Henry to keep her off my hands. [*He disappears through the window*]~~.

~~*The parlormaid answers the bell. Pickering sits down in Doolittle's place*~~.

~~MRS HIGGINS. Ask Miss Doolittle to come down, please.~~

~~THE PARLORMAID. Yes, maam. [*She goes out*]~~.

~~MRS HIGGINS. Now, Henry: be good.~~

~~HIGGINS. I am behaving myself perfectly~~.

~~PICKERING. He is doing his best, Mrs Higgins.~~

~~*A pause. Higgins throws back his head; stretches out his legs; and begins to whistle.*~~

~~MRS HIGGINS. Henry, dearest, you don't look at all nice in that attitude.~~

~~HIGGINS [*pulling himself together*] I was not trying to look nice, mother.~~

~~MRS HIGGINS. It doesn't matter, dear. I only wanted to make you speak~~.

~~HIGGINS. Why?~~

~~MRS HIGGINS. Because you can't speak and whistle at the same time.~~

~~*Higgins groans. Another very trying pause*~~.

~~HIGGINS [*springing up, out of patience*] Where the devil is that girl? Are we going to wait here all day?~~

MRS HIGGINS GOES OVER TO THE DOUBLE DOORS, OPENS THEM, AND ADMITS ELIZA. THE CAMERA FOLLOWS ELIZA FROM BEHIND AS SHE WALKS INTO THE ROOM.

Eliza enters, sunny, self-possessed, and giving a staggeringly convincing exhibition of ease of manner. She carries a little workbasket, and is very much at home. Pickering is too much taken aback to rise.

~~LIZA. How do you do, Professor Higgins? Are you quite well?~~

~~HIGGINS [*choking*] Am I— [*He can say no more*]~~.

LIZA. ~~But of course you are: you are never ill~~. [*AS ELIZA ENTERS, SHE IGNORES HIGGINS: SHE TURNS TO COLONEL PICKERING, SMILING*]. GOOD MORNING, ~~So glad to see you again~~, Colonel Pickering. [*He rises hastily; and they shake hands*]. Quite chilly this morning, isn't it? [*SHE IS SEWING CASUALLY, AND WALKING VERY PROPERLY*]. [*THE CAMERA FOLLOWS HER CLOSELY AS SHE SITS DOWN, AND NOTICES HIGGINS*]. OH! HOW DO YOU DO, PROFESSOR HIGGINS? ARE YOU QUITE WELL? BUT OF COURSE YOU ARE: YOU ARE NEVER ILL. [*HIGGINS STANDS FUMING, WITH HIS HANDS ON HIS HIPS*]. [*ELIZA TURNS BACK TO PICKERING, TOUCHES THE SEAT NEXT TO HER*]. WON'T YOU SIT DOWN, COLONEL PICKERING? [~~*She sits down on his left*~~. *He sits beside her*].

HIGGINS. Don't you dare try this game on me. ~~I taught it to you; and it doesn't take me in.~~ Get up and come home; and don't be a fool.

Eliza takes a piece of needlework from her basket, and begins to stitch at it, without taking the least notice of this outburst.

MRS HIGGINS. Very nicely put, indeed, Henry. No woman could resist such an invitation.

HIGGINS. ~~You let her alone, mother~~. Let her speak for herself. ~~You will jolly soon see whether she has~~ THERE ISN'T an idea that I haven't put into her head ~~or a word that I haven't put into her mouth.~~ I tell you I have created this thing out of the squashed cabbage leaves ~~of~~ IN Covent Garden; and now she pretends to play the fine lady with me.

~~MRS HIGGINS [*placidly*] Yes, dear; but you'll sit down, won't you?~~

~~*Higgins sits down again, savagely.*~~

LIZA [*to Pickering, taking no apparent notice of Higgins, and working away deftly*]. Will you drop me altogether now that the experiment is over, Colonel Pickering?

PICKERING. Oh ~~don't.~~ You musn't think of it as an experiment. ~~It shocks me, somehow.~~

LIZA. Oh, I'm only a squashed cabbage leaf—[*HIGGINS THROWS DOWN HIS PAPER IN A RISING FURY*].

PICKERING [*impulsively*] No.

LIZA [*continuing quietly*]—but I owe so much to you that I should be very unhappy if you forgot me.

~~PICKERING. It's very kind of you to say so, Miss Doolittle~~.

LIZA. ~~It's not because you paid for my dresses. I know you are generous to everybody with money. But~~ it was from you that I learnt really nice manners; and that is what makes me a lady, isn't it?

HIGGINS [*INTERRUPTING*]. HAH!

~~LIZA. You see it was so very difficult for me with the example of Professor Higgins always before me. I was brought up to be just like him, unable to control myself, and using bad language on the slightest provocation~~. ~~And I should never have known that ladies and gentlemen didn't behave like that if you hadn't been there~~.

~~HIGGINS. Well!!~~

~~PICKERING. Oh, that's only his way, you know. He doesn't mean it~~.

LIZA. ~~Oh, *I* didn't mean it either, when I was a flower girl. It was only my way~~. ~~But you see I did it; and~~ that's what makes the difference after all.

~~PICKERING. No doubt. Still, he taught you to speak; and I couldn't have done that, you know~~.

~~LIZA [*trivially*] Of course: that is his profession~~.

~~HIGGINS. Damnation!~~

LIZA [*continuing*] ~~It was just like learning to dance in the fashionable way: there was nothing more than that in it. But~~ do you know what began my real education?

PICKERING. ~~What?~~ NO?

LIZA [*stopping her work for a moment*] Your calling me Miss Doolittle that day when I first came to Wimpole Street. That was the beginning of self-respect for me. [*She resumes her stitching*]. ~~And there were a hundred little things you never noticed, because they came naturally to you. Things about standing up and taking off your hat and opening doors—~~

~~PICKERING. Oh, that was nothing.~~

~~LIZA. Yes: things that shewed you thought and felt about me as if I were something better than a scullery-maid; though of course I know you would have been just the same to a scullery-maid if she had been let into the drawing room. You~~ [[In the play version, the word "you" is emphasized.]] ~~never took off your boots in the dining room when I was there~~.

~~PICKERING. You mustn't mind that. Higgins takes off his boots all over the place~~.

LIZA. ~~I know. I am not blaming him. It is his way, isn't it? But it made such a difference to me that you didn't do it. You see, really and truly, apart from~~

~~the things anyone can pick up (the dressing and the proper way of speak-ing, and so on~~), the difference between a lady and a flower girl is not how she behaves, but how she's treated. [*QUICK CUT TO DOOLITTLE LISTENING AT THE DOOR IN THE NEXT ROOM; THEN CUT BACK TO ELIZA*]. I KNOW I shall always be a flower girl to Professor Higgins, because he always treats me as a flower girl and always will.

THROUGHOUT ALL OF THIS, HIGGINS IS STANDING WITH HIS BACK TURNED TO THE CAMERA, READING A NEWS-PAPER.

MRS HIGGINS. DON'T GRIND YOUR TEETH, HENRY.

LIZA [*CONTINUING*] But I know I can be a lady to you, because you always treat me as a lady, and always will.

~~MRS HIGGINS. Please don't grind your teeth, Henry.~~

PICKERING. Well, this is really very nice of you TO SAY SO, Miss Doolittle.

LIZA. I should like you to call me Eliza, now, if you would.

PICKERING. Thank you. Eliza, of course. [*HE PATS HER HAND VERY AFFECTIONATELY*].

LIZA. And I should like Professor Higgins to call me Miss Doolittle.

HIGGINS. ~~I'll see you damned first.~~ [*HE JUMPS UP IN A RAGE*].

MRS HIGGINS. Henry! Henry!

~~PICKERING [*laughing*] Why don't you slang back at him? Don't stand it. It would do him a lot of good.~~

~~LIZA. I can't. I could have done it once; but now I can't go back to it~~. [[In the play version, this sentence occurs here: "Last night, when I was wandering about, a girl spoke to me; and I tried to get back into the old way with her: but it was no use."]] ~~You told me, you know, that when a child is brought to a foreign country, it picks up the language in a few weeks, and forgets its own. Well, I am a child in your country. I have forgotten my own language, and can speak nothing but yours. That's the real break-off with the corner of Tottenham Court Road. Leaving Wimpole Street finishes it.~~

PICKERING [*much alarmed*] Oh! ~~but you're coming back to Wimpole Street, aren't you?~~ You'll forgive Higgins?

HIGGINS ~~[*rising*]~~ Forgive! Will she, by George! Let her go. Let her find out how she can get on without us. IN THREE WEEKS She will relapse into the gutter ~~in three weeks~~ without me at her elbow.

~~*Doolittle appears at the centre window*~~. *CUT TO DOOLITTLE COMING IN FROM THE NEXT ROOM. With a look of dignified reproach at Higgins, he comes slowly and silently to his daughter, who, ~~with her back to the window,~~ is unconscious of his approach.*

PICKERING. ~~He's incorrigible, Eliza.~~ You won't relapse, will you, ELIZA?

LIZA. No: ~~not now.~~ Never again. ~~I have learnt my lesson.~~ I don't believe I could utter one of the old sounds if I tried. [*THE CAMERA PANS TO ELIZA. Doolittle touches her on the left shoulder. She drops her work, losing her self-possession utterly at the spectacle of her father's splendor*]. A-a-a-a-ah-ow-ooh!

HIGGINS [*with a crow of triumph*] Aha! ~~Just so. A-a-a-a-ahowooh! A-a-a-a-ahowooh! A-a-a-a-ahowooh!~~ Victory! Victory! ~~[*He throws himself on the divan, folding his arms, and spraddling arrogantly*]~~.

EVERYONE SHOUTS AT ONCE: HIGGINS, MENACINGLY, COMES CLOSER AND CLOSER TO ELIZA, WITH HIS FINGER RAISED INTO HER FACE, SHOUTING HER "A-a-a-a-ahowooh!" SOUND SIX TIMES, EACH TIME CLOSER TO HER. ELIZA TRIES TO RUN AWAY; SHE BUSTLES ABOUT, SQUEALING, BUT ALWAYS VERY LADY-LIKE. MRS HIGGINS SHOUTS OVER THE DIN.

MRS HIGGINS. HENRY! HENRY! LOOK, HENRY!

PICKERING [*SHOUTING TOO*]. YOU CAN'T JUST PASS OVER HER!

~~DOOLITTLE. Can you blame the girl? Don't look at me like that, Eliza. It ain't my fault. I've come into some money~~.

~~LIZA. You must have touched a millionaire this time, dad.~~

~~DOOLITTLE. I have. But I'm dressed something special today. I'm going to St~~. ~~George's, Hanover Square. Your stepmother is going to marry me.~~

~~LIZA [*angrily*] You're going to let yourself down to marry that low common woman!~~

~~PICKERING [*quietly*] He ought to, Eliza. [*To Doolittle*] Why has she changed her mind?~~

~~DOOLITTLE [*sadly*] Intimidated, Governor. Intimidated. Middle class morality claims its victim. Won't you put on your hat, Liza, and come and see me turned off?~~

~~LIZA. If the Colonel says I must, I~~—~~I'll [*almost sobbing*] I'll demean myself. And get insulted for my pains, like enough.~~

~~DOOLITTLE. Don't be afraid: she never comes to words with anyone now, poor woman! respectability has broke all the spirit out of her~~.

~~PICKERING [*squeezing Eliza's elbow gently*] Be kind to them, Eliza. Make the best of it.~~

~~LIZA [*forcing a little smile for him through her vexation*] Oh well, just to shew there's no ill feeling. I'll be back in a moment. [*She goes out*]~~.

~~DOOLITTLE [*sitting down beside Pickering*] I feel uncommon nervous about the ceremony, Colonel. I wish you'd come and see me through it.~~

~~PICKERING. But you've been through it before, man. You were married to Eliza's mother.~~

~~DOOLITTLE. Who told you that, Colonel?~~

~~PICKERING. Well, nobody told me. But I concluded—naturally—~~

~~DOOLITTLE. No: that ain't the natural way, Colonel: it's only the middle class way. My way was always the undeserving way. But don't say nothing to Eliza. She don't know: I always had a delicacy about telling her.~~

~~PICKERING. Quite right. We'll leave it so, if you don't mind.~~

~~DOOLITTLE. And you'll come to the church, Colonel, and put me through straight?~~

~~PICKERING. With pleasure. As far as a bachelor can.~~

~~MRS HIGGINS. May I come, Mr Doolittle? I should be very sorry to miss your wedding.~~

~~DOOLITTLE. I should indeed be honored by your condescension, maam; and my poor old woman would take it as a tremenjous compliment. She's been very low, thinking of the happy days that are no more.~~

~~MRS HIGGINS [*rising*] I'll order the carriage and get ready. [*The men rise, except Higgins*]. I shan't be more than fifteen minutes. [*As she goes to the door Eliza comes in, hatted and buttoning her gloves*]. I'm going to the church to see your father married, Eliza. You had better come in the brougham with me. Colonel Pickering can go on with the bridegroom.~~

~~*Mrs Higgins goes out. Eliza comes to the middle of the room between the centre window and the ottoman. Pickering joins her.*~~

~~DOOLITTLE. Bridegroom. What a word! It makes a man realize his position, somehow. [*He takes up his hat and goes towards the door*].~~

~~PICKERING. Before I go, Eliza, do forgive Higgins~~ [[The play version has "him" instead of "Higgins."]] ~~and come back to us.~~

~~LIZA. I don't think dad~~ [[The play version has "papa" instead of "dad."]] ~~would allow me. Would you, dad?~~

~~DOOLITTLE [*sad but magnanimous*] They played you off very cunning, Eliza, them two sportsmen. If it had been only one of them, you could have nailed him. But you see, there was two; and one of them chaperoned the other, as you might say. [*To Pickering*] It was artful of you, Colonel; but I bear no malice: I should have done the same myself. I been the victim of one woman after another all my life, and I don't grudge you two getting the better of Liza~~ [[In the play version, Doolittle calls her "Eliza" here.]] ~~I~~

~~shan't interfere. It's time for us to go, Colonel. So long, Henry. See you in St. George's, Eliza. [*He goes out*]~~.

~~PICKERING [*coaxing*] Do stay with us, Eliza. [*He follows Doolittle*]~~.

~~*Eliza goes out on the balcony to avoid being alone with Higgins. He rises and joins her there. She immediately comes back into the room and makes for the door; but he goes along the balcony*~~ [[The play version has the word "quickly" in the stage directions.]] ~~*and gets his back to the door before she reaches it.*~~

~~HIGGINS. Well, Eliza, you've had a bit of your own back, as you call it. Have you had enough? and are you going to be reasonable? Or do you want any more?~~

~~LIZA. You want me back only to pick up your slippers and put up with your tempers and fetch and carry for you.~~

~~HIGGINS. I haven't said I wanted you back at all.~~

~~LIZA. Oh, indeed. Then what are we talking about?~~

~~HIGGINS. About you, not about me. If you come back I shall treat you just as I have always treated you. I can't change my nature; and I don't intend to change my manners. My manners are exactly the same as Colonel Pickering's.~~

~~LIZA. That's not true. He treats a flower girl as if she was a duchess.~~

~~HIGGINS. And I treat a duchess as if she was a flower girl.~~

~~LIZA. I see. [*She turns away composedly, and sits on the ottoman, facing the window*]. The same to everybody.~~

~~HIGGINS. Just so.~~

~~LIZA. Like father.~~

~~HIGGINS [*grinning, a little taken down*] Without accepting the comparison at all points, Eliza, it's quite true that your father is not a snob, and that he will be quite at home in any station of life to which his eccentric destiny may call him. [*Seriously*] The great secret, Eliza, is not having bad manners or good manners or any other particular sort of manners, but having the same manner for all human souls: in short, behaving as if you were in Heaven, where there are no third class carriages, and one soul is as good as another.~~

~~LIZA. Amen. You are a born preacher.~~

~~HIGGINS [*irritated*] The question is not whether I treat you rudely, but whether you ever heard me treat anyone else better.~~

~~LIZA [*with sudden sincerity*] I don't care how you treat me. I don't mind your swearing at me. I shouldn't~~ [[The play version has "don't" instead of "shouldn't."]] ~~mind a black eye: I've had one before this. But [*standing up and facing him*] I won't be passed over~~.

HIGGINS. ~~Then get out of my way; for I won't stop for you~~. You talk about me as if I were a ~~motor~~ bus.

LIZA. So you are a motor bus: all bounce and go, and no consideration for anyone.

[[Insert no. 3 comes in here in the sound track version. The transposed lines appear on pages 106 and 107 of the printed movie version, pages 181–182 in this appendix.]]

LIZA. ~~But~~ I can do without you: don't think I can't.

~~HIGGINS. I know you can. I told you you could~~.

~~LIZA [*wounded, getting away from him to the other side of the ottoman with her feet to the hearth*] I know you did, you brute. You wanted to get rid of me~~.

~~HIGGINS. Liar~~.

~~LIZA. Thank you. [*She sits down with dignity*]~~.

HIGGINS. You never asked yourself, I suppose, whether *I* could do without you.

LIZA ~~[*earnestly*] Don't you try to get round me~~. [*IN A CLOSE-UP SHOT, ELIZA SPINS AROUND ANGRILY, THEN SOFTENS*]. You'll have [[In the play version, the word "have" is emphasized.]] to do without me.

HIGGINS [*arrogant*] I can do without anybody. [HE JUMPS UP]. I have my own soul: my own spark of divine fire. But [*with sudden humility*] I shall miss you, Eliza. [*He sits down near her on the ottoman*]. ~~I have learnt something from your idiotic notions~~: I confess that humbly and gratefully. And I have grown accustomed to your voice and appearance. I EVEN like them, rather.

LIZA. Well, you have THEM both ~~of them~~ on your gramophone and in your book of photographs. ~~When you feel~~ AND IF YOU'RE lonely ~~without me~~, you can turn the machine on. It's got no feelings to hurt. [*THE CAMERA IS FOCUSED ON THE BACK OF ELIZA'S HEAD*].

HIGGINS. I can't turn your soul on. ~~Leave me those feelings; and you can take away the voice and the face. They are not you~~.

SHE TURNS DIRECTLY INTO THE CAMERA, AND HISSES.

LIZA. Oh, you are a devil. You can twist the heart in a girl as easy as some could twist her arms to hurt her. ~~Mrs Pearce warned me. Time and again she has wanted to leave you; and you always got round her at the last minute. And you don't care a bit for her. And you don't care a bit for me~~.

~~HIGGINS. I care for life, for humanity; and you are a part of it that has come my way and been built into my house. What more can you or anyone ask?~~

~~LIZA. I won't care for anybody that doesn't care for me~~.

~~HIGGINS. Commercial principles, Eliza. Like [*reproducing her Covent Garden pronunciation with professional exactness*] s'yollin voylets [selling violets]~~, ~~isn't it?~~

~~LIZA. Don't sneer at me. It's mean to sneer at me~~.

~~HIGGINS. I have never sneered in my life. Sneering doesn't become either the human face or the human soul. I am expressing my righteous contempt for Commercialism. I don't and won't trade in affection. You call me a brute because you couldn't buy a claim on me by fetching my slippers and finding my spectacles. You were a fool: I think a woman fetching a man's slippers is a disgusting sight: did I ever fetch your slippers? I think a good deal more of you for throwing them in my face. No use slaving for me and then saying you want to be cared for: who cares for a slave? If you come back, come back for the sake of good fellowship; for you'll get nothing else. You've had a thousand times as much out of me as I have out of you; and if you dare to set up your little dog's tricks of fetching and carrying slippers against my creation of a Duchess Eliza, I'll slam the door in your silly face.~~

~~LIZA. What did you do it for if you didn't care for me?~~

~~HIGGINS [*heartily*] Why, because it was my job.~~

~~LIZA. You never thought of the trouble it would make for me~~.

~~HIGGINS. Would the world ever have been made if its maker had been afraid of making trouble? Making life means making trouble. There's only one way of escaping trouble; and that's killing things. Cowards, you notice, are always shrieking to have troublesome people killed~~.

~~LIZA. I'm no preacher: I don't notice things like that. I notice that you don't notice me.~~

[[These lines, which we will call insert no. 3, come in here in the play version and in the printed movie version, but are moved in the sound track version to the place noted on page 180 in this appendix.]]

HIGGINS ~~[*jumping up and walking about intolerantly*] Eliza: you're an idiot~~. ~~I waste the treasures of my Miltonic mind by spreading them before you.~~ Once for all, understand that I go my way and do my work without caring twopence what happens to either of us. ~~I am not intimidated, like your~~

~~father and your stepmother.~~ So you can come back or go to the devil: which EVER you please.

LIZA. What am I to come back for?

HIGGINS [*bouncing up on his knees on the ottoman and leaning over it to her*] For the fun of it. That's ~~why~~ WHAT I took you on FOR.

LIZA [*with averted face*] And you ~~may~~ CAN throw me out tomorrow if I don't do everything you want me to?

HIGGINS. ~~Yes;~~ and you ~~may~~ CAN walk out tomorrow if I don't do everything you want me to do.

LIZA. And live with my stepmother?

HIGGINS. Yes, or sell flowers.

~~LIZA. Oh! if I only could go back to my flower basket! I should be independent of both you and father and all the world! Why did you take my independence from me? Why did I give it up? I'm a slave now, for all my fine clothes~~.

HIGGINS. ~~Not a bit. I'll adopt you as my daughter and settle money on you if you like~~. Or would you rather marry Pickering?

LIZA [*looking fiercely round at him*] I wouldn't marry you if you asked me; and you're nearer my age than what he is.

HIGGINS [*gently*] Than he is: ~~not "than what he is."~~

LIZA [*losing her temper and rising*] I'll ~~talk~~ SPEAK as I like. You're not my teacher now. [*HIGGINS GRINS, AS ELIZA WALKS ANGRILY OVER TO THE WINDOW*].

~~HIGGINS [*reflectively*] I don't suppose Pickering would, though. He's as confirmed an old bachelor as I am.~~

LIZA. ~~That's not what I want; and don't you think it. I've always had chaps enough wanting me that way. Freddy Hill writes to me twice and three times a day, sheets and sheets.~~

~~HIGGINS [*disagreeably surprised*] Damn his impudence! [*He recoils and finds himself sitting on his heels*]~~.

~~LIZA. He has a right to if he likes, poor lad. And he does love me~~.

~~HIGGINS [*getting off the ottoman*] You have no right to encourage him.~~

~~LIZA. Every girl has a right to be loved~~.

~~HIGGINS. What! By fools like that?~~

~~LIZA. Freddy's not a fool. And if he's weak and poor and wants me, maybe he'd make me happier than my betters that bully me and don't want me.~~

~~HIGGINS. Can he make anything of you? That's the point~~.

~~LIZA. Perhaps I could make something of him. But I never thought of us making anything of one another; and you never think of anything else. I only want to be natural.~~

~~HIGGINS. In short, you want me to be as infatuated about you as Freddy? Is that it?~~

~~LIZA. No, I don't. That's not the sort of feeling I want from you. And don't you be too sure of yourself or of me. I could have been a bad girl if I'd liked. I've seen more of some things than you, for all your learning. Girls like me can drag gentlemen down to make love to them easy enough. And they wish each other dead the next minute~~.

~~HIGGINS. Of course they do. Then what in thunder are we quarrelling about?~~

LIZA [*much troubled*] I want a little kindness. I know I'm a common ignorant girl, ~~and you a book-learned gentleman;~~ but I'm not dirt under your feet. What I done [*correcting herself*] what I did was not for the dresses and the taxis: I did it because we were pleasant together and BECAUSE I come—came—to care for you; ~~not to want you to make love to me~~, and not forgetting the difference between us, but more friendly like, NOT TO WANT YOU TO MAKE LOVE TO ME.

DURING THE CONVERSATION, THE CAMERA ALTERNATES IN QUICK CLOSE-UPS BACK AND FORTH BETWEEN ELIZA AND HIGGINS.

HIGGINS. Well, of course, ELIZA. That's ~~just~~ EXACTLY how I feel. And how Pickering feels. Eliza: you're a fool. [*HIGGINS SHAKES HIS HEAD SADLY*].

LIZA. That's not a proper answer to give me [*she sinks on the chair at the writing-table in tears*].

HIGGINS. ~~It's all you'll get until you stop being a common idiot. If you're going to be a lady, you'll have to give up feeling neglected if the men you know don't spend half their time snivelling over you and the other half giving you black eyes. If you can't stand the coldness of my sort of life, and the strain of it, go back to the gutter. Work til you're more a brute than a human being; and then cuddle and squabble and drink til you fall asleep. Oh, it's a fine life, the life of the gutter. It's real: it's warm: it's violent: you can feel it through the thickest skin: you can taste it and smell it without any training or any work. Not like Science and Literature and Classical Music and Philosophy and Art.~~ You find me cold, unfeeling, selfish, don't you? Very well: THEN ~~be off with you to the sort of people you like.~~ Marry some sentimental hog or other with ~~lots of money, and~~ a thick pair of lips to kiss you with and a thick pair of boots to kick you with. If you can't appreciate what you've got, you'd better get what you can appreciate.

LIZA. I WON'T CARE FOR ANYONE WHO DOESN'T CARE FOR ME.

HIGGINS [*EXASPERATED*]. *OH ELIZA, YOU'RE AN IDIOT!*

LIZA [*desperate*] Oh, ~~you are a cruel tyrant.~~ I can't ~~talk~~ SPEAK to you: you turn everything against me: ~~I'm always in the wrong. But you know very well all the time that you're nothing but a bully.~~ You know VERY WELL I can't go back to the gutter, as you call it, and that I have no real friends in the world but you and the Colonel. ~~You know well I couldn't bear to live with a low common man after you two; and it's wicked and cruel of you to insult me by pretending I could.~~ You think I must go back to Wimpole Street because I have nowhere else to go but father's. But don't you be too sure that you have me under your feet to be ~~trampled on~~ BULLIED and talked down. I'll marry Freddy, I will, as soon as I'm able to support him. [[In the play version, the phrase reads: ". . . as soon as he's able to support me."]]

HIGGINS [*thunderstruck*] ~~Freddy!!!~~ WHAT!!! that young fool! YOU SHALL MARRY AN AMBASSADOR! YOU SHALL MARRY THE VICE-ROY OF INDIA. I WON'T HAVE MY MASTERPIECE THROWN AWAY ON FREDDY! [[In the play version, Higgins's response is very much as it is in the sound track version: "[*Sitting down beside her*] Rubbish! you shall marry an ambassador. You shall marry the Governor-General of India or the Lord-Lieutenant of Ireland, or somebody who wants a deputy-queen. I'm not going to have my masterpiece thrown away on Freddy."]] ~~That poor devil who couldn't get a job as an errand boy even if he had the guts to try for it! Woman: do you not understand that I have made you a consort for a king?~~

~~LIZA. Freddy loves me: that makes him king enough for me. I don't want him to work: he wasn't brought up to it as I was.~~ [[This entire last exchange was omitted from the play version, too.]]

LIZA. YOU THINK I LIKE YOU TO SAY THAT. BUT I HAVEN'T FORGOTTEN WHAT YOU SAID A MINUTE AGO. IF I CAN'T HAVE KINDNESS, I'LL HAVE INDEPENDENCE. [[In the play version, Eliza's response is the same as in the sound track version, except she adds the phrase, "I won't be coaxed round as if I was a baby or a puppy."]]

HIGGINS. INDEPENDENCE? THAT'S MIDDLE-CLASS BLASPHEMY. WE ARE ALL OF US DEPENDENT ON ONE ANOTHER, EVERY SOUL ON EARTH.

LIZA [*RISING DETERMINEDLY*]. I'LL LET YOU SEE WHETHER I'M DEPENDENT ON YOU. IF YOU CAN PREACH, I CAN TEACH. I'll go and be a teacher. [[This last exchange is the same in the play version as in the sound track version.]]

HIGGINS. What'll you teach, in heaven's name?

LIZA. What you taught me. I'll teach phonetics.

~~HIGGINS. Ha! Ha! Ha!~~

LIZA. I'll offer myself as an assistant to ~~that hairyfaced Hungarian~~ PROFESSOR KARPATHY. [[In the play version, the sentence reads: "I'll offer myself as an assistant to Professor Nepean."]]

HIGGINS [*rising in a fury*] What! ~~That imposter!~~ that humbug! THAT IMPOSTER! that toadying ignoramus! ~~Teach him my methods! my discoveries!~~ You take one step in his direction and I'll wring your neck. [*He lays hands on her; GRABS HER BY THE SHOULDERS*]. Do you hear?

LIZA [*defiantly non-resistant*] Wring away. What do I care? I knew you'd strike me ~~some~~ ONE day. [*He lets her go, AND GROANS,* ~~*stamping with rage at having forgotten himself, and recoils so hastily that he stumbles back into his seat on the ottoman*~~]~~. Aha!~~ Now I know how to deal with you. Oh, what a fool I was not to think of it before! ~~You can't take away the knowledge you gave me. You said I had a finer ear than you. And I can be civil and kind to people, which is more than you can. Aha!~~ [*SHE LAUGHS DEEPLY, purposely dropping her aitches to annoy him*]. That's done you, Enry Iggins, it az. Now I don't care that [*snapping her fingers*] for your bullying and your ~~big~~ FINE talk. ~~I'll advertize it in the papers that your duchess is only a flower girl that you taught, and that she'll teach anybody to be a duchess just the same in six months for a thousand guineas.~~ Oh, when I think of myself crawling under your feet and being trampled on and called names, when all the time I had only to lift up my finger to be as good as you ARE, I could just kick myself. [*DURING THE WHOLE OF THIS EXUBERANT SPEECH OF ELIZA'S THE CAMERA SHOOTS HER FROM A VERY LOW POSITION, MAKING HER LOOM LARGE OVER HIGGINS, MAKING HER LOOK VERY SUPERIOR*]. [[In the play version, Eliza does not drop her aitches in the preceding speech, and the word "that" is emphasized as she snaps her fingers.]]

HIGGINS [*wondering at her*] ~~You damned impudent slut, you! But its better than snivelling; better than fetching slippers and finding spectacles, isn't it? [*Rising*]~~ By George, Eliza, I said I'd make a woman of you; and I have. I like you like this.

LIZA. Yes: ~~you turn round and~~ make up to me now that I'm not afraid of you, and can do without you.

HIGGINS. Of course I do, you little fool. Five minutes ago you were like a millstone round my neck. Now you're a tower of strength: a consort battleship. [*CLOSE-UP OF ELIZA'S FACE, LOOKING STARTLED AT BEING CALLED A BATTLESHIP*]. ~~You and I and Pickering will be three old bachelors~~ [[The play version has the word "together" here]] ~~instead of only two men and a silly girl. [*Mrs Higgins returns, dressed for the wedding. Eliza instantly becomes cool and elegant*]~~.

~~MRS HIGGINS. The carriage is waiting, Eliza. Are you ready?~~

~~LIZA. Quite. Is the Professor coming?~~

~~MRS HIGGINS. Certainly not. He can't behave himself in church. He makes remarks out loud all the time on the clergyman's pronunciation~~.

LIZA. ~~Then I shall not see you again, Professor.~~ Goodbye, PROFESSOR HIGGINS. [*She goes to the door. HE FROWNS. CLOSE-UP OF ELIZA'S FACE: SHE TURNS UP HER NOSE AND LEAVES. THE DOOR SLAMS BEHIND HER*].

~~MRS HIGGINS [*coming to Higgins*] Goodbye, dear~~.

~~HIGGINS. Goodbye, mother. [*He is about to kiss her, when he recollects something*]. Oh, by the way, Eliza, order a ham and a Stilton cheese, will you? And buy me a pair of reindeer gloves, number eights, and a tie to match that new suit of mine.~~ [[The play version has the phrase here, "at Eale & Binman's."]] ~~You can choose the color. [*His cheerful, careless, vigorous voice shews that he is incorrigible*]~~.

~~LIZA [*disdainfully*] Number eights are too small for you if you want them lined with lamb's wool. You have three new ties that you have forgotten in the drawer of your washstand. Colonel Pickering prefers Double Gloucester to Stilton; and you don't notice the difference. I telephoned Mrs Pearce this morning not to forget the ham. What you are to do without me I cannot imagine. [*She sweeps out*]~~. [[In the play version, as in the sound track version, this entire speech of Eliza's is omitted. In the play version, she simply responds: "Buy them yourself."]]

~~MRS HIGGINS. I'm afraid you've spoilt that girl, Henry. I should be uneasy about you and her if she were less fond of Colonel Pickering~~.

~~HIGGINS. Pickering! Nonsense: she's going to marry Freddy. Ha Ha! Freddy! Freddy! Ha ha ha ha ha!!!!! [*He roars with laughter as the play ends*]~~. [[The end of the printed movie version.]]

[[In the play version the last two speeches read as follows:

MRS HIGGINS. I'm afraid you've spoilt that girl, Henry. But never mind, dear: I'll buy you the tie and gloves.

HIGGINS [*sunnily*] Oh, don't bother. She'll buy 'em all right enough. Goodbye. [*They kiss. Mrs Higgins runs out. Higgins, left alone, rattles his cash in his pocket; chuckles; and disports himself in a highly self-satisfied manner*]. The end of the play version.]]

HIGGINS IS ALL ALONE IN HIS MOTHER'S HOUSE. A HORN IS HEARD FROM THE STREET BELOW. FREDDY IS WAITING FOR ELIZA: ELIZA COMES OUT OF THE HOUSE AND GETS INTO FREDDY'S CAR. HIGGINS RUNS OUT OF THE HOUSE INTO THE STREET, JUST IN TIME TO SEE ELIZA AND FREDDY PULL AWAY. CUT TO ELIZA LOOKING SADLY OUT OF THE CAR WINDOW. CUT BACK TO A CLOSE-UP OF HIGGINS'S DISTURBED FACE, AS THE MUSIC CHANGES FROM FAST, EXCITED MUSIC, TO A ROMANTIC ECHO OF THE THEME OF THE BALLROOM SCENE. HIGGINS BEGINS TO WALK SLOWLY ALONG THE STREET. FADE-OUT AND FADE-IN TO HIGGINS WALKING VERY QUICKLY ALONG THE STREET, ACCOMPANIED NOW BY EXCITED MUSIC. HE CHANGES HIS DIRECTION. IN A SERIES OF QUICK FADES, HIGGINS IS SEEN WALKING EXCITEDLY, BUMPING INTO PEOPLE, GROWING FURIOUS. THE CAMERA ZOOMS UPWARD, DEPRESSING ALL BENEATH IT. HIGGINS RUSHES INTO HIS OWN HOUSE. QUICK FADE-OUT AND FADE-IN TO HIGGINS ENTERING HIS HOUSE, THE EXCITING MUSIC CHANGING BACK TO THE ECHO OF THE THEME OF THE BALLROOM SCENE AS HE ENTERS HIS HOUSE. HIGGINS CHARGES INTO HIS LIVING ROOM, FURIOUSLY BEGINS SMASHING THE PHONOGRAPH RECORDS. CLOSE-UP TO THE SWITCH ON THE PHONOGRAPH AS HIGGINS ACCIDENTALLY TURNS IT ON. ELIZA'S VOICE IS HEARD COMING OUT OF THE PHONOGRAPH:

ELIZA'S VOICE. AH-AH-AH-AH-OW-OW-OO-OO!! I AIN'T DIRTY: I WASHED MY FACE AND HANDS AFORE I COME, I DID.

HIGGINS'S VOICE. I SHALL MAKE A DUCHESS OF THIS DRAGGLETAILED GUTTERSNIPE.

ELIZA'S VOICE. AH-AH-AH-OW-OW-OO!

HIGGINS'S VOICE. IN SIX MONTHS . . . [*HIGGINS SWITCHES*

OFF THE PHONOGRAPH. CLOSE-UP OF HIGGINS'S SORROWFUL FACE].

ELIZA ENTERS THE ROOM, UNSEEN BY HIGGINS. HE HEARS HER VOICE, SPEAKING WITH PERFECT LADY-LIKE DICTION, SOFT, GENTLE, LOVINGLY.

ELIZA. I WASHED MY FACE AND HANDS BEFORE I CAME.

AS HIGGINS TURNS TO LOOK AT ELIZA, THE BALLROOM THEME BEGINS ONCE MORE. HIGGINS LOOKS AT ELIZA TENDERLY. CUT TO A CLOSE-UP OF ELIZA, LOOKING BACK AT HIM. HIGGINS JUST BEGINS TO SMILE; THEN HE RECOLLECTS HIMSELF, AND SAYS STERNLY, AS THE CAMERA LOOKS ONLY AT THE BACK OF HIS HEAD:

HIGGINS. WHERE THE DEVIL ARE MY SLIPPERS, ELIZA?

AS THE BALLROOM THEME SWELLS INTO A CRESCENDO, A FADE-OUT FROM THE BACK OF HIGGINS'S HEAD. THE LILTING MUSIC OF THE BALLROOM WALTZ IS HEARD AS "THE END" AND THE CAST ARE FLASHED UPON THE SCREEN.

APPENDIX D

The Entire Screen Play For A Projected Film Version Of *Arms And The Man* By Bernard Shaw

This previously unpublished screen play is the whole of Shaw's adaptation of *Arms and the Man* for the screen. He wrote this scenario for Gabriel Pascal in 1941, nine years after the first screen version of this play. But the Pascal film was never produced. The original of this document, signed by Shaw, is in the personal files of Miss Marjorie Deans, London.

A cold afternoon in November 1855. The battlefield of Slivnitza. Cannon thunder and smoke. Shells bursting. In the foreground a shell hole and a machine-gun section. A company of Serbian troops, commanded by Bluntschli, a Swiss officer, is waiting to come into action, intent on the guns.

BLUNTSCHLI [*scanning through his field-glasses*] What is that cavalry regiment doing there?

A couple of Austrian sub-lieutenants rise and use their glasses in the same direction.

FIRST SUB. It looks to me as if they were going to charge us, sir.

BLUNTSCHLI. Charge a battery of machine-guns! They couldn't be such damned fools.

2ND SUB. They *are*.

1ST SUB. No mistake about it, sir. Those Bulgarian idiots are capable of anything.

2ND SUB. They know no more about war than a cat knows of a Holiday.

BLUNTSCHLI. Well, we shall just make holes in them, poor devils. Yes: there's no mistake: They're coming for us. [*To the gunners*] Now children: don't be afraid of the horses: don't move an inch: have your guns ready: and don't loose off until you can see the whites of the horses' eyes. Then let them have it. How are we off for ammunition?

A sergeant rushes in with utter dismay in his countenance.

SERGEANT. Captain: they've sent us the wrong belts. The guns won't work.

BLUNTSCHLI. Damnation! [*Peremptorily*] Run for it. Save himself who can. [*The gunners spring up and abandon their guns and rush away*].

1ST LIEUT. They don't even know how to charge, the fools! They're galloping all the way and waving their silly swords.

2ND LIEUT. Their horses will be tired before they reach us.

BLUNTSCHLI. No matter: they will be fresh enough to do for us. And my revolver isn't loaded, confound it.

1ST LIEUT. Same here.
2ND LIEUT. Same here.
BLUNTSCHLI. Nothing for it but a bunk. Off with you! That is an order. [*The two lieutenants salute and run off. The cavalry charge sweeps down, with wild cheering and flourishing of sabres, Sergius Saranoff leading three yards in front. Bluntschli draws his sword and jumps into the shell-hole. Close-up of Bluntschli crouching in shell-hole. As before—the charge passes, cheering madly. Sounds of the fugitives being cut down. Bluntschli comes out of the shell-hole; looks through his glasses after the rout and slaughter: then in the opposite direction at a body of Bulgarian boot, who are following up the cavalry: shrugs his shoulders; sheathes his sword; and walks off to the right without hurrying himself in the least.*]

Late evening. A road approaching a Bulgarian village. Masses of brambles, thistles, gorse and weeds of all sorts border the roadway on the far side. Bulgarian infantry tramp along the road towards the village, singing a Bulgarian marching song, tired and dusty, but flushed with victory. Petkoff and Saranoff with them on horseback. The villagers rush out to meet them, cheering, throwing flowers (the girls showering them on Saranoff), handing cucumbers and apples, and kissing the soldiers who are natives of the village. The soldiers tramp on, keeping their formation as best they can. The villagers turn and go back into the village with them. The road is left deserted. The cheering and singing fade into the distance. From the apparently impenetrable thornbrake Bluntschli emerges cautiously, his uniform torn and his face and hands scratched and soiled by the thorns. His plight looks pretty desperate. He looks cautiously up and down the road. An oldish peasant woman comes along, pulling a barrow full of loaves of bread. Bluntschli draws his revolver and hides until she is close to him, then springs out at her.
THE WOMAN [*recognising his uniform*] Serbian! [*She begins screaming*].
BLUNTSCHLI [*covering her with the revolver*] Silence: not a word. [*The woman gasps and throws up her hands, silent and terrified*].
BLUNTSCHLI. Now listen, mother. I am not a Serb: I am a Swiss. I will not harm you; but I am hungry, and you must sell me bread. I will pay for it: see! [*He holds up a silver coin as big as a half-crown*] The price of ten loaves. I take one. *The woman drops her hands and eyes the money greedily. He replaces his pistol in its case: takes a loaf from the barrow and throws the coin into it.*
BLUNTSCHLI. Now off home with you; and say nothing. They will kill you if they find out that you have sold bread to an enemy. [*He hurries back into the brush, eating the loaf ravenously*].
The woman looks for the coin in the barrow; pockets it; trundles the barrow off towards the village as fast as she can. A distant burst of cheering accompanies her retreat.

In the Village. The square before the church. The church steps serve as a platform on which stand Petkoff, Saranoff, and the Mayor, a podgy little man in red gown, chain of office, and three cornered hat. He is attended by a gigantic beadle, in whatever is the Bulgarian equivalent to a cocked hat and gold-braided cape and trousers, carrying a mace on his shoulder, and a big bell in his disengaged hand. The soldiers are drawn up along the foot of the steps between the speakers and the crowd, which is excited and very noisy.

THE BEADLE [*makes a fearful clamor with his bell, in stentorian tones*] Silence! Si-i-i-lensss! Silence for the Worshipful the Mayor. [*The noise stops. All listen*].

THE MAYOR. Fellow citizens. I have glorious news for you. A battle, the like of which has never been fought in the history of the world, has been fought at Slivnitza. [*Cheers from the crowd, which knows all about it, but wants to hear speeches*].

THE BEADLE [*as before*] Silence! Silence! [*Clangs his bell*].

THE MAYOR. On that field Bulgaria has faced the invading hosts of our deadly enemies the Serbs. [*Cries of "Swine"*]. They were as the sands of the sea in number. The all-devouring Austrian empire armed them, officered them, fed them, promised them victory. What had we to oppose these millions of ruthless foes? Two hundred men.

VOICE FROM THE CROWD. Two thousand.

THE BEADLE [*clanging*] Silence! Do you hear? Silence!

Tumult. The interrupter, kicked and hustled, has to fly for his life.

THE MAYOR. Two hundred men. A handful against a host. Yes, fellow citizens; but the two hundred were Bulgarians. [*Cheers*]. By whom were these Bulgarians led? Was it by those Russian generals who have come here to teach Bulgarians how to fight? No, fellow citizens: the cowardly Russian orders were defied. [*Cheers*]. We were led to a glorious victory by our fellow countryman Sergius Saranoff, who has not a drop of blood in his veins that is not true blue Bulgarian of the best. There he stands. [*Tremendous cheering; the girls throw all the flowers they have left at Saranoff, who looks stern and irresponsive*].

THE MAYOR [*at the top of his voice*] He will now address you.

THE BEADLE. Silence for the Right Honourable His Excellency Sergius Saranoff. [*Clanging*] Silence, silence! [*The tumult ceases as Saranoff steps forward. All listen eagerly*].

SERGIUS. My Mayor: I am not a hero [*cries of "You are" in which the girls join enthusiastically*]. I tell you I am not. There can be no single hero in a nation where all are heroes. [*Cheers, suppressed by the beadle by a stroke of his bell*]. Why was I first in the charge that won the battle for us? I was no braver than the rest; but my horse is the fastest in Bulgaria: he cost me twenty thousand levas. [*Cheers and laughter*]. Cheer till you are hoarse, I will not accept a single cheer or flower that is not shared by every man that rode with me that day at Slivnitza. [*He steps back amid thunders of applause*].

THE BEADLE [*clanging*] Silence! Silence for the Worshipful the Mayor!

THE MAYOR. I call on Commander Petkoff.

THE BEADLE. Silence for honourable and gallant Commander Petkoff.

PETKOFF [*stepping forward*] Citizens: we have won a battle; but the war is not over. I shall not sleep in my bed at home for six months yet: we have that much fighting still before us, and perhaps more. But however long it lasts you must keep a sharp lookout for Serbian runaways. I have just heard that one of your old women has been robbed within a hundred yards of the village by a scoundrel in Serbian uniform. You all know her: you buy your bread from her. She was on her way here with her basket of loaves peacefully and lawfully as she had a perfect right to do when a cowardly swine sprang from the bushes, flung her brutally to the ground and trampled on her until she lost her senses. When she recovered the fellow was gone and her basket was empty: he has not left the poor woman a single crumb. Hunt that man down; and see that he gets what he deserves. He cannot be far off. You of the Home Guard: away with you. [*With loud boos and execrations, the able-bodied men rush off, and the meeting breaks up*].

Night. Full moon. A street in a small Bulgarian town. Only one of the houses has pretensions and has two storeys. One of its upper windows is lighted up, and has a balcony over the porch, which is a structure of trellis work covered with flowering creepers. There is a mounting-block beside the door. Mountain tops, glittering with snow in the moonlight, are visible beyond the low-roofed houses opposite. Bluntschli, a hunted fugitive, footsore, hungry, and utterly weary, steals in. He looks carefully about to satisfy himself that the town is asleep and no one is in sight. He collapses on the mounting-block, elbows on knees, head buried on his hands, dead beat. The lighted window is opened. He starts up and blots himself against the wall, watching the balcony. Raina appears in her nightdress, and posts herself there, gazing at the snowy mountains, and looking distinctly operatic, like Elsa in Lohengrin. Bluntschli stares at her. Distant shots break the quiet of the night. Raina at the sound of the shots blows out her candle, and jumps into bed. Bluntschli has returned to his seat on the mounting-block; but he is less dejected, and is looking curiously up at the closed window. The shots startle him: he springs up, keenly alert, looking up and down the street. A mob of soldiers appear, "wild, drunk, and furious," as Louka presently describes them, searching for imaginary fugitives in every corner, and firing recklessly at shadows. A couple of them see Bluntschli in the middle of the street and fire at him. He darts to the side of the portal farthest from them for cover. Peeping out, he sees that when they have reached the house they will catch him. He climbs the trellis and gets over into the balcony, where he crouches out of sight. Change back to Raina's darkened room, and she in bed. The text of the play begins with Bluntschli breaking in. The remainder of Act I follows.

Continuation from the end of Act I:

CATHERINE. The poor dear! Raina!!!

RAINA. Well, he is quite harmless. And I can sleep in your room. He can have my bed for the night. He will be all right when he has had a good breakfast.

CATHERINE [*aghast*] A good breakfast! And what are we to do with him then, pray? Give him up to our soldiers?

RAINA. Never. They would kill him. We must not betray him: the guest is sacred. We must help him to escape.

CATHERINE. Don't be ridiculous, child. This isn't an opera: it's real life. How could he escape in that uniform?

RAINA. Oh, there are lots of father's old clothes in the blue closet. Father will never miss them.

CATHERINE. I never heard of such a thing. But I suppose you must have your way: now that I see the poor creature lying there helpless I don't feel I should like to see him murdered. But look at the mess he is making of your bed with his boots. His spurs will tear the sheets to pieces.

RAINA. Yes: we must pull them off. [*She seizes one of the boots and begins pulling it off*].

CATHERINE. Take care of the spurs. [*She sets to work on the other boot*].

Bluntschli groans and snores protestingly, but does not wake. The boots come off simultaneously; and the two ladies are left sitting on the floor, each hugging a military boot.

Catherine's Bedroom. There is a big double bed in which Catherine is fast asleep, and a little one in which Raina has slept. It is now empty. Raina enters in her dressing-gown, with an old suit of clothes on her arm.

RAINA. Mother: get up, get up. It's nearly nine. [*She shakes the sleeper*].

CATHERINE [*rubbing her eyes*] Eh? What? What have you got there?

RAINA. Clothes for the man.

CATHERINE. What man?

RAINA. The man last night. Wake up, mother: you're half asleep still. The man that came in at my window.

CATHERINE [*sitting up*] We must get rid of him. Has he had his breakfast?

RAINA. I should think he has. He has eaten your breakfast and mine too on top of his own. I did not know that a man could be such a pig. His mouth was too full to speak to me.

CATHERINE. Where is he?

RAINA. In father's snuggery, undressing himself. Do you think these things will do? [*Showing Catherine the clothes*].

CATHERINE. Yes: just the thing. Your father is always asking for that old coat, and disgracing us by wearing it when we have visitors. I'll tell him the moths have eaten it and we have had to burn it.

RAINA. We shall have to burn the man's uniform, or bury it or something. I will take these to him. [*She goes out with the clothes, Catherine getting out of bed meanwhile and putting on her slippers*].

Raina's Bedroom. The bed is badly disordered as Bluntschli had left it earlier. Raina enters, carrying the clothes, which she puts down on the bed while she goes to the chest of drawers, from which she takes out a packet of cabinet photographs and a red pencil. She picks out four of the photographs, and holds them up like a hand at cards, considering which to choose. Close-up of the four photographs in her hand showing that they are portraits of herself in different poses. As before, she selects one, and begins to write on it. The marks made by the pencil not being black enough, she puts it in her mouth and licks the lead. She resumes her writing. Close-up of the selected pose, inscribed "Raina to her chocolate-cream soldier, a Souvenir." As before, she puts the inscribed photo-

graph into the side-pocket of the coat, smiling to herself complacently, gathers up the clothes, and goes out.

A Bulgarian postchaise (or diligence) is waiting at the porch. Louka is watching from an upper window. The door opens; Raina and Catherine come out and stand on the threshold. Bluntschli comes out between them: a ridiculous spectacle in an old smoking-cap and jacket, and Bulgarian civvies that do not fit him too well.

BLUNTSCHLI [*with his characteristic crisp decision accentuated*] Gracious ladies: my eternal gratitude. Not a word about me. You would be shot for not giving me up. [*He jumps into the vehicle*] Avanti! [*Or its Bulgarian equivalent if we can discover it*].

The driver, startled by the command, which comes like a pistol-shot, cracks his whip, which has a lash four feet long or thereabouts, and sets his horses off at a full gallop. The two women turn and stare at one another, completely taken aback. Close-up of Raina and Catherine in the doorway.

CATHERINE. The brute! Eternal gratitude indeed!

RAINA. Could we really be shot for saving a man's life?

CATHERINE. In war-time anybody can be shot for anything or nothing. He said it just to shut our mouths in case we wanted to give him away.

RAINA. What! Betray him! After all we did for him!

CATHERINE. Serbians are all like that: They think everybody as treacherous as themselves. [*She turns and goes in*].

RAINA [*following her*] He's not a Serb: he's a Swiss.

A Council Chamber. Noon. A table with big inkstands at the ends and one in the middle. The plenipotentiaries of the conflicting States, including Petkoff and Saranoff (for Bulgaria) are seated round the table. Officials stand behind them. All look their glummest. In the middle a white statue of Peace, ten feet high, spreads its wings over the scene. In its left hand is a wreath held out to the sitters. Its right hand is behind it, invisible. The chief official has a sheet of vellum in his hand. In dead silence he places it before each plenipotentiary in turn. They sign, finishing with Petkoff and Sergius, who find writing their names a bit of a job.

THE CHIEF OFFICIAL [*gathering the signed document*] Your Excellencies will no doubt find it advisable to appear on the balcony and inform the people that the peace is concluded.

The plenipotentiaries rise, and follow the official out, almost scowling at one another. The other officials go out at the back, leaving the room empty. A distant outburst of cheering announces that the crowd has heard the joyful news. The statue turns slowly around and reveals its right hand held behind its back. The hand holds a revolver. The cheering continues.

Change to Act II of the play.

Continuation of Act II:

BLUNTSCHLI. Well, if I must, I must.

NICOLA [*appearing at the top of the steps, and bowing formally*] Lunch is served. [*He remains with drooping head while they pass him*].

CATHERINE. Captain Bluntschli is staying to lunch, Nicola.

NICOLA. Yes, madam: his place is laid.

CATHERINE. Then let us go in.

Catherine and Raina go into the house, the men following, and Bluntschli leading, Petkoff and Sergius mildly insisting on his precedence as guest.

A Spacious Flagged Kitchen. The table, with a meal set out for five persons, is piled with accessory foods: baskets of bread, melons, pickles, a cold ham, hors d'oeuvres of all sorts. At the back two enormous vats. Everything indicates that Petkoff is a prosperous farmer in a country where everything is home-made, big, rough, and plentiful. The fireplace has neither grate nor coals: it burns great logs; and over it hangs a huge pot on a chain, a novelty in the shape of a gleaming tin roasting jack, and a pile of plates and dishes. (Close-up) Louka takes three fat roast fowls from the jack, puts them on a dish, bastes them from the dripping pan, and hands them to Nicola, who places them on the table. The five guests enter in the order in which they have left the garden. Petkoff takes his seat before the fowls as head of the household. Catherine indicates that Bluntschli is to sit next to Raina, Sergius taking the chair at her other hand. She herself sits next to her husband.

PETKOFF [*taking up a huge carving knife and hone and shouting very unceremoniously*] For what we are about to receive may the Lord make us truly thankful. [*He sharpens the knife noisily, as if it was a scythe, and cuts a fowl in halves at one stroke and puts one half on the top plate of the pile before him*]. Half a fowl to begin with, Bluntschli?

BLUNTSCHLI [*as Nicola places it before him*] Thank you.

LOUKA [*coming behind Bluntschli, with a large black saucepan*] Veg?

BLUNTSCHLI [*helping himself from the saucepan*] Thank you.

LOUKA [*incredulously*] No sausages!!!?

BLUNTSCHLI. Well, perhaps one small one. [*He helps himself*].

PETKOFF. Raina: will you share a bird with Sergius, or would you rather have a whole one?

RAINA [*vexed*] Oh papa, you will make Captain Bluntschli think I am a boa-constrictor. Half will be quite enough to begin with. [*Petkoff carves accordingly. Nicola takes it to Raina. Then Louka mutely presents the saucepan, from which Raina takes a stupendous helping of miscellaneous vegetables. She adds three sausages. Close-up of this incident, giving Bluntschli's stealthy look at the steaming plate*].

PETKOFF [*to Catherine*] Kit: you will split a bird with Sergius as usual, eh?

CATHERINE. Yes: I have no appetite to-day.

PETKOFF. Good! That leaves a whole one for me. [*He carves; Catherine and Sergius are served, Louka presenting the saucepan to each in silence and then replacing it at the fire. Petkoff dumps the remaining fowl on his own plate and sets to work with knife and fork. Close-up of Raina pulling a leg off her half-chicken with her fingers and gnawing it greedily, Bluntschli again noting this refinement in some dismay*].

All are busy eating.

PETKOFF. Nicola!

NICOLA. Yes, Mayor.

PETKOFF. Take the table out of the scullery and put in the library.

NICOLA. Yes, Mayor.

PETKOFF. And take the pens and ink and paper off the desk in my office and put them on the table. We'll go up there when we've finished eating; and [*to Bluntschli*] you will show us how to get those troops to Philipopolis, won't you?

BLUNTSCHLI. Yes: it won't be difficult. I know the route.

SERGIUS. You know everything, I think.

Change to Beginning of Act III.

No changes of location are needed in the 3rd Act beyond the usual close-up, mediums, and full shots.

It is a mistake to interrupt the play by changes of scene after the audience has become interested in the characters and story.

(Signed) G. Bernard Shaw,
Ayot St. Lawrence,
Welwyn, Herts.
3rd September 1941

SOURCES

Introduction and *The Fascination of the Serpent's Eye*

"The Big Parade," *Literary Digest*, LXXXIX (June 12, 1926), 29.

Carter, Huntly. *The New Spirit of the Cinema*. London: Harold Shaylor, 1930.

Church, Hayden. "Shaw May Come Here in Movies," *The New York World*, December 5, 1926.

Colbourne, Maurice. *The Real Bernard Shaw*. Toronto: J. M. Dent and Sons, Ltd., 1930.

Deans, Marjorie. *Meeting at the Sphinx: Gabriel Pascal's Production of Bernard Shaw's Caesar and Cleopatra*. London: MacDonald and Company, Ltd., no date.

Fowler, Gene. *Good Night, Sweet Prince*. New York: The Viking Press, 1943.

Gernsheim, Helmut. "GBS and Photography," *Photographic Journal: Section A*, XCI (January, 1951), 31–36.

Hall, Mordaunt. "G.B.S.'s Talking Shadow," *The New York Times*, July 1, 1928.

———. "G. Bernard Shaw Acts in Movietone," *The New York Times*, June 26, 1928.

———. "The Screen," *The New York Times*, September 7, 1929.

Irvine, William. *The Universe of G.B.S.* New York: Whittlesey House, 1949.

Knight, Arthur. *The Liveliest Art*. New York: The Macmillan Company, 1957.

MacCormac, John. "Bernard Shaw on Films," *The New York Times*, May 27, 1928.

Mander, Raymond, and Mitchenson, Joe. *Theatrical Companion to Shaw*. New York: Pitman Publishing Company, 1955.

Marriott, R. B. "Films Are Not Children's Picture Books: Bernard Shaw Talks About 'St. Joan' Film," *The Era*, CI (May 5, 1938), 1.

Mayer, Arthur. *Merely Colossal*. New York: Simon and Schuster, 1953.

"Mr. Shaw and Mr. Menjou," *The New York Times*, June 3, 1928.

Mycroft, Walter Charles. "Shaw—and the Devil to Pay," *Films and Filming*, V (February, 1959), 14, 30, 31.

Patch, Blanche. *Thirty Years with G.B.S.* London: Victor Gollancz, Ltd., 1951.

"Russian Film Banned," *The Times* (London), February 25, 1930.

Saroyan, William. "My Visit with G.B.S.," *The New Republic*, LXXIII (July 2, 1946), 80.

Shaw, George Bernard, and Bishop, G. W. "The Living Talkies: An Interview," *Theatre Guild Magazine*, VII (November, 1929), 32.

Shaw, George Bernard, and Henderson, Archibald. "The Drama, The Theatre, and The Films," *The Fortnightly Review*, CXVI n.s. (September 1, 1924), 289–302.

Shaw, George Bernard. "*Arms and the Man* on the Screen," *Malvern Festival Book*, July, 1932, reprinted in West, E. J. (ed.). *Shaw on Theatre*. New York: Hill and Wang, 1958.

———. "The Art and Talking for the Talkies," *World Film News*, I (November, 1936), 6, 7.

———. "The Cinema as a Moral Leveller," *The New Statesman: Special Supplement on the Modern Theatre*, III (June 27, 1914), 1, 2.

———. "Education and the Cinematograph," *The Bioscope: Educational Supplement No. 2*, XXIII (June 18, 1914), i, ii.
———. "Efficient for Evil," [Letter to the Editor] *The Times* (London), February 17, 1930.
———. "Films, Plays, and G. B. Shaw—an Interview," *FAME: The Box Office Check-Up*, (1937), pp. 22, 26.
———. "G.B.S. on Film Censorship," *The Listener*, XIII (January 30, 1935), 200.
———. "My First Talkie," *Malvern Festival Book*, August, 1931, reprinted in West, E. J. (ed.). *Shaw on Theatre*. New York: Hill and Wang, 1958.
———. *Our Theatre in the Nineties*. 3 vols. London: Constable and Company, Ltd., 1932.
———. *Pygmalion*. New York: Dodd, Mead and Company, 1939.
———. "A Relief from the Romantic Film," *The Illustrated London News*, LXXXI (December 3, 1927), 1004.
———. "*Saint Joan* Banned: Film Censorship in the United States" [Letter to the Editor], *The New York Times*, September 14, 1936.
———. "Shaw's Rules for Play Producers," *The Strand*, CXVII (July, 1949), 18–25.
———. "The Theatre and the Film," *The Referee*, September 4, 1921, p. 5.
———. "Views on Censorship," *British Film Journal*, I (April-May, 1928), 65, 66.
———. "What I Think About the Film Industry," *Daily Film Renter*, XIX (January 1, 1946), 5.
———. "What the Film May Do to the Drama," *Metropolitan Magazine*, XLII (May, 1915), 23, 54.
"G. B. Shaw in Talking Film; May Be Seen in America," *The New York Times*, December 29, 1926.
"Shaw Approves 'Dawn'," *The New York Times*, February 19, 1928.
"Shaw Defends 'The Big Parade'," *The New York World*, May 23, 1926.
"Shaw Finally Allows Play to Be a Talkie," *The New York Times*, August 8, 1930.
"Shaw Finds Talkies Opening New Field," *The New York Times*, May 19, 1929.
"Shaw for Talking Movies," *The New York Times*, July 20, 1928.
"Shaw Hails Lenin as the Pathfinder," *The New York Times*, July 28, 1931.
"Shaw to Appear in Film," *The New York Times*, May 29, 1928.
Thorndike, Russell. *Sybil Thorndike*. London: T. Butterworth, 1929.
Warren, Low. *The Film Game*. London: T. Werner Laurie, Ltd., 1937.

GBS the Screen Writer

Bakshy, Alexander. "Shaw's First Movie," *The Nation*, CXXXII (February 4, 1931), 135, 6.
Crowther, Bosley. "G. B. Shaw's Disciple," *The New York Times*, October 23, 1938.
Deans, Marjorie. *Meeting at the Sphinx: Gabriel Pascal's Production of Bernard Shaw's Caesar and Cleopatra*. London: MacDonald and Company, Ltd., no date.
Delacorte, Valerie. "G.B.S. in Filmland," *Esquire*, LXII (December, 1964), 150–153, 288–292.
"A Dutch Film of 'Pygmalion'," *The Times* (London), March 3, 1937.
Fowler, Gene. *Good Night, Sweet Prince*. New York: The Viking Press, 1943.
"GBS Hits Hollywood," *London Sunday Disptach*, March 1, 1931.
"Goldwyn Raps 'Greedy' Critic," *The New York American*, October 11, 1926.
Henderson, Archibald. *Bernard Shaw: Playboy and Prophet*. New York: D. Appleton and Company, 1932.

"Lasky Offer of $75,000 Tempts G. B. Shaw," *The New York Times*, November 18, 1926.
Lejeune, C. A. "Prelude to the Battle," *The New York Times*, July 21, 1940.
Marriott, R. B. "Films Are Not Children's Picture Books: Bernard Shaw Talks About 'St. Joan' Film," *The Era*, CI (May 5, 1938), 1.
"Memo: From G.B.S. to S.G.," *The New York Times*, September 27, 1936.
"Mr. Shaw and Mr. Menjou," *The New York Times*, June 3, 1928.
Mycroft, Walter Charles. "Shaw—and the Devil to Pay," *Films and Filming*, V (February, 1959), 14, 30, 31.
Nicoll, Allardyce. *Film and Theatre*. New York: Thomas Y. Crowell Company, 1936.
"$1,000,000 Refused by Shaw Because Tax is Too High," *The New York American*, March 28, 1920.
Pascal, Gabriel. "Shaw as a Scenario Writer," in Winsten, S. (ed.). *G.B.S. 90*. New York: Dodd, Mead and Company, 1946, pp. 255–260.
Patch, Blanche. *Thirty Years with G.B.S.* London: Victor Gollancz, Ltd., 1951.
"Pola Negri to Screen Shaw's 'Cleopatra'," *The New York Times*, December 1, 1928.
Reynolds, H. K. "Shaw Finds Himself Failing," *The New York American*, October 9, 1926.
———. "U.S. Movies Capture Shaw at $100,000," *The New York American*, November 14, 1926.
St. John, Christopher (ed.). *GBS and Ellen Terry: A Correspondence*. New York: G. P. Putnam's Sons, 1931.
"Says RKO Beat British," *The New York Times*, November 26, 1933.
Shaw, George Bernard, and Bishop, G. W. "The Living Talkies: An Interview," *Theatre Guild Magazine*, VII (November, 1929), 32.
Shaw, George Bernard, and Henderson, Archibald. "The Drama, The Theatre, and The Films," *The Fortnightly Review*, CXVI n.s. (September 1, 1924), 289–302.
Shaw, George Bernard. "Bernard Shaw Centenary," *Cine Technician*, XXII (August, 1956), 123. (Reprinted from *Cine Technician* of Autumn, 1936).
———. "Films, Plays, and G. B. Shaw—An Interview," *FAME: The Box Office Check-Up*, (1937), pp. 22, 26.
"Shaw Can't Recall Scenario Rejection," *The New York Times*, October 12, 1926.
"Shaw Cold Shoulders U.S. Film Rights Buyer," *The New York World*, February 23, 1926.
"Shaw Denies Tale of Rejected Play," *The New York Evening Post*, October 12, 1926.
"Shaw Disdainful at Movie Colony," *The New York Times*, March 29, 1933.
"Shaw Finally Allows Play to be a Talkie," *The New York Times*, August 8, 1930.
"Shaw Goes Shavian to Kid Yankees for Being Asleep," *The New York World*, May 23, 1928.
"Shaw Helps Direct Talkie," *The New York Times*, October 28, 1930.
"Shaw Picks to Pieces £10,000 Movie Offer," *The New York Times*, May 27, 1921.
"Shaw Ready to Give Films Chance to Portray Works," *The New York Herald Tribune*, March 12, 1928.
"Shaw Says Americans Do Well When Shown," *The New York Times*, March 2, 1931.
"Shaw Talkie Disappoints," *The New York Times*, January 13, 1931.
"Shaw Wins Suit on 'Chocolate Soldier' Film," *The New York Times*, March 22, 1927.
West, E. J. (ed.). *Shaw on Theatre*. New York: Hill and Wang, 1958.
Winsten, Stephen. *Jesting Apostle: The Life of Bernard Shaw*. London: Hutchinson and Company, 1956.

———. *Shaw's Corner.* London: Hutchinson and Company, 1952.
Wood, Alan. *Mr. Rank.* London: Hodder and Stoughton, 1952.

UNPUBLISHED MATERIAL:

Letter from Louis Calvert to Shaw, dated August 20, 1915 (in the Hanley Collection).
Letter from Shaw to J. E. Vedrenne, dated June 11, 1927 (in the Hanley Collection).
Cablegram from Mary Pickford to Shaw, dated February 6, 1930 (in the Hanley Collection).
Cablegram from Shaw to Mary Pickford, undated (in the Hanley Collection).
Letter from Shaw to Gene Tunney, dated Easter Sunday, 1930 (in the files of the Shaw Society of Chicago).
Copy of Contract between Shaw and British International Pictures for *How He Lied to Her Husband,* dated August 18, 1930 (in the Hanley Collection).
Copy of Contract between Shaw and British International Pictures for *Arms and the Man,* dated July 7, 1932 (in the Hanley Collection).
Cablegram from Kenneth Macgowan to Shaw, dated November 10, 1933 (in the RKO archives).
A series of letters between Shaw and Eberhard K. Klagemann, Dr. Paul Koretz, and Siegfried Trebitsch, dated throughout 1934 and 1935 (in the Hanley Collection).
Copy of Contract between Shaw and Klagemann Films, dated February 16, 1935 (in the Hanley Collection).
Letter from Shaw to Blanche Patch, dated March 29, 1935 (in the Hanley Collection).
Letter from Shaw to Siegfried Trebitsch, dated March 28, 1940 (in the Hanley Collection).
Letter from Shaw to Blanche Patch, dated January 1, 1946 (in the Hanley Collection).
Letter from Marjorie Deans to Donald P. Costello, dated March 7, 1959 (in my files).
Letter from Marjorie Deans to Donald P. Costello, dated June 15, 1959 (in my files).
Letter from Mrs. Valerie Pascal Delacorte to Donald P. Costello, dated August 20, 1959 (in my files).
Letter from Blanche Patch to Donald P. Costello, dated May 15, 1960 (in my files).
Letter from Cecil Lewis to Donald P. Costello, dated June 14, 1960 (in my files).

Pygmalion

Alicoate, Jack (ed.). *The 1939 Film Daily Year Book of Motion Pictures.* New York: The Film Daily, 1939.
Asquith, Anthony. "Shakespeare, Shaw on the Screen," *Cine Technician,* IV (November-December, 1938), 123, 4.
Chappelow, Allen (ed.). *Shaw the Villager and Human Being: A Biographical Symposium.* London: Charles Skilton, Ltd., 1961.
Crowther, Bosley. "G. B. Shaw's Disciple," *The New York Times,* October 23, 1938.
Davy, Charles. "Films," *The London Mercury,* XXXIX (November, 1938), 63.
Deans, Marjorie. *Meeting at the Sphinx: Gabriel Pascal's Production of Bernard Shaw's Caesar and Cleopatra.* MacDonald and Company, Ltd., no date.
Delacorte, Valerie. "G.B.S. in Filmland," *Esquire,* LXII (December, 1964), 150–153, 288–292.
Howard, Leslie Ruth. *A Quite Remarkable Father.* New York: Harcourt, Brace and Company, 1959.
Langner, Lawrence. *G.B.S. and the Lunatic.* New York: Atheneum, 1963.

Mannock, P. L. "Shaw Shows 'Em," *London Daily Herald,* October 7, 1938.
Marriott, R. B. "Films Are Not Children's Picture Books: Bernard Shaw Talks About 'St. Joan' Film," *The Era,* CI (May 5, 1938), 1.
Nugent, Frank S. "G. B. Shaw Surrenders With Honor," *The New York Times,* December 11, 1938.
Orme, Michael. "The World of the Cinema," *The Illustrated London News,* CIII (September 17, 1938), 510.
Pascal, Gabriel. "Shaw as a Scenario Writer," in Winsten, S. (ed.). *G.B.S. 90.* New York: Dodd, Mead and Company, 1946, pp. 255–260.
Patch, Blanche. *Thirty Years with G.B.S.* London: Victor Gollancz, Ltd., 1951.
Pearson, Hesketh. *G.B.S. A Postscript.* London: Collins, 1951.
Platt, David. "What G. B. Shaw Said About Hollywood Films," *The Daily Worker,* November 3, 1950.
"Pygmalion," *The Motion Picture Review Digest,* IV (March 27, 1939), 75, 76.
Roman, Robert C. "GBS on the Screen," *Films in Review,* XI (August-September, 1960), 406–418.
Shaw, Bernard, and Lipscomb, W. P., and Lewis, Cecil. *Pygmalion.* Produced as a motion picture by Gabriel Pascal, 1938.
Shaw, Bernard. "Films, Plays, and G. B. Shaw—an Interview," *FAME: The Box Office Check-Up,* (1937), pp. 22, 26.
———. *Pygmalion.* New York: Dodd, Mead and Company, 1939.
———. *Pygmalion.* Baltimore: Penguin Books, 1941.
"Shaw's 'Barbara' Set," *Variety,* CXXXVI (November 15, 1939), 14.
Sheean, Vincent. "My Last Visit with Shaw," *The Atlantic,* CLXXXVII (January, 1951), 19–24.
Variety, Vols. CXXXIII, CXXXIV (December-June, 1939).
West, E. J. "Hollywood and Mr. Shaw: Some Reflections on Shavian Drama-into-Cinema," *Educational Theatre Journal,* V (October, 1953), 220–232.
Winsten, Stephen. *Jesting Apostle: The Life of Bernard Shaw.* London: Hutchinson and Company, 1956.
———. *Shaw's Corner.* London: Hutchinson and Company, 1952.
Wood, Alan. *Mr. Rank.* London: Hodder and Stoughton, 1952.
Wright, Basil. "Pygmalion," *The Spectator,* CLXI (October 14, 1938), 603.
Zinnser, Jesse. "Pygmalion," *Cue,* VII (December 3, 1938), 42.

UNPUBLISHED MATERIAL:
Letter from firm of J. D. Langton and Passmore, representing Columbia Pictures Corporation, to Gabriel Pascal, dated September 17, 1937 (in the Hanley Collection).
Gaupp, Charles John, Jr. "A Comparative Study of the Changes in 15 Film Plays Adapted from Stage Plays," Unpublished Ph.D. dissertation, Department of Speech, State University of Iowa, 1950.
Thomas, Frank E., Jr. "An Examination of Four Plays by Bernard Shaw Adapted to the Film Medium," Unpublished Master's dissertation, Department of English, Cornell University, 1955.
Letter from Cecil Lewis to Donald P. Costello, dated June 14, 1960 (in my files).

Major Barbara

Alicoate, Jack (ed.). *The 1942 Film Daily Year Book of Motion Pictures.* New York: The Film Daily, 1942.

"Click of 'Candida' Revival Cues Pascal's M-G Film; Cornell or Garson to Star," *Variety*, CXLVII (June 10, 1942), 1.
Delacorte, Valerie. "G.B.S. in Filmland," *Esquire*, LXII (December, 1964), 150–153, 288–292.
Hartung, Philip T. "For the Brain; For the Heart," *The Commonweal*, XXXIV (May 30, 1941), 136.
Lejeune, C. A. "London's Second Wind, *The New York Times*, August 25, 1940.
———. "Spring Finds London's Film Studios Active," *The New York Times*, May 28, 1944.
"Major Barbara," *Time*, XXXVII (June 2, 1941), 80.
" 'Major Barbara' Filming by Pascal Stalled by Air Raids," *Variety*, CXL (September 25, 1940), 13.
"Mr. Shaw, Script Writer," *Theatre Arts*, XXV (September, 1941), 655.
Mycroft, Walter Charles. "Shaw—and the Devil to Pay," *Films and Filming*, V (February, 1959), 14, 30, 31.
"Pascal Here on Exeter," *The New York Times*, February 4, 1941.
"Pascal's 'Major Barbara' Gives Idea of London's Film Production Woes," *Variety*, CXXXIX (September 2, 1941), 80.
Patch, Blanche. *Thirty Years with G.B.S.* London: Victor Gollancz, Ltd., 1951.
Pryor, Thomas M. "By Way of Report," *The New York Times*, September 28, 1941.
Shaw, Bernard. *Major Barbara.* New York: Dodd, Mead and Company, 1941.
———. *Major Barbara.* Produced as a motion picture by Gabriel Pascal, 1941.
———. *Major Barbara: A Screen Version.* Baltimore: Penguin Books, 1951.
Variety, Vols. CXLII, CXLIII, CXLIV, CXLV (March-December, 1941).
Whitebait, William. "Major Barbara, at the Odeon," *The New Statesman and Nation*, XXI (April 12, 1941), 387.
Winsten, Stephen. *Jesting Apostle: The Life of Bernard Shaw.* London: Hutchinson and Company, 1956.
Wood, Alan. *Mr. Rank.* London: Hodder and Stoughton, 1952.

UNPUBLISHED MATERIAL:
Letter from Shaw to John Wardrop, dated April 14, 1941 (in the files of The Shaw Society of Chicago).

Caesar and Cleopatra and *Afterword*

[Advertisements for *Caesar and Cleopatra*], *The New York Times*, September 3, September 4, September 7, 1946.
Anstey, Edgar. "Caesar and Cleopatra," *The Spectator*, CLXXV (December 21, 1945), 519.
Asquith, Anthony. "The Importance of Being Faithful," *Theatre Arts*, XXXVII (April, 1953), 73, 74.
———. "The Play's the Thing," *Films and Filming*, V (February, 1959), 13.
Barker, Felix. *The Oliviers.* Philadelphia: J. B. Lippincott, 1953.
"Cost of 'Caesar' to be Raised in Commons," *The Daily Film Renter*, XIX (January 16, 1945), 3.
"Court Circular," *The Times* (London), December 14, 1945.
Deans, Marjorie. *Meeting at the Sphinx: Gabriel Pascal's Production of Bernard Shaw's Caesar and Cleopatra.* MacDonald and Company, Ltd., no date.

Delacorte, Valerie. "G.B.S. in Filmland," *Esquire,* LXII (December, 1964), 150–153, 288–292.
Hartung, Philip T. "Happy Birthday, GBS," *The Commonweal,* XLIV (August 16, 1946), 434.
Hoffman, Theodore. "Thrown to the Lions," *The New Republic,* CXXVIII (June 15, 1953, 22, 23.
Jacobson, Sol. "Androcles in Hollywood," *Theatre Arts,* XXXVI (December, 1952), 66–69.
Lerner, Alan Jay. "*Pygmalion* and *My Fair Lady,*" *The Shaw Bulletin,* I (November, 1956), 4, 5.
McCarten, John. "The Current Cinema," *The New Yorker,* XL (June 29, 1957), 58.
Manvell, Roger. *Twenty Years of British Film: 1925–1945.* London: The Falcon Press, Ltd., 1946.
Mycroft, Walter Charles. "Shaw—and the Devil to Pay," *Films and Filming,* V (February, 1959), 14, 30, 31.
"Pascal to Make Shaw Films in U.S.," *The Times* (London), February 5, 1947.
Patch, Blanche. *Thirty Years with G.B.S.* London: Victor Gollancz, Ltd., 1951.
Roman, Robert C. "The Devil's Disciple," *Films in Review,* October, 1959, p. 17.
"Shavian History in Technicolor," *The Times* (London), December 12, 1945.
Shaw, Bernard. *Caesar and Cleopatra.* New York: Brentano's, 1913.
———. *Caesar and Cleopatra.* Produced as a motion picture by Gabriel Pascal, 1945.
"Three More Shaw Films," *The Times* (London), August 1, 1946.
Variety, Vols. CLXI, CLXII, CLXIII, CLXIV (December, 1945-November, 1946).
Winnington, Richard. "Caesar and Cleopatra," *News Chronicle,* December 12, 1940.
Winsten, Stephen. *Days with Bernard Shaw.* London: Hutchinson and Company, 1949.
———. *Jesting Apostle: The Life of Bernard Shaw.* London: Hutchinson and Company, 1956.
———. *Shaw's Corner.* London: Hutchinson and Company, 1952.
Wood, Alan. *Mr. Rank.* London: Hodder and Stoughton, 1952.

UNPUBLISHED MATERIAL:
Letter from Shaw to Eberhard K. Klagemann, dated October 29, 1935 (in the Hanley Collection).
Shaw, Bernard. "Caesar and Cleopatra: Final Shooting Script." Independent Producers' Ltd., Gabriel Pascal Production, June 1, 1944 (in the Theatre Collection, New York Public Library).
Letter from Mrs. Valerie Pascal Delacorte to Donald P. Costello, dated August 20, 1959 (in my files).
Letter from Christopher Mann to Arthur L. Mayer, dated November 14, 1961 (in the files of Mr. Mayer, New York).
Letter from Evelyn Goodavage, Secretary to Vice President of United Artists Corporation, to Arthur L. Mayer, dated December 11, 1961 (in the files of Mr. Mayer, New York).

INDEX